SEXUAL ASSAULT ON CAMPUS

Fair adjudication of campus sexual assault is one of the most divisive issues facing the United States. Victims contend that schools aren't doing enough to protect them, and accused students complain that they are presumed guilty. *Sexual Assault on Campus: Defending Due Process* begins by critically assessing the extent of the problem, before explaining why the criminal justice system has been unable to respond adequately. The book discusses the Department of Education's attempts to force schools to take campus assault seriously and uses original data in assessing the fairness of adjudication in the wake of the 2011 "Dear Colleague Letter." It also includes excerpts from interviews with complainants, accused students, and administrators, which offer readers a first-hand account of these proceedings. Finally, the book provides a critical, in-depth look at the Title IX regulations put in place by the Trump Administration, with detailed recommendations for how they can be improved.

Tamara Rice Lave is a Professor of Law at the University of Miami. She was the reporter for the ABA Criminal Justice Section Task Force on College Due Process Rights and Victim Protections. She has advised both sides in Title IX hearings. Lave is also a former public defender.

T0381916

CAMBRIDGE STUDIES ON CIVIL RIGHTS AND CIVIL LIBERTIES

This series is a platform for original scholarship on US civil rights and civil liberties. It produces books on the normative, historical, judicial, political, and sociological contexts for understanding contemporary legislative, jurisprudential, and presidential dilemmas. The aim is to provide experts, teachers, policymakers, students, social activists, and educated citizens with in-depth analyses of theories, existing and past conditions, and constructive ideas for legal advancements.

General Editor: Alexander Tsesis, *Loyola University, Chicago*

Sexual Assault on Campus

DEFENDING DUE PROCESS

TAMARA RICE LAVE
University of Miami

CAMBRIDGE
UNIVERSITY PRESS

University Printing House, Cambridge CB2 8BS, United Kingdom

One Liberty Plaza, 20th Floor, New York, NY 10006, USA

477 Williamstown Road, Port Melbourne, VIC 3207, Australia

314–321, 3rd Floor, Plot 3, Splendor Forum, Jasola District Centre,
New Delhi – 110025, India

103 Penang Road, #05–06/07, Visioncrest Commercial, Singapore 238467

Cambridge University Press is part of the University of Cambridge.

It furthers the University's mission by disseminating knowledge in the pursuit of
education, learning, and research at the highest international levels of excellence.

www.cambridge.org
Information on this title: www.cambridge.org/9781108843577
DOI: 10.1017/9781108919180

First published 2022

A catalogue record for this publication is available from the British Library.

Library of Congress Cataloging-in-Publication Data
NAMES: Lave, Tamara Rice, author.
TITLE: Campus sexual assault : defending due process / Tamara Rice Lave,
University of Miami.
DESCRIPTION: 1. | Cambridge, United Kingdom ; New York, NY : Cambridge
University Press, 2022. | Series: Cambridge studies on civil rights and civil liberties |
Includes index.
IDENTIFIERS: LCCN 2022010288 | ISBN 9781108843577 (hardback) | ISBN 9781108919180
(ebook)
SUBJECTS: LCSH: Rape – Law and legislation – United States. | Rape in universities
and colleges – United States. | Sexual harassment in universities and colleges – United
States. | Campus violence – Law and legislation – United States. | Women college
students – Crimes against – United States. | Dur process of law – United States. | Civil
rights – United States. | Kinsman, Erica. | BISAC: LAW / Constitutional
CLASSIFICATION: LCC KF9329 .L38 2022 | DDC 345.73/02532–dc23/ENG/20220429
LC record available at https://lccn.loc.gov/2022010288

ISBN 978-1-108-84357-7 Hardback
ISBN 978-1-108-82590-0 Paperback

For Atalanta

Contents

Tables

Acknowledgments

Thank you to those who agreed to be interviewed for this book. Your first-hand experience is of critical importance.

I am grateful to Charlton Copeland, Mary Ann Franks, Matt Gallaway, Aya Gruber, David Harris, Shep Melnick, Pablo Rueda, Peter Smuts, Alexander Tsesis, and Bob Weisberg for their invaluable feedback on this manuscript. I am also thankful to Gabriel (Jack) Chin, Donna Coker, Charlton Copeland, Caroline Corbin, Michael Froomkin, Patrick Gudridge, Osamudia James, Olatunde Johnson, Edward Rubin, Steve Schnably, Scott Sundby, and Bob Weisberg for their help on the law review articles that eventually became Chapters 3, 4, and 5.

My work benefitted immensely from the insights of my colleagues on the ABA Task Force: Andrew Boutros, Pamela J. Bernard, Carrie Bettinger-Lopez, Robert M. Cary, Laura L. Dunn, Cynthia P. Garrett, Marcos E. Hasbun, Janet P. Judge, Bridget M. Maricich, Robin Rachel Runge, Lauren Schoenthaler, Brenda V. Smith, Mary P. Koss, and Elise Lopez.

Many thanks to my fantastic research assistants who aided with this project: Andres Chinchilla, Jessica Duque, Shanise Lawrence, Ashley Meyer, Toni Ramos, Andrea Sinner, and Dexter Whitley.

I am most appreciative for the hard work of my wonderful assistants, Maria Briz and Tina Sutton.

I am indebted to my mother for her support, especially for taking care of my daughter during the many early mornings and late nights it took to write this book.

I am beholden to my father who taught me to be fearless in the pursuit of truth and justice.

Introduction

The Hunting Ground recounts the story of Erica Kinsman.[1] On December 7, 2012, Erica, then a freshman at Florida State University (FSU), reported to campus police that she had been raped by an unknown male. Erica was transported to the hospital where her injuries were photographed, and samples were taken to test for the presence of semen. One month later, Erica told the investigating officer that she recognized the man who raped her from one of her classes. His name: FSU football sensation and future Heisman Trophy winner, Jameis Winston.[2]

Despite the identification, it took eleven months for Jameis' DNA to be tested and compared with the semen found on Erica's underwear.[3] In the meanwhile, the FSU police secured a copy of the Tallahassee report, which they gave to administrators in the Athletic Department, who then turned it over to Jameis' lawyer.[4] He was able to secure signed affidavits from two of Jameis' friends who both swore that they had seen Jameis and Erica having consensual sex. Claiming he would be unable to secure a conviction, the prosecutor chose not to file criminal charges.[5]

Soon after, Jameis won the Heisman and led FSU to a national championship. Although existing Title IX guidelines required that allegations of sexual assault be resolved quickly, Jameis' conduct hearing did not take place until twenty-four months after the purported attack, and he was ultimately found not responsible.[6] Erica sued, and FSU agreed to pay $950,000 to settle the case. The University did not admit fault, but it agreed to provide five years of sexual assault awareness programs and to publish the results.[7]

The experience was painful for Erica. She was harassed and dropped out of FSU, which had been her dream school since she was a little girl. "All these people were praising him; they were calling me a slut, a whore . . . I kind of just want to know like, why me?"[8]

Exactly two years after Erica was raped, on December 7, 2014, San Diego State University (SDSU) sophomore, Francisco Sousa, met Jane Doe[9] at an off-campus party. Although Jane would later claim otherwise, text messages show that they planned on meeting at the event. At one point, Francisco led Jane by the hand to the bathroom where she orally copulated him. Francisco contended that the sex was consensual; indeed, he said that she had done it to him before. Despite a picture of the two kissing a few weeks earlier and flirtatious text messages stretching for several weeks before and then immediately after the alleged attack,[10] Jane told the police that she did not know Francisco well. She said the sex was forced. Two days after the party, San Diego Police arrested Francisco for forcible oral copulation and false imprisonment.[11] He bailed out the next day and was never charged with a crime.[12]

The University, however, suspended Francisco and issued a community Safety Alert naming him as the suspect in an alleged assault.[13] When Francisco asked to review the basis of the allegations against him, the Title IX Investigator refused, telling him that "he would not be entitled to a hearing on the Title IX portion of the matter, he would not have the right to confront his accuser, he had no right to direct participation of counsel, she would make findings of fact and reach conclusions of law and mete out a sanction, and he would not be entitled to an appeal."[14]

On nine different occasions, from December 12, 2014 to March 12, 2015, Francisco sent letters requesting information about the charges against him. On April 2, after sixteen months of waiting, Francisco filed a writ in Superior Court, requesting that SDSU be ordered to provide notice of the allegations and evidence against him as well as a reasonable opportunity to provide responsive evidence.[15] Soon after, SDSU dismissed the charges against him.[16] Francisco sued, and SDSU agreed to pay him $10,000 – an amount to not burden taxpayers but help compensate his parents for the money they had spent on attorney fees.[17] As part of the deal, SDSU agreed to provide its police and Title IX office with additional training in handling sexual assault, and it reduced his arrest to a detention. Francisco had this to say about the experience:

> It's unreal to see how my life was drastically changed due to a false accusation and how it has and will impact me in 1, 2, 10, 30 years, when I'm looking for a job or my kids google their dad's name. The [woman's] lies and the misdeeds of San Diego State can't ever be erased, nor the damage caused ever heal, but I am glad that is all over, and I am vindicated.[18]

High-profile cases like those of Erika Kinsman and Francisco Sousa brought a much-needed spotlight to how schools have handled campus rape in the wake of the 2011 Dear Colleague Letter (DCL). In that letter, the Department of Education, Office for Civil Rights (OCR) under President Barack Obama called the statistics on sexual violence "deeply troubling and a call to action for the nation."[19] The Office for Civil Rights reminded universities that sexual violence constitutes a form of discrimination under Title IX.[20] It told schools that in order to be in compliance, they had to change disciplinary proceedings to more effectively hold rapists accountable.[21] Some applauded OCR's efforts,[22] but others contended that universities went too far in sacrificing the rights of the accused.[23]

In 2016, Donald J. Trump was elected the 45th President of the United States. Eight months later, the Department of Education (DOE) formally rescinded the 2011 Dear Colleague Letter and undertook to draft new procedural regulations.[24] On May 6, 2020, after almost a year and a half spent reviewing over 124,000 public comments, the DOE released its new rule on Title IX sexual harassment. The new regulations made major changes to Title IX adjudication, including beefing up procedural protections in Title IX hearings. For example, they required postsecondary schools to have adjudicatory hearings with live witnesses and cross-examination.

Some celebrated the new rule. The Foundation for Individual Rights in Education (FIRE) released a statement that said: "Advocates for free speech and due process on campus won one of their biggest-ever victories today with the finalization of long-awaited new Department of Education Title IX regulations."[25] Others were more critical. The advocacy group Know Your IX damned the new regulations: "Today the Department of Education released its final rule on Title IX, which guts student survivors' rights and tips the scales of school sexual misconduct cases in favor of perpetrators and schools that wish to sweep sexual violence under the rug."

In 2020, Joe Biden was elected President. Less than three months after his inauguration, Biden formally began the process of undoing the new Title IX rule.

In *Sexual Assault on Campus: Defending Due Process*, I dive headfirst into this emotional and highly charged issue. Victims like Erica Kinsman contend that schools aren't doing enough to protect them. They are infuriated by the refusal to take campus sexual assault seriously, especially if it is perpetrated by a star athlete. Accused students, like Francisco Sousa, are outraged by the fact that they are presumed guilty. They can't meaningfully defend themselves when they are denied the most basic of procedural protections.

I argue that robust procedural protections – the kind guaranteed in the new Title IX rule – are important not just to the Franciscos of the world, but also to the Ericas. Schools can be biased against both victims and the accused, and these regulations help to ensure that schools will adequately investigate both sides and then allow each to present and challenge evidence. Unfortunately, the new rule also dramatically limits what counts as actionable sexual harassment under Title IX, and I argue that many of those changes should be undone.

My book is grounded in careful legal analysis and unrelenting empirical investigation – relying on both published studies and original data as well as interviews with complainants, accused students, and Title IX personnel, which are interwoven throughout. My book is also informed by my experience in advising both sides in Title IX hearings. I have advised women who were raped, and men who were falsely accused. I have even tackled Title IX from an administrative perspective. Foundational to the book is the understanding that both sides matter, and the injustice both perceive is real.

The book proceeds as follows:

In Chapter 1, I examine the problem of campus sexual assault in the United States. I critically discuss major recent studies that measure the incidence and prevalence of campus rape and sexual assault, including the 2007 National Institute of Justice Study, the 2014 Bureau of Justice Statistics Study, the 2015 Association of American Universities Campus Climate Survey, the 2016 Campus Climate Validation Study, and the most recent 2019 Association of American Universities Study. I then explain why, for a long time, the criminal justice system could not respond to what was happening on campus because it wasn't a crime. I close by discussing attempts at reform and explain why those have been largely unsuccessful at addressing campus rape.

In Chapter 2, I trace how a piece of legislation, Title IX of the 1972 Education Amendments, became the primary vehicle for addressing campus sexual assault. Title IX prohibits discrimination on the basis of sex in any educational program or activity that receives federal financial assistance. Although the legislation was intended to increase educational opportunities for women, it quickly became a means for increasing athletic opportunities, and then later a tool for combatting sexual violence. I begin with a brief explanation of the administrative process before moving in chronological order through actions by the DOE and the courts. I then explain why even once sexual assault was recognized as a form of discrimination it still took a long time to extend Title IX to peer assault.

In Chapter 3, I investigate the problematic beginnings of the 2011 Dear Colleague Letter (DCL) issued by the OCR under President Obama.

I explain how the DCL misrepresented existing data, violated the Administrative Procedure Act by changing the law without going through notice and comment, and flouted existing norms. In the process, I provide an in-depth discussion of the changes brought about by the DCL, including mandating a lower standard of proof in sexual assault hearings.

In Chapter 4, I provide original data on the way sexual assault was adjudicated across the country in the wake of the Dear Colleague Letter. I present data gathered from eighty-five of the top colleges and universities over a twenty-seven-month period, from October 2014 to January 2017. I ask about rights deemed fundamental in a criminal trial including: the right to a live hearing, the right to question the opposing party, the right to appeal, and the right to remain silent.

In Chapter 5, I evaluate the fairness of DCL-influenced proceedings under two theories: violation of procedural due process and breach of contract for failure to comport with basic procedural fairness. The first, which is grounded in the U.S. Constitution, provides a stronger basis for recovery. However, it requires state action, which means it is probably only available to public school students. I argue that under either theory, the procedural protections are inadequate.

In Chapter 6, I discuss Title IX under Secretary DeVos. I begin by describing how the DOE quickly broke from its predecessor before recounting the two-year process of promulgating new regulations. I then turn to the first of a two-chapter deeper dive into changes made to Title IX. Here, I focus on how the new regulations narrow what counts as actionable sexual harassment and weaken oversight of schools by the DOE. I contend that most of these changes are deeply problematic and should be reversed.

In Chapter 7, I conduct part two of my deeper dive into the new regulations, but here I focus on the changes made to the investigation and adjudication of sexual assault. I explain the ways in which the new procedures differ from those under the 2011 Dear Colleague Letter, and how they better protect complainants and the accused. In considering the fairness of the new procedures, I compare them to the consensus recommendations of the 2017 American Bar Association Criminal Justice Section Task Force on Campus Due Process and Victim Protection. I also offer suggestions for how schools can implement the new regulations in a way that is compliant with the new regulations but better protects the rights of victims and the accused.

I conclude by arguing that President Biden should leave the new rule largely intact and not reinstate the 2011 Dear Colleague Letter, as he has promised to do. The new rule isn't perfect; indeed, in this final chapter I review my recommendations for improvement. It is, however, a tremendous step forward for victims and the accused, both the Ericas and the Franciscos.

NOTES

1. Erica Kinsman is being called by name because she publicly identified herself in a documentary first shown at the Sundance Film Festival entitled, *The Hunting Ground*. Tyler Kingkade, Erica Kinsman, Woman Who Accused Jameis Winston of Rape, Goes Public for the First Time, Huffington Post (Jan. 26, 2015, 12:38 PM), www.huffingtonpost.com/2015/01/26/erica-kinsman-jameis-winston_n_6539916.html/.

2. OFFICER CLAYTON FALLIS, INCIDENT REPORT, TALLAHASSEE POLICE DEPARTMENT (Dec. 7, 2012), www.talgov.com/uploads/public/documents/assets/news/tpd-documents.pdf/.

3. Email from Erica Buckley, Investigator, to Jill Allison (Nov. 27, 2013, 12:53 PM) (on file with author); JILL ALLISON, REPORT FROM FLA. DEP'T. OF LAW ENF'T. (Dec. 2, 2013) (on file with author).

4. Kevin Vaughan, *Documents: Police, FSU Hampered Jameis Winston Investigation*, FOXSPORTS (Oct. 10, 2014, 4:23 PM), www.foxsports.com/college-football/story/jameis-winston-florida-state-tallahassee-police-hindered-investigation-documents-101014.

5. One of the reasons given was that Erica Kinsman had semen from two sources, Jameis Winston and another person. Erica explained that the other person was her boyfriend, but that explanation did not change the prosecutor's decision. Julie Montanaro, *FSU QB Jameis Winston Won't Face Charges*, WCTV (Dec. 6, 2013), www.wctv.tv/sports/headlines/BREAKING-231816891.html.

6. Jerry Hinnen, *Jameis Winston's Conduct Hearing Concludes on Its Second Day*, CBSSPORTS.COM (Dec. 3, 2014), www.cbssports.com/college-football/news/jameis-winstons-fsu-conduct-hearing-concludes-on-its-second-day/.

7. Marc Tracy, *Florida State Settles Suit over Jameis Winston Rape Inquiry*, N.Y. TIMES, (Jan. 25, 2016).

8. Marissa Payne, *Erica Kinsman, Who Accused Jameis Winston of Rape, Tells Her Story in New Documentary "The Hunting Ground,"* WASHINGTON POST (Feb. 19, 2015, 5:16 PM), www.washingtonpost.com/news/early-lead/wp/2015/02/19/erica-kinsman-who-accused-jameis-winston-of-rape-tells-her-story-in-new-documentary-the-hunting-ground/https://www.washingtonpost.com/news/early-lead/wp/2015/02/19/erica-kinsman-who-accused-jameis-winston-of-rape-tells-her-story-in-new-documentary-the-hunting-ground/.

9. Not her real name.

10. Letter from Michael D. McGlinn, Att'y for Francisco Sousa, to Dr. Lee Mintz, Dir., Ctr. for Student Rights and Responsibilities, San Diego State 2 (Mar. 12, 2015) [hereinafter Letter from McGlinn] (on file with author at 2–3).

11. Michael Fleeman, *Arrest Made in San Diego Rape, One of a String Near College Campus*, REUTERS (Dec. 10, 2014, 4:11 PM), www.reuters.com/art icle/2014/12/10/us-usa-rape-california-idUSKBN0JO2AQ20141210.

12. Angie Lee & Richard Allyn, *SDSU Sex Assault Suspect Out on Bail*, CBS8.COM (Dec. 10, 2014, 6:23 PM), www.cbs8.com/story/27599987/sds u-sex-assault-suspect-out-on-bail.

13. *Notice of Interim Suspension* from Eric Rivera, Vice President for Student Affairs, San Diego State Univ., to Francisco Sousa (Dec. 9, 2013), www .avoiceformalestudents.com/wp-content/uploads/2015/04/Petition-for-Writ-of-Mandate-Francisco-Sousa-San-Diego-State-University-filed-2015–4–2.pdf.

14. Letter from McGlinn, *supra* note 10, at 4.

15. Petition for Writ of Mandate at 6–7, Sousa v. San Diego State Univ., No. 37–2015–00011119-CU-WM-CTL (Cal. Super. Ct. Apr. 2, 2015).

16. Gary Warth, *SDSU Lifts Suspension against Student*, SAN DIEGO UNION TRIBUNE (Sept. 1, 2015).

17. Gary Warth, *SDSU to Pay $10K Settlement to Former Student Accused of Sexual Assault*, SAN DIEGO UNION TRIBUNE (Apr. 4, 2017).

18. Dorian Hargrove, *San Diego State Pays Francisco Damages for False Accusation Bunging: SDSU Will Send Campus Police for More Detailed Training on Sex Assault*, SAN DIEGO READER (Apr. 29, 2017), www.sandiegoreader.com/news/2017/apr/29/ticker-san-diego-sta te-pays-sousa-damages-false/.

19. Letter from Russlyn Ali, Assistant Sec'y for Civil Rights, Office for Civil Rights, U.S. Dep't. of Educ., to Title IX Coordinators 2 (Apr. 4, 2011), www2.ed.gov/about/offices/list/ocr/letters/colleague-201104.pdf.

20. *Dear Colleague Letter*, *supra* note 19, at 1.

21. *Id.* at 1–3, 7–14.

22. *See* Michelle J. Anderson, *Campus Sexual Assault Adjudication and Resistance to Reform*, 125 YALE L.J. (2016); Lavinia M. Weizel, Note, *The Process That Is Due: Preponderance of the Evidence as the Standard of Proof for University Adjudications of Student-on-Student Sexual Assault Complaints*, 53 B.C.L. REV. 1613, 1642–1655 (2012); Amy Chmielewski, Note, *Defending the Preponderance of the Evidence Standard in College Adjudications of Sexual Assault*, 2013 BYU EDUC. & L.J. 143, 149–174 (2013).

23. *See* William A. Jacobsen, *Accused on Campus: Charges Dropped, but the Infamy Remains*, LEGAL INSURRECTION (May 16, 2015, 8:30 PM), http:// legalinsurrection.com/2015/05/accused-on-campus-charges-dropped-but-the-infamy-remains/; *see also* Ryan D. Ellis, Note, *Mandating Injustice: The Preponderance of the Evidence Mandate Creates a New Threat to Due Process on Campus*, 32 REV. LITIG. 65, 80–81 (2013); Barclay Sutton Hendrix, Note, *A Feather on One Side, a Brick on the Other:*

Tilting the Scale Against Males Accused of Sexual Assault in Campus Disciplinary Proceedings, 47 GA. L. REV. 591, 599 (2013); Stephen Henrick, Note, *A Hostile Environment for Student Defendants: Title IX and Sexual Assault on College Campuses,* 40 N. KY. L. REV. 49 (2013); Naomi Shatz, *Feminists, We Are Not Winning the War on Campus Sexual Assault,* HUFFINGTON POST (Oct. 29, 2014, 6:44 PM), www.huffingtonpost.com/naomi-shatz/feminists-we-are-not-winn_b_6071500.html.

24. Letter from Candice Jackson, Acting Sec'y for Civil Rights, U.S. Dep't. of Educ., to U.S. Dep't of Educ., Office for Civil Rights, www2.ed.gov/about/offices/list/ocr/letters/colleague-title-ix-201709.pdf.

25. Daniel Burnett, *Education Dept. Issues New Title IX Regs with Crucial Campus Due Process Protections, Adopts Supreme Court Sexual Harassment Definition,* FIRE (May 6, 2020), www.thefire.org/breaking-education-dept-issues-new-title-ix-regs-with-crucial-campus-due-process-protections-adopts-supreme-court-sexual-harassment-definition/.

1

The Problem

For most of the history of this country, rape was defined as "the carnal knowledge of a female, forcibly and against her will."[1] That means that, until relatively recently, the legal definition of rape simply didn't include most of what was happening on campus. It wasn't rape to have sex with a sorority sister who was intoxicated from drinking or doing drugs. Nor was it rape to penetrate someone even after they repeatedly said "no."

Since the 1970s, reformers have been successful in expanding the definition of rape and removing procedural barriers to conviction, but victims both on and off campus continue to face an uphill battle. If they report, and the vast majority do not, the police often think they are lying. Should the case somehow reach the prosecutor's office, two common characteristics in campus rape cases – that the victim was drinking and attacked by someone she knew – make charging and ultimately conviction less likely. The end result: an almost complete failure of accountability and justice.

I begin this chapter by presenting research on the incidence of campus rape and sexual assault. I then explain why, for a long time, the criminal justice system could not respond to what was happening on campus. I close by discussing attempts at reform and explain why they have been largely unsuccessful in addressing campus rape. An important caveat – I make no claims that college students have it worse than other victims of sexual assault. To the contrary, I have written elsewhere about how certain people, especially Black women with a criminal record, are less likely to be believed by the police and prosecutors.[2] This neglect is a serious problem that needs to be wrestled with; however, it is not the focus of this book.

1.1 INCIDENCE OF CAMPUS RAPE AND SEXUAL ASSAULT

In the last few years, there have been several major studies on the incidence of campus rape and sexual assault, but for a long time there was absolutely nothing. Although the Federal Bureau of Investigation (FBI) has been compiling national arrest data on rape since 1930, it has never provided information on the context in which the rape occurred. The National Crime Victimization Survey, administered by the Department of the Census on behalf of the Department of Justice, Bureau of Justice Statistics, has been gathering detailed information about crime incidents, including unreported crime, since 1972. But it wasn't until the Violence Against Women Act of 1994 that the Attorney General was mandated with "provid[ing] for a national baseline study to examine the scope of the problem of campus sexual assaults and the effectiveness of institutional and legal policies in addressing such crime and protecting victims."[3] It's no surprise that a search on the LexisNexis database using the terms "campus rape" and "school rape" found zero relevant articles before 1980.[4]

In considering the studies in this chapter, it is important to keep in mind a few things: how the definition of rape has changed over time; the percentage of women who indicate they have been raped or sexually assaulted; the consistently low percentage who report their victimization to any authority, attributes about victims including relationship with offender, and, where available, information on how many assaults are actually connected with a school. For a comparison of all the studies, see Appendix A.

1.2 EARLY STUDIES: 1957–1977

There were a few early nongovernmental, nonnationally representative studies, but they were of so called "erotic aggressiveness," and they showed an alarming level of what we would now recognize as criminal behavior. The first study I am aware of – *Male Sex Aggression on a University Campus* – was published in the American Sociological Review in 1957.[5] Kirkpatrick and Kanin distributed an eight-page questionnaire to females in twenty-two varied university classes on one campus. The women were asked about "five degrees of erotic aggressiveness, namely attempts at 'necking,' 'petting' above the waist, 'petting' below the waist, sex intercourse, and attempts at sex intercourse with violence or threats of violence" from September 15, 1954 to May 15, 1955.[6]

Overall, 162 of the 291 women (55.7 percent) reported being "offended" at least once during the academic year at some level of erotic intimacy. More specifically, 20.9 percent were "offended by forceful attempts at intercourse" and 6.2 percent by "aggressively forceful attempts at sex intercourse in the course of which menacing threats or coercive infliction of physical pain were employed."[7] Kirkpatrick and Kanin wrote that, "[w]hile for some girls offensive experience was no doubt trivial, considerable mention was made of fear and guilt reactions."[8] The 162 women reported a total of 1,022 offensive episodes, or an average of 6.3 episodes per offended woman. Kirkpatrick and Kanin explicitly did not ask the women whether the men were successful: "In the interest of gaining full co-operation the questionnaire was carefully devised to avoid probing the sex conduct of the female respondents."[9]

The mean age of the offended girls was younger than that of the nonoffended, 18.8 as opposed to 19.0 years. Kirkpatrick and Kanin hypothesized the reason why: "[t]he difference could be due either to prudishness of younger students or to their assumed exploitability."[10]

Very few women reported what happened to the authorities, and perhaps counterintuitively, the more serious the conduct, the less likely they were to report. Twenty-three women who experienced aggressive necking and petting above the waist reported, as compared with four women who experienced aggressive petting below the waist, and zero women who experienced attempted intercourse and attempted intercourse with violence.[11]

Twenty years later, Kanin tried to replicate and extend the prior study. In 1977, Kanin and Parcell published *Sexual Aggression: A Second Look at the Offended Female*. Similar to the earlier study, they interviewed female students in twenty-three varied classes at a large Midwestern state university (282 usable questionnaires).[12] As before, the questions were focused on male sex aggression, but the female had to also "perceive the male efforts as offending and displeasing."[13]

Although Kanin and Parcell hypothesized that the "various social movements that stress sex-role egalitarianism, intrasex communication, and a more permissive sexuality" might have impacted the incidence of male sexual aggression, they found that it was about the same as in their earlier study.[14] One half of women (143) reported that they were offended by male sexual aggression at some level during the 1971–72 academic year, and they reported being involved in 725 episodes, or an average of 5.1 per offended female during this same period. Of the offended women, 23.8 percent experienced aggressive intercourse, and 2.7 percent experienced aggressive intercourse with menacing or physical pain.[15] Of all respondents, 69.2 percent reported being offended since entering college, and 63.5 percent were offended during high school.[16] Including all aggressive experience from high school to the present survey, 83 percent reported aggression at some level of erotic intimacy. Kanin and Parcell also found that those who reported being offended were more likely to be habitual victims. Unfortunately, Kanin and Parcell did not provide information on how many women reported their victimization to authorities.

They did, however, compare the relationship between offender and offended across the two studies. In the earlier study, they found that "the more advanced aggressions tended to be reported by those involved in the more durable pairings, i.e., steady and regular dates, pinned, and engaged."[17] With necking excluded, only 30 percent of episodes were reported for casual pairings.[18] The later study, however, had a "radically different pattern in that the majority of episodes are reported for casual pairings."[19]

It is telling how Kanin and Parcell describe their findings. The fact that a woman may have eventually become compliant seems to make it acceptable even if she was "forcibly rendered sexually superable." Conduct short of sexual intercourse doesn't seem to matter, and sexual intercourse – even if accomplished with aggression – may not be rape.

> With respect to the various levels of intimacy, the percentages of successful episodes were as follows: kissing, 36.2%; intercourse, 29.2%; intercourse with violence, 100.0%. However, the meaning of these figures is not at all clear. They do not tell us whether the female was forcibly rendered sexually superable and subsequently, compliant or whether the entire event was characterized by duress. The only significance that can be attributed to "success" is obviously associated with the level of aggression. To succeed in kissing or sexually touching a refractory female may be a rather fleeting and innocuous type of accomplishment, but success at achieving intercourse, regardless of the brevity of the experience, is indeed a phenomenon of a significantly different caliber, psychologically, socially, and legally. Approximately 32% of the intercourse aggressions were reported to be successful. It is unfortunate that we cannot elaborate further on the character of these episodes so as to possibly reveal something on the order of a rape index.[20]

1.3 1987: THE FIRST STUDY ON A NATIONALLY REPRESENTATIVE SAMPLE

Starting in the 1980s, there was an increase in research on campus rape. This included articles on gang rape,[21] rape by fraternity brothers,[22] and acquaintance rape.[23] The first study on the incidence of campus rape on a nationally representative sample of higher education students was done by Koss, Gidycz, and Wisniewski in 1987.[24] A self-reporting questionnaire (which contained a ten-item Sexual Experiences Survey (SES)) was given to 6,159 students (3,187 female and 2,972 male) enrolled in thirty-two schools, asking them about the incidence of sexual aggression over the prior twelve-month period. The questions on rape were based on the State of Ohio's 1980 definition: "vaginal intercourse between male and female, and anal intercourse, fellatio, and cunnilingus between persons regardless

of sex" if accomplished through force or threat of force or the administration of any drug or other intoxicant, which substantially impairs the
other person's judgment or control, for the purpose of preventing
resistance.[25]

They were specifically asked, "Have you had sexual intercourse when you
didn't want to because a man gave you alcohol or drugs." That question was
based on Ohio law, which held that it wasn't rape unless there was "intention
by the perpetrator to use drugs to incapacitate the victim."[26] Since then, many
states have broadened their definition of rape, and in 2007, Koss et al. revised
the SES to focus only on the state of the victim. The language became:
"taking advantage of me when I was too drunk or out of it to stop what was
happening."[27]

Although the definition of rape in many states is gender neutral, Koss
et al. focus on female victims and male perpetrators "because women
represent virtually 100% of reported rape victims ... [and] the FBI definition
of rape that is used in victimization studies ... limits the crime of rape to
female victims."[28] Koss et al. found 15.4 percent of college women reported
experiencing rape, and 12.1 percent reported attempted rape, since age 14.[29]
There were differences among institutions, with 14 percent of women from
private colleges and 17 percent of women from major universities reporting
being raped as compared with 7 percent from religiously affiliated
institutions.[30] Koss et al. also measured victimization rates over a six-
month period. They found a victimization rate of 83 per 1,000 women
who experienced rape or attempted rape.[31] Under the more restrictive
Uniform Crime Reporting (UCR) definition at the time (carnal knowledge
of a female, forcibly and against her will), the combined victimization rate
was 38 per 1,000.[32]

Just as with other studies, the women who were raped were young. The
mean age was 18.5 years.[33] The mean age of the men who reported an act of
sexual aggression was the same.[34]

Only 27 percent of the women who had experienced an act that met legal
definitions of rape perceived it as such, and just 5 percent reported it to the
police.[35] Perhaps most troubling, 41 percent of the women who were raped
expected to experience something similar in the future.[36] Consistent across
other studies, 84 percent of the perpetrators of legal rape were acquaintances,
and 57 percent were dating partners.[37]

Of the men who committed legal rape, just one perceived his behavior as
rape, whereas 84 percent stated that "it definitely was not rape."[38] Forty-
seven percent expected to engage in a similar act of aggression in the
future.[39]

1.4 INCREASED ATTENTION AND RESEARCH: 1990–2020

The 1990s marked a significant increase in attention to campus rape. In 1992, Congress amended the Student Right-to-Know and Campus Security Act of 1990 to include the Campus Sexual Assault Victims' Bill of Rights, which requires colleges and universities to provide basic rights to sexual assault victims and develop and publish policies on awareness and prevention of sexual assault.[40] Six years later, the Act (renamed the Jeanne Clery Disclosure of Campus Security Policy and Campus Crime Statistics Act) was amended again to mandate more reporting of campus crime (including maintaining a daily public crime log) and to require extensive security provisions.[41] In 1999 and 2000, the US Department of Justice awarded a combined 14.7 million dollars to forty-one post-secondary institutions to combat sexual harassment, domestic violence, and stalking.[42] Fisher et al. (2000) provided insight into what prompted this shift:

> During the past decade, concern over the sexual victimization of female college students has escalated. In part the interest in this problem has been spurred by increasing attention to the victimization of women in general; until the relatively recent past, female victims received very little attention. However, this is no longer true. Terms such as "date rape" and "domestic violence" have entered the public lexicon and signify the unprecedented, if still insufficient, notice given to women who have been victimized. Attention to the sexual victimization of college women, however, also has been prompted by the rising fear that college campuses are not ivory towers but, instead, have become hot spots for criminal activity.[43]

Between 2000 and 2020, there were several major studies on the prevalence, nature, and reporting of campus sexual misconduct. Only two were nationally representative, and I will discuss them first. I will then turn to studies that examine sexual assault in nonnationally representative samples. These are valuable studies, but advocates have misused their findings to make sweeping claims about the number of students being sexually assaulted across all US colleges and universities.

1.4.1 *National Studies*

1.4.1.1 National College Women Sexual Victimization (NCWSV) Study (2000)

Fisher et al.'s study was based on a telephone survey conducted on a randomly selected, national sample of 4,446 women who were enrolled in a two or four-year college or university course in the fall of 1996.[44] Participants were interviewed between February and May 1997 about any victimization they had suffered since school began in fall 1996.[45] There was an 85.6 percent response rate.[46]

Fisher et al. measured several different kinds of victimization, including completed and attempted rape. They used a narrower definition than that used by Koss et al. thirteen years before: "Unwanted completed penetration by force or the threat of force. Penetration includes penile-vaginal, mouth on your genitals, mouth on someone else's genitals, penile-anal, digital-vaginal, digital-anal, object-vaginal, and object-anal."[47] They found that 1.7 percent of the sample had experienced a completed rape, and an additional 1.1 percent had experienced an attempted rape.[48] That meant the victimization rate was 27.7 rapes or attempted rapes per 1,000 students, which is equivalent to 1 in 36 college women.[49] They cautioned however that the incidence rate only reflected a seven-month period, and the victimization would likely climb if it measured the course of a college career: "Over the course of a college career – which now lasts an average of 5 years – the percentage of completed or attempted rape victimization among women in higher educational institutions might climb to between one-fifth and one-quarter."[50] Fisher et al. did not explain how they came up with this estimate, and it appears that they might have simply multiplied 1 in 36 by $(5{\times}12)/7$, which equals 0.238 or 24 percent.[51] This methodology assumes a constant risk of victimization, which is problematic because studies show that the risk of being sexually assaulted is greatest for younger students.[52]

There were a few findings of particular note. Most rapes – 66.3 percent of completed rapes and 54.9 percent of attempted rapes – occurred off campus.[53] Ninety-six percent of completed rapes and 91.9 percent of attempted rapes were perpetrated by known offenders, either classmates (35.5%, 43.5%), friends (34.2%, 24.2%), boyfriends/ex-boyfriends (23.7%, 14.5%), or acquaintances of the victim (2.6%, 9.7%).[54] Of these, classmates were the only offenders who were clearly associated with the school. Less than 5 percent of all rapes were reported to law enforcement.[55] Among the factors that consistently increased the risk of sexual victimization was frequently drinking enough to get drunk.[56]

1.4.1.2 National Crime Victimization Survey (2014)

In 2014, Sinozich and Langton from the Bureau of Justice Statistics used data from the National Crime Victimization Survey (NCVS) to analyze rape and sexual assault among females aged 18–24 between 1995 and 2013.[57] The definition of rape was broader than the Fisher et al. study and includes unlawful penetration or attempted penetration through psychological coercion or physical force.[58]

The NCVS had a higher response rate (88 percent for eligible persons) than any of the other studies, which means there is less chance of nonresponse bias.[59]

Although Sinozich and Langton found that women between the ages of 18 and 24 had a higher rate of rape and sexual assault than all other age groups, they still found a much lower incidence than other studies: 6.1 per 1,000 female post-secondary students were the victims of rape and sexual assault for the period between 1995 and 2013.[60] Looking only at rape: they found 2.0 per 1,000 female post-secondary students were raped, and 1.5 per 1,000 were the victims of attempted rape.[61] In 78 percent of cases, the assailant was known by the victim.[62]

Unlike other studies, Sinozich and Langton did not find a significant difference in the rate of victimization by age for female college students.[63] For female noncollege students, however, they found that the rate of victimization was lower for 22–24-year-olds as compared with those between the ages of 18 and 21.[64]

Many advocates have argued that college campuses pose a particular risk for women, but NCVS numbers showed the opposite to be true. Sinozich and Langton found that the rate of rape and sexual assault was 1.2 times *higher* for nonstudents compared with students (7.6 per 1,000 as compared with 6.1 per 1,000).[65] Both groups had low reporting rates: 32 percent of nonstudents reported to the police as compared with 20 percent of students.[66] When asked why they hadn't reported, 26 percent of students and 23 percent of nonstudents stated that they thought the incident was a personal matter, and 20 percent of both stated a fear of reprisal. Twelve percent of student victims and 5 percent of nonstudent victims stated that the incident was not important enough to report.[67]

Sinozich and Langton also found that 1.4 per 1,000 male students between the ages of 18 and 24 had been the victim of rape or sexual assault as compared with 6.1 per 1,000 of female students.[68] Male nonstudents were less likely than male students to be the victim of sexual assault, 0.3 per 1,000.[69]

1.4.2 *Nonnationally Representative Studies*

1.4.2.1 Campus Sexual Assault (CSA) Survey (2007)

You have probably heard of the 2007 Campus Sexual Assault (CSA) Survey. Assistant Secretary for Civil Rights Russlyn Ali referred to it in the 2011 Dear Colleague Letter as justification for reducing procedural protections for students accused of sexual misconduct. She wrote:

> The statistics on sexual violence are both deeply troubling and a call to action
> for the nation. A report prepared for the National Institute of Justice found

that about 1 in 5 women are victims of completed or attempted sexual assault while in college.[70]

Yet Ali's "1 in 5" claim is misleading because the CSA is not a nationally representative study. Instead, Krebs, Lindquist, Warner, Fisher, and Martin conducted an anonymous, web-based survey of undergraduate students in the winter of 2006 at two large, public universities.[71] A total of 5,446 women responded,[72] which constituted a response rate of 42.2 percent and 42.8 percent respectively.[73] They later acknowledged that their response rate was "relatively low (42%) . . . (and) it is possible that nonresponse bias had an impact on our prevalence estimates, whether positive or negative."[74]

Krebs et al. distinguished between sexual assault accomplished through physical force or threats of physical force versus incapacitation.[75] Sexual assault included both battery (unwanted sexual contact) and rape (oral, vaginal, anal, or object penetration).[76] Of the women, 19 percent – and 26.3 percent of senior women – *at those two schools* reported experiencing completed or attempted sexual assault since entering college.[77] Focusing only on rape – 3.4 percent of respondents experienced penetration through physical force, and 8.5 percent experienced penetration through intoxication.[78] Also worth mentioning, although Krebs et al. noted that "date rape drugs" have received a lot of attention in the media, just 0.6 percent of the undergraduate women studied reported being sexually assaulted after being given a drug without knowledge or consent since entering college.[79]

Krebs et al. then looked for risk factors for various types of sexual assault. Experiencing physically forced sexual assault before college was significantly associated with being a victim of forced sexual assault in college.[80] They also found that "women who are victimized during their college career are most likely to be victimized early during their college tenure."[81] Specifically, they found that sophomores had the highest "past 12 month" prevalence estimates of sexual assault.[82] Other risk factors included the frequency with which women reported getting drunk or using marijuana.[83] Attending fraternity parties was positively associated with being a victim of incapacitated sexual assault.[84]

Consistent with other studies, Krebs et al. found that most victims had been assaulted by someone they knew,[85] and most did not report to law enforcement. Only 2 percent of those who experienced intoxicated sexual assault and 13 percent of those who experienced forced sexual assault reported to police or campus security.[86] Most (56% of physically forced and 67% of incapacitated) explained that they did not report because they did not think it was serious enough.[87] A very small number reported that their assailant received any disciplinary action from the university or was arrested, prosecuted, charged, or convicted.[88] Just 32 percent of victims of forced sexual assault were satisfied with how the reporting was handled, and 17.2 percent regretted having reported.[89]

1.4.2.2 Association of American Universities Campus Climate Survey, 2015 (Revised 2017)

The Revised 2017 Association of American Universities (AAU) Campus Climate Survey[90] is another frequently misused study. Headlines in prominent publications like the *New York Times*, the *Los Angeles Times*, and *Newsweek* proclaimed that 1 in 4 undergraduate women experienced sexual assault while in college.[91] However, the revised 2017 AAU study is not nationally representative, and it actually finds significant differences across institutions.[92]

In 2014, members of the AAU contracted with Westat to determine the incidence, prevalence, and characteristics of incidents of sexual assault and misconduct.[93] Twenty-seven Institutes of Higher Education (IHE) participated in the first survey, which was given at the end of the spring 2015 semester.[94] The overall response was 19.3 percent, with a total of 150,072 students participating.[95] As the authors acknowledged, if victims are more likely to respond to a survey on sexual assault then the results would be biased to overestimate the amount of rape and sexual assault. To test this, they conducted three different assessments of nonresponse bias. The results weren't good: "Two of these three analyses provide evidence that nonresponders tended to be less likely to report victimization. This implies that the survey estimates related to victimization and selected attitude items may be biased upwards (i.e., somewhat too high)."[96]

Cantor et al. asked questions about sexual touching[97] and nonconsensual penetration[98] by physical force,[99] threats of physical force, or incapacitation.[100] They also included questions on nonconsensual sexual contact by absence of affirmative consent, harassment, intimate partner violence, and stalking. Cantor et al. gathered data from (1) female students; (2) male students; and those identifying as (3) transgender, genderqueer, or gender nonconforming, questioning, or not listed (TGQN); and (4) decline to state.[101]

Of seniors 16.5 percent reported completed nonconsensual penetration or sexual touching by force or incapacitation since entering the IHE.[102] The rates were highest for senior females (26.1%, which serves as the basis for the misleading 1 in 4 number) and senior TGQN (29.5%).[103] Of senior males 6.3 percent reported such experiences.[104] Focusing only on rape – 11.3 percent of senior females, 12.6 percent of TGQN, and 2.5 percent of senior males reported being a victim of nonconsensual penetration involving physical force or incapacitation.[105]

As previously mentioned, there was a marked difference in reported victimization across the different IHEs. Cantor et al. found that rates of unwanted sexual penetration and touching ranged from 13 percent to 30 percent across the twenty-seven IHEs.[106] These differences led Cantor et al. to criticize estimates like 1 in 4:

> Overall, these comparisons illustrate that estimates such as "1 in 5" or "1 in 4" as a global rate across all IHEs is at least oversimplistic, if not misleading. None of the studies that generate estimates for specific IHEs are nationally representative. The above results show that the rates vary greatly across institutions.[107]

Table 1.1 below provides detailed information about the characteristics of victims who have experienced nonconsensual sexual contact involving physical force or incapacitation since entering college.[108] Breaking down victims into different subgroups, bisexuals (25.3%), American Indians or Alaska Natives (15.1%), Hispanics (12.2%), and the disabled (21.4%) experienced the most nonconsensual sexual contact since entering college.[109] Across all groups, TGQN students experienced the most.[110]

Finally, like many other studies, Cantor et al. found that younger students were more likely to experience sexual misconduct. Of freshmen females 16.9 percent reported sexual contact by physical force or incapacitation, which declined steadily by year to a low of 11.1 percent of seniors.[112] They also found that most did not report their victimization. Just 25.5 percent of students who had experienced forcible penetration and 13.3 percent of students who had experienced penetration by intoxication reported to at least one program on the university list.[113] A total of 58.6 percent of those who experienced penetration by force and 62.1 percent who experienced penetration by incapacitation explained that they did not think it was serious enough to report, and 23.3 percent and 27.0 percent respectively did not want the person to get into trouble.[114]

1.4.2.3 Campus Climate Survey Validation Study (CCSVS) (2016)

In 2014, the Office on Violence Against Women funded the Bureau of Justice Statistics to develop and test a pilot campus climate survey.[115] The Bureau of Justice Statistics (BJS) then contracted with an outside research company to collaborate on the design and implementation of the Campus Climate Survey Validation Study (CCSVS). The survey created focused on the 2014–2015

TABLE 1.1 *Percentage of Students Experiencing Nonconsensual Sexual Contact Involving Physical Force or Incapacitation since Entering College by Gender and Victim Characteristics.*[111]

	Total	Woman	Man	TGQN
Sexual Orientation				
Heterosexual	10.8%	18.1%	3.6%	9.2%
Gay or Lesbian	13.7%	18.5%	12.1%	18.4%
Bisexual	25.3%	31.7%	11.1%	24.3%
Ethnicity				
Hispanic	12.2%	17.9%	5.5%	33.3%
Not Hispanic	11.6%	19.0%	4.2%	19.9%
Race				
White	13.0%	21.0%	4.7%	21.6%
Black or African American	13.1%	18.2%	5.5%	28.9%
Asian	7.7%	13.1%	2.9%	17.6%
American Indian or Alaska Native	15.1%	23.4%	6.4%	20.1%
Native Hawaiian or other Pacific Islander	12.2%	21.2%	3.8%	22.6%
Disability				
Yes	21.4%	31.6%	8.7%	34.4%
No	11.3%	18.4%	4.2%	20.0%

academic year.[116] Once the survey was complete, twenty-four schools were selected to participate, and nine accepted.[117] The nine schools differed among key dimensions like size and public versus private. "Importantly, neither this sample of nine schools nor the data collected from the students attending them are intended to be nationally representative of all college students or institutions of higher education."[118] A total of 23,000 undergraduate students took the survey with an average response rate across all nine schools of 54 percent for females and 40 percent for males.[119] Minimal bias was detected.[120]

Krebs et al. found that the prevalence rate[121] for completed sexual assault among undergraduate females during the 2014–2015 academic year averaged 10.3 percent across the nine IHEs, with a range of 4.2 percent to 20 percent.[122] Sexual assault included completed sexual battery[123] (prevalence rate averaged 5.6% across the nine IHEs, with a range of 1.7% to 13.2%)[124] and completed rape[125] (prevalence rate averaged 4.1% across the nine IHEs, with a range of 2.2% to 7.9%).[126] Researchers also estimated the prevalence rate for completed sexual assault since entering undergraduate school and across lifetime, but they urged caution in interpreting these results.[127]

Unlike the 2015 AAU Campus Climate Survey, Krebs et al. found that across most schools, rates of sexual assaults for white and nonwhite students in the female sample were not statistically distinguishable.[128] For two schools, however, the prevalence rate was *higher* for white as compared with nonwhite students.[129] Similar to the 2015 AAU Campus Climate Survey, the prevalence of sexual assault was higher at the nine schools for nonheterosexual as compared with heterosexual female students.[130]

The victimization numbers were lower for men. The prevalence of completed sexual assault among undergraduate men during the 2014–2015 academic year ranged from 1.4 percent to 5.7 percent with an average of 3.1 percent.[131] Breaking that down further, the average prevalence rate for sexual battery was 1.7 percent (0.4%–3.3%), and the average prevalence rate for completed rape was 0.8 percent (0.3%–1.4%).[132]

In describing the tactics used to accomplish sexual assault, female undergraduates reported that 24.9 percent of the time they were incapacitated and unable to provide consent or stop what was happening; 23.7 percent of the time physical force was used against them, and 4.9 percent of the time the person threatened to hurt them or someone they cared about.[133] A person touched or grabbed their sexual body parts 85.4 percent of the time.[134] Victims perceived the offender was under the influence of alcohol or drugs in 59 percent of rape incidents, and they themselves reported using alcohol or drugs in 63 percent of cases in which they had been raped.[135]

Only 9 percent of rapes were perpetrated by strangers.[136] The rest were perpetrated by an acquaintance, friend of a friend, or someone that the victim had just met (53%); someone the victim had seen or heard about but not talked to (7.7%), a current or ex-dating partner or spouse (23%), or current or ex-friend or roommate (16%).[137]

Across all nine schools, 4.3 percent of sexual batteries and 12.5 percent of rapes were reported by the victim to any official.[138] Just 1.1 percent of sexual batteries and 4.2 percent of rape incidents were reported to law enforcement.[139] For those that reported to law enforcement, victims considered the official to be helpful in 53 percent of rape incidents and 69 percent of sexual battery incidents.[140]

Krebs et al. made findings that are worth emphasizing. Only 33 percent of rape incidents and 28 percent of sexual battery incidents took place on campus, and just 55 percent of the rape offenders and 56 percent of the sexual battery offenders were affiliated with the school as students, professors, or other employees.[141] That means a significant percentage of what is being experienced by college students potentially should not be characterized as *campus* sexual assault.

1.4.2.4 Campus Climate Survey on Sexual Assault and Misconduct, 2019
(revised 2020)

RAINN (Rape, Abuse, & Incest National Network) – "the nation's largest anti-sexual violence organization" – misleadingly cites the 2019 Campus Climate Survey for the proposition that, "[a]mong undergraduate students, 26.4% of females, and 6.8% of males experience rape or sexual assault through physical force, violence, or incapacitation."[142] This characterization makes it sound like the 2019 study is nationally representative when it explicitly is not. As Krebs et al. explain: "The variation across schools emphasizes the importance of not generalizing from these 33 schools to a larger population (e.g., national). The schools participating in the survey were not randomly selected, and the rates discussed in this report should not be seen as representing student populations beyond this group of schools."[143]

The 2019 AAU Campus Climate Survey is still important, but its significance should not be overstated. This time there were thirty-three schools and 181,752 students – 108,221 undergraduates and 73,531 graduate and professional respondents.[144] The final response rate was 21.9 percent – 17.5 percent for males and 26.1 percent for females.[145] Just as in 2015, Cantor et al. asked questions about nonconsensual sexual contact by physical force, threats of physical force, or incapacitation. They also included questions on nonconsensual sexual contact by absence of affirmative consent, harassment, intimate partner violence, and stalking.

Cantor et al. found that for the twenty-one schools that had participated in both studies, the rate of nonconsensual sexual contact by physical force or incapacitation increased for undergraduate women (from 23.4 to 26.4%), graduate and professional women (from 8.4 to 10.8%), and for undergraduate men (from 5.5 to 6.9%).[146] The changes for TGQN students decreased, but the changes were not statistically significant.[147] As before, there was significant variation across institutions.

Cantor et al. found that 18.1 percent of 4th year students or higher reported nonconsensual penetration or sexual touching by force or incapacitation since entering the IHE.[148] The percentages were highest for senior females (32.8%) and senior TGQN (28.9%). Of senior males, 8.9 percent reported such experiences. Focusing only on rape – 9.4 percent of 4th year students or higher reported being a victim of nonconsensual penetration involving physical force or incapacitation.[149] The percentages were higher for senior females (18%) and senior TGQN (14.9%) as compared with senior men (4.2%).[150]

Importantly, there was a marked difference in reported victimization across the different IHEs. Cantor et al. found that rates of nonconsensual sexual contact by force or inability to consent for undergraduate women ranged from 14 to 32 percent across the thirty-three IHEs.[151] Cantor et al. write, "Many of the differences in prevalence rates across schools are not statistically significant. Nonetheless, there is a wide range of prevalence rates across schools."[152]

Cantor et al. also study the percentage of students who experienced penetration by sexual touching involving physical force or inability to consent or stop what was happening, by victim characteristics and gender. The results are similar to the 2015 study, however there is one notable change. There were more white students (14.7%) who reported experiencing unwanted penetration or sexual touching as compared with black students (12.7%).[153] In addition, just as before, Cantor et al. found that younger students were more likely to experience nonconsensual sexual contact.[154] They also found that most students did not report their victimization. Women who experienced nonconsensual penetration made contact with a program or resource in 29.5 percent of incidents as compared with TGQN students (42.9% of incidents) and male students (17.8% of incidents).[155] When asked why the women did not seek help, 20.0 percent said they could handle it themselves, 16.8 percent didn't think it was serious enough to warrant getting help, and 15.9 percent felt embarrassment or shame or that it would be too emotionally difficult to get assistance.[156]

1.5 SUMMARY

These studies give us valuable information on the prevalence, nature, and reporting of campus sexual misconduct in the United States.

For those who doubt whether campus sexual assault is a serious problem, these studies convincingly show that it is. However, this discussion also highlights how these studies have been distorted by politicians and advocates. The CSA study (cited for the "1 in 5" figure) and the AAU Campus climate survey (cited for the "1 in 4" figure) both specifically state that they are not nationally representative. Indeed, the authors of the 2007 CSA study were so taken aback by the misuse of their study that they published an essay in *Time Magazine* to "set the record straight."[157] In it, they emphasized that the "1-in-5 statistic is *not* a nationally representative estimate of the prevalence of sexual assault." Similarly, the authors of the 2015 AAU Campus Climate Survey emphasized that their study was not nationally representative, and that there was a marked difference in reported victimization across the different IHEs. "Overall these comparisons illustrate that estimates such as '1 in 5' or '1 in 4' as a global rate, across all IHEs is at least oversimplistic, if not misleading."[158]

The only two studies that are nationally representative found much lower rates of victimization, however they included only force and not intoxication in their definition of unwanted sexual touching and penetration. The 2000 NCWSV found that 1.7 percent of the sample had experienced a completed rape, and 1.1 percent had experienced an attempted rape. That meant the victimization rate was 27.7 rapes or attempted rapes per 1,000 students. Their findings are equivalent to 1 in 36 college women. They cautioned however that the incidence rate only reflected a seven-month period and might climb much higher. The 2014 NCVS study found 6.1 per 1,000 postsecondary female students (or 1 of 132) were the victims of rape or sexual assault each year.

These studies also provide important information about the nature of campus rape and sexual assault. Among other things, they suggest who is at greater risk: non gender conforming individuals followed by women, younger students, bisexuals, disabled students, and certain racial and ethnic groups. They also provide overwhelming evidence that most sexual assaults are committed by someone the victim knows, and most victims do not report their rape or sexual assault to authorities, including the police.

Finally, these studies pose a foundational critique for how we describe the problem. Krebs et al. found that only 33 percent of rape incidents and 28 percent of sexual battery incidents took place on campus, and just 55 percent of the rape offenders and 56 percent of the sexual battery offenders were affiliated with the school. These findings suggest that almost half of all sexual assaults might not even merit being called *campus* sexual assault.

1.6 THE INADEQUATE RESPONSE FROM THE CRIMINAL JUSTICE SYSTEM

Sexual assault on campus continues to be a serious problem, albeit not to the levels commonly believed. Yet, the criminal justice system has not responded effectively. As I will explain, part of the reason for early inaction had to do with the definition of rape, but even with reforms, prosecution remains unlikely.

1.6.1 *The Early Definitional Hurdle*

For most of the history of this country, rape was defined as "the carnal knowledge of a female, forcibly and against her will."[59] Since "carnal knowledge" means, "the slightest penetration of the sexual organ of the female (vagina) by the sexual organ of the male (penis)," even the violent sodomy of a male student wouldn't count. This historic definition also eliminated other kinds of penetration, regardless of how brutally they were accomplished. Requiring the use of force, in turn, meant that it wasn't rape to have sex with a student who was passed out from drinking[160] or for a professor to copulate with a student after first threatening to fail her if she didn't comply. Nor was it rape to penetrate someone even after they repeatedly said, "no."

On top of that, proof of resistance was needed to show that force was used "over and above the coercion implicit in denying freedom of sexual choice"[161] *and* to prove that the penetration was against the woman's will.[162] It wasn't sufficient for a woman to say that she didn't want to have sex because "[a]lthough a woman may desire sexual intercourse, it is customary for her to say, 'no, no, no' (although meaning 'yes, yes, yes') and to expect the male to be the aggressor."[163] "Scars of struggle," as Susan Schwartz put it, "provided visible corroboration of a woman's word, which was suspect."[164] The resistance requirement meant that even if a fraternity brother confessed to holding a cheerleader down, it wouldn't be rape unless she could show that she was physically injured from trying to fight him off.

A prompt reporting requirement posed another hurdle. Just as it was supposedly the "natural instinct" of every woman to resist, so was it "so natural as to almost be inevitable that a female upon whom the crime has been committed will make immediate complaint thereof to her mother or other confidential friend."[165] Not doing so, the Utah Supreme wrote " ... tends to discredit her as a witness, and may raise an inference against the truth of the charge."[166] Although this section is now under revision, the Model Penal Code – an influential model statute drafted over a ten-year period by notable criminal law scholars, judges, and practitioners – has since its inception contained a prompt complaint rule that barred prosecution for a sexual offense if a competent adult failed to notify law enforcement within three months of the offense.[167] Some jurisdictions instituted a short statute of limitations for sexual assault cases; others allowed the judge to instruct the jurors that they should draw an inference against a complainant who did not quickly report.[168]

On top of all this, many states and the Model Penal Code required corroborating evidence. That meant a rape conviction could not be sustained on the word of the victim alone; there had to be extrinsic corroborating evidence. The justification for the corroboration requirement, as explained in a 1970 article in the *University of Pennsylvania Law Review*, was the special danger posed in rape cases:

> The incidence of false accusations and the potential for unjust convictions are perhaps greatest with sexual offenses. Women often falsely accuse men of

sexual attacks to extort money, to force marriage, to satisfy a childish desire for notoriety, or to attain personal revenge. Their motives include hatred, a sense of shame after consenting to illicit intercourse, especially when pregnancy results, and delusion.[169]

The corroboration requirement meant that no matter how compelling and believable a victim might be, nothing could happen without additional evidence, which was unlikely to be available given the fact that most campus assault happens behind closed doors, with no one else present.

Even if a campus assault met all of these requirements, proving it in a court of law would still be difficult. Jurors were often given so-called cautionary instructions based on Lord Hale's seventeenth-century warning that rape "is an accusation easily to be made and hard to be proved, and harder to be defended by the party accused, tho never so innocent."[170] They were told that there had to be corroborating evidence, or independent evidence to prove that she was telling the truth. In addition to all of that, a woman's sexual history and manner of dress were all admissible to discredit her.

And that's assuming the woman reported at all. A 1980 report on sexual harassment of students from the National Advisory Council on Women's Educational Programs explained why students didn't report even extreme abuse. The fear that drove them not to report is the same fear that induced them to submit or at least not actively resist. Under the law at the time, they were then deemed to have consented:

> For the most part, (sexual crimes and misdemeanors) go unreported, even when they are extreme – such as forced sexual intercourse – because of the student-victim's fear of the consequences of reporting the incidents to <u>any</u> authority. That fear often introduces a form of consent into the acts, to the extent that the students do not resist strenuously and often continue their association with the perpetrator despite stress, anxiety or fear. This frequently robs the acts, especially those involving force, of their criminality. Consent is an absolute defense against charges of rape, for example, and cooperation of any type (including passive resistance) is likely to be construed as "consent" in the absence of physical danger. Although the perpetrator involved may have the power to destroy the student's academic career – and thus dramatically change the course of the student's life – such acts are not likely to be viewed as presenting "physical" danger, but only "psychological coercion," which is generally considered an insufficient form of force to establish rape.

1.7 RAPE REFORM

In response to widespread criticism, starting in the mid-1970s, significant reforms were made to rape law at both the state and federal level.[171] Redefining rape was one notable change. Not only was there an expansion in who could be raped to include men and wives by their husbands, but rape became easier to prove as a matter of law. The proof of resistance requirement was repealed after advocates showed that resistance could put a victim in greater danger, and the corroboration requirement has been almost entirely removed as well.[172] (Texas stands out for still requiring corroborating evidence if a rape was not reported within a year.[173]) In most states, the prompt complaint mandate has been removed.[174] Rape was also extended to include penetration achieved by means other than force, such as by fraud or intoxication.

There were also efforts to make the adjudicatory process less traumatic. Rape shield laws were enacted to exclude evidence of the victim's clothing and prior sexual history unless the judge ruled that it was relevant to a particular case. Most states abolished cautionary jury instructions that had explicitly cast doubt on the veracity of the victim's testimony.[175] Attention was also directed to making police more responsive and empathetic to victims.

These changes have achieved some success, but not to the degree reformers had hoped. In particular, they haven't had much of an impact on prosecuting the kind of rape taking place on campus. Clay-Warner and Burt found that rapes committed after 1989 were more likely to be reported than those committed before 1975, but aggravated rape is still more likely to be reported as compared with simple rape despite the fact that both are deemed serious crimes post reform.[176] An aggravated rape has extrinsic violence (use of a weapon or infliction of injury), multiple assailants, or no prior relationship between the victim and the defendant.[177] A simple rape has none of these elements.

1.7.1 *Impact of These Reforms on Campus Sexual Assault*

The first big hurdle for prosecution of campus rape cases, even after reform, is the low level of reporting. The studies discussed earlier convincingly show that the vast majority of campus rape and sexual assault victims do not report what happened to the police. Not reporting makes prosecution almost impossible. The police are gatekeepers to the criminal justice system in the United States. It is their responsibility to investigate crimes, make arrests, and recommend cases for prosecution. If the police don't know about a crime, there is almost no pathway to prosecution.

Even if a student reports a sexual assault to the police, and even if the event constitutes a crime, it was and still is unlikely to go very far. That's because the average campus assault doesn't meet the common conception of a rape.

The image of a rapist remains a stranger lurking in the bushes; it's not an All-American track star or a friend down the hall. Controlling for where there was an identified suspect, Tasca et al. found that cases where the victim was assaulted by a stranger were 9.123 times more likely to result in an arrest as compared with cases where the victim was assaulted by an acquaintance or relative.[178] Frazier and Haney found that in cases where there was an identified suspect, police were more likely to refer a stranger case for prosecution as opposed to an acquaintance rape.[179] That finding is consistent with a 2008 study by Felson and Pare in which victims of sexual assault were more likely to complain about their interaction with the police when the offender was someone they knew.[180] In those cases, the victims reported that the police showed too much leniency, expressed disbelief or skepticism, and treated them with insensitivity.

If alcohol and/or drugs are involved, as they often are on campus, that creates even more of a hurdle. In 1951, the influential former Magistrate and criminal law expert Morris Ploscowe wrote, "When a woman drinks with a man to the point of intoxication, she practically invites him to take advantage of her person. She should not be permitted to yell when she is sober, 'I was raped!'"[181] Although that statement was made seventy years ago, recent studies show that police officers blame the woman for having consumed alcohol or drugs instead of the man for taking advantage of a person who was under the influence. Spohn et al. found that detectives were three times more likely to unfound a reported crime (classify it as false or baseless) if there were questions about the victim's character or reputation, which included information such as the victim having a pattern of drug or alcohol abuse.[182] Jordan found that in 33 percent of the cases that the police said were false, they identified the fact that the person was drunk or stoned as a factor in their analysis.[183] This is a striking finding since studies show that people are more likely to be raped when they are under the influence,[184] and laws across the country either specifically state that intoxication vitiates consent to sex or allow proof of intoxication to show the person was raped due to being "mentally incapacitated" or "physically helpless."[185]

Most campus rapes take place while one or both of the people are intoxicated,[186] and yet many people think that being intoxicated undermines a person's victimhood. For example, a study from the early 1980s found that an offender was deemed less responsible when he had been drinking, whereas a victim was deemed more responsible for the rape when she was drunk. She was also liked less and seen as being more immoral and more aggressive.[187] A later study found similar results. Subjects were asked questions about the responsibility of women drinking cola vs. alcohol in a sexual encounter. Researchers found that as compared with the woman drinking cola, the one drinking alcohol was rated as "more aggressive and impaired, less socially skillful, and more sexually predisposed." She was seen as "more sexually available, and as more likely to engage in foreplay behaviors and intercourse than the cola drinking woman."[188] Almost ten years later, the same double standard persisted. A 1997 study found rape victims were seen as more responsible for being drunk, and they found a perpetrator less responsible if he was drunk.[189]

But it's not just alcohol or drugs that pose a problem for victim credibility. That same 1997 study found that subjects were more likely to discount a woman's later resistance if she had agreed to let the perpetrator drive her home and/or invited him into her apartment.[190] What a victim was wearing also makes a difference. Studies show that people were more likely to blame the victim in an acquaintance rape situation if she was wearing a short skirt as opposed to a longer one.[191] One study found that a difference of three inches in skirt length affected whether the victim was deemed responsible.[192] All of this makes it very difficult to successfully prosecute the lion's share of campus sexual misconduct.

1.8 CONCLUSION

For many years, the unconsented sex happening on campus was not a crime. Even with a change in the definition of rape and a removal of other barriers to conviction, the criminal justice system has still proven inadequate at addressing the problem. Something else was needed. That something else is Title IX. The next chapter describes how a law aimed at addressing inequality in education became used as a vehicle for addressing campus sexual assault.

APPENDIX 1.A: *Comparison of Studies on Campus Sexual Assault*

Study	Year	Type	Definition of Rape	Incidence and prevalence	Special findings
Kirkpatrick and Kanin	1957	Questionnaire to women in 22 varied university classes (291 respondents) Not nationally representative	Forceful attempt at intercourse Aggressively forceful attempts at sex intercourse in the course of which menacing threats or coercive infliction of physical pain employed	55.7% reported being offended by attempt at erotic intimacy during academic year 20.9% offended by forceful attempts at intercourse during academic year 6.2% offended by aggressively forceful attempts at intercourse during academic year	No women who experienced attempted intercourse or attempted intercourse with violence reported to authorities Mean age of the offended girls was younger than that of the nonoffended, (18.8 vs. 19.0)
Kanin and Parcell	1977	Questionnaire to women at large midwestern university (282 respondents) Not nationally representative	Aggressively expended male effort at sexual intercourse Male effort at sexual intercourse where menacing threats or physical pain were employed	23.8% of the offended women experienced aggressive intercourse 2.7% experienced intercourse with menacing or physical pain	69.2% reported experiencing male sexual aggression since entering college Majority of sexually aggressive episodes reported for casual pairings; the rest were more durable pairings.

Study	Year	Sample	Definition	Findings	Outcomes
Koss et. al study	1987	Nationally representative sample of 6,159 male and female students enrolled in 32 institutions representative of diversity of higher education settings across U.S. National level study	Vaginal intercourse between male and female, and anal intercourse, fellatio, and cunnilingus between persons regardless of sex if accomplished through force or threat of force or the administration of any drug or other intoxicant, which substantially impairs the other person's judgment or control, for the purpose of preventing resistance	15.4% of females experienced rape (12.1% attempted rape) since age 14. 83 per 1,000 females experienced rape or attempted over prior six-month period	5% reported rape to the police. 27% perceived it was rape. Average age of female victim 18.5. 84% of perpetrators were acquaintances, and 57% were dating partners. One man who committed legal rape viewed it as such. 84% did not. 47% expected to engage in a similar act in the future
National College Women Sexual Victimization Study (NCWSV)	2000	National sample of 4,446 women enrolled in 2 or 4 year college. 85.6% response rate. Nationally representative	Unwanted completed penetration by force or threat of force. Penetration includes penile-vaginal, mouth on your genitals, mouth on someone else's genitals,	1.7% experienced completed rape over seven-month period. 1.1% experienced attempted rape over seven-month period. 27.7 rapes or attempted rapes per 1,000	Less than 5% of completed and attempted rapes reported to police. 66.3% of completed rapes and 54.9% of attempted rapes happened off campus

Study	Year	Type	Definition of Rape	Incidence and prevalence	Special findings
			penile-anal, digital-vaginal, digital anal, object-vaginal, and object-anal.	students, 1 in 36 women over seven-month period	96% of completed rapes and 91.9% of attempted rapes were perpetrated by offenders known to victim
Campus Sexual Assault (2007)	2007	Anonymous web-based survey to under-graduate students at two large, public universities (5,446 women) 42% response rate Not nationally representative	Oral, vaginal, anal, or object penetration through force or victim incapacitation	3.4% of respondents experienced rape through physical force; 8.5% experienced rape through intoxication since entering college	2% of those who experienced intoxicated sexual assault and 13% of those who experienced forced sexual assault reported to law enforcement Sophomores had the highest "past 12 month" prevalence estimates of sexual assault Most victims assaulted by someone they knew
National Crime Victimization Survey	2014	Data gathered as part of a large national study conducted by the	Unlawful penetration of a person against the will of the victim,	6.1 per 1,000 female post-secondary students victims of rape or	33% of nonstudents reported to the police

32

		Department of the Census on nonfatal crimes reported and not reported to the police against persons age 12 or older 88% response rate Nationally representative	with use or threatened use of force, or attempting such an act Rape includes psychological coercion and physical force, and forced sexual intercourse means vaginal, anal, or oral penetration by the offender Rape also includes incidents where penetration is from a foreign object . . . against males and females, and both heterosexual and homosexual rape	sexual assault between 1997 and 2013.	20% of students reported to the police Did not find a significant difference in the rate of victimization by age for female college students
AAU Campus Climate Survey	2015 (revised 2017)	Twenty-seven Institutes of Higher Education (IHEs) participated in the first survey.	Nonconsensual penetration by physical force, threats of physical force, or incapacitation	11.3% of senior females, 2.5% of senior men, and 12.6% of TGQN reported being a victim of	25.5% of students who experienced forcible penetration and 13.3% of students who experienced rape by

Study	Year	Type	Definition of Rape	Incidence and prevalence	Special findings
		150,072 students participated 19.3% response rate Not nationally representative		nonconsensual penetration involving physical force or incapacitation while in college	intoxication reported to authority 16.9% of freshmen females reported sexual contact by physical force or incapacitation, which declined steadily by year to a low of 11.1% of seniors
CCSVS	2016	Nine schools, 23,000 undergraduates 54% female response rate 40% male response rate Not nationally representative	Any unwanted and nonconsensual penetrative act, including oral sex, anal sex, sexual intercourse, or sexual penetration with a finger or object	Average of 4.1% of undergraduate females and 0.8% of undergraduate males across the nine IHEs experienced rape in the 2014–2015 academic year	Average of 12.5% of rapes were reported to any official across the nine IHEs Average of 4.2% of rapes reported to law enforcement Only 9% of rapes were perpetrated by strangers 33% of rapes and 28% of sexual batteries took place on campus 55% of rape and 56% of sexual battery offenders were affiliated with the school

| AAU Campus Climate Survey | 2019 (revised 2020) | 33 schools, 181,752 students
21.9% response rate
17.5% male response rate
26.1% female response rate
Not nationally representative | Same as from 2015 study | 18% of senior females, 4.2% of senior men, and 14.9% of senior TGQN reported being a victim of nonconsensual penetration involving physical force or incapacitation while in college | 29.5% of women who experienced nonconsensual penetration reported to a program or resource.
42.9% of TGQN students reported 17.8% of male students reported
Younger students were more likely to experience nonconsensual sexual contact |

NOTES

1. Rape, BLACK'S LAW DICTIONARY (6th ed., 2009); Vivian Berger, *Man's Trial, Woman's Tribulation: Rape Cases in the Courtroom*, 77 COLUMBIA L.R. 1, 1–103 (1977).
2. *See* Tamara Rice Lave, *The Prosecutor's Duty to Imperfect Rape Victims*, 49 TEX. TECH. L. REV. 219 (2016); TAMARA RICE LAVE, *Police Sexual Violence*, in THE CAMBRIDGE HANDBOOK ON POLICING IN THE UNITED STATES 392 (Tamara Rice Lave & Eric J. Miller, eds., 2019).
3. 42 U.S.C. § 14012 (1994); 103 H.R. 4092 § 1610 (a).
4. Before 1970, there were seventy results on campus and rape, but none of these pertained to rape on campus. There were also fifty-four articles about school rape, but none pertained to rape at schools. From 1971 to 1980 there were ten articles on campus rape, but none about rape on campus. In the same time period, there were sixty-five articles on school rape, but none were about rape in schools. Lexis search conducted on February 26, 2021.
5. Clifford Kirkpatrick & Eugene Kanin, *Male Sex Aggression on a University Campus*, 22 AMERICAN SOCIO. REV. 52, 53 (1957).
6. *Id.*
7. *Id.*
8. *Id.*
9. *Id.*
10. *Id.*
11. *Id.* at 56.
12. Eugene J. Kanin & Stanley R. Parcell *Sexual Aggression: A Second Look at the Offended Female*, 6 ARCHIVES OF SEXUAL BEHAVIOR, 67, 68 (1977).
13. *Id.* at 68.
14. *Id.* at 75.
15. *Id.* at 69.
16. *Id.* at 69.
17. *Id.* at 73.
18. *Id.*
19. *Id.*
20. *Id.* at 70.
21. Julie K. Ehrhart & Bernice R. Sandler, *Campus Gang Rape: Party Games?* Ass'n of American Colleges, Project on the Status and Education of Women (1985), https://files.eric.ed.gov/fulltext/ED267667.pdf.
22. Patricia Yancey Martin & Robert A. Hummer, *Fraternities and Rape on Campus*, 3 GENDER & SOCIETY SPECIAL ISSUE: VIOLENCE AGAINST WOMEN 457, 457–473 (1989).

23. Laurie Neff, *Acquaintance Rape on Campus: The Problem, the Victims, and Prevention*, NASPA JOURNAL (1988), www.tandfonline.com/doi/abs/10.1080/00220973.1988.11072044?journalCode=uarp19.

24. Mary P. Koss, Christine A. Gidycz, & Nadine Wisniewski, *The Scope of Rape: Incidence and Prevalence of Sexual Aggression and Victimization in a National Sample of Students in Higher Education*, 55(2) JOURNAL OF CONSULTING AND CLINICAL PSYCH., 162, 164 (1987). "Because of the assumptions on which the sampling plan was based and the institutional hesitancy to participate, the sample was not absolutely representative. However, within the limitations of our assumptions, it was a close approximation of the higher education enrollment" (p. 164).

25. Koss, Gidycz, & Wisniewski, *supra* note 24, at 166. The 1980 Ohio definition of rape is broader than the FBI's at the time: carnal knowledge of a female, forcibly and against her will. The FBI definition remained the same until 2013 when it became, "Penetration, no matter how slight, of the vagina or anus with any body part or object, or oral penetration by a sex organ of another person, without the consent of the victim." *Frequently Asked Questions about the Change in the UCR Definition of Rape*, FBI (2014), https://ucr.fbi.gov/recent-program-updates/new-rape-definition-frequently-asked-questions.

26. Mary P. Koss et al., *Revising the SES: A Collaborative Process to Improve Assessment of Sexual Aggression and Victimization*, 31 PSYCHOLOGY OF WOMEN QUARTERLY, 357, 358 (2007).

27. *Id.* at 358.

28. Koss, Gidycz, & Wisniewski, *supra* note 24, at 163.

29. *Id.* at 166.

30. *Id.* at 166.

31. *Id.* at 168.

32. *Id.* at 168.

33. Mary P. Koss et al., *Hidden Rape: Incidence and Prevalence of Sexual Aggression and Victimization in a National Sample of Students in Higher Education*, NAT. INSTITUTE OF MENTAL HEALTH (Aug. 1985), https://files.eric.ed.gov/fulltext/ED267321.pdf.

34. *Id.* at 19.

35. *Id.* at 19.

36. *Id.* at 19.

37. *Id.* at 19.

38. *Id.* at 19.

39. *Id.* at 19.

40. 20 U.S.C. § 1092 (1992).

41. 20 U.S.C. § 1092 (1998).

42. Bonnie S. Fisher, Francis T. Cullen, & Michael G. Turner, *The Sexual Victimization of College Women*, U.S. DEP'T. OF JUST. (2000), www .ojp.gov/pdffiles1/nij/182369.pdf.

43. *Id.* at 1.

44. *Id.* at 3.

45. *Id.* at 7.

46. *Id.* at 4.

47. *Id.* at 8.

48. *Id.* at 10.

49. *Id.* at 10.

50. *Id.* at 10.

51. They assume that many students now go to college for five years, which equals sixty months. They then take their seven-month estimate of 1/36 and multiply it by the number of months they are estimating (60) divided by the number of months they have already estimated (7). That equals 1/36 x 60/7 = 0.238 or 24%.

52. *See* Kirkpatrick & Kanin, *supra* note 4 (1957); Kanin & Parcell *supra* note 12 (1977); Koss, Gidycz, & Wisniewski, *supra* note 24; CHRISTOPHER P. KREBS ET AL., THE CAMPUS SEXUAL ASSAULT (CSA) STUDY, FINAL REPORT TO THE NATIONAL INSTITUTE OF JUSTICE, NAT. INSTITUTE OF JUST. (2007), www.ojp.gov/pdffiles1/nij/grants/221153.pdf /; DAVID CANTOR ET AL., REPORT ON THE AAU CAMPUS CLIMATE SURVEY ON SEXUAL ASSAULT AND SEXUAL MISCONDUCT, ASSOC. OF AMERICAN UNIVERSITIES (Sept. 21, 2015) (revised 2017), www.aau.edu /sites/default/files/%40%20Files/Climate%20Survey/AAU_Campus_Cli mate_Survey_12_14_15.pdf; DAVID CANTOR ET AL., REPORT ON THE AAU CAMPUS CLIMATE SURVEY ON SEXUAL ASSAULT AND SEXUAL MISCONDUCT THE UNIVERSITY OF NORTH CAROLINA CHAPEL HILL, ASSOC. OF AMERICAN UNIVERSITIES (Sept. 16, 2019), https://s afe.unc.edu/wp-content/uploads/sites/1110/2020/06/University-of-North-Carolina-at-Chapel-Hill_Report-and-Appendices-.pdf/.

53. Fisher, Cullen, & Turner, *supra* note 42, at 20.

54. *Id.* at 17–19.

55. *Id.* at 23. When asked why, 65.4% of victims of completed rape and 76.5% of victims of attempted rape said that they didn't think it was serious enough to report. Other reasons given were fear of reprisal by assailant and others (39.5% and 25%); fear of being treated hostilely by police (24.7% and 8.8%); police wouldn't think it was serious enough (27.2% and 33.8%); lack of proof that it happened (42% and 30.9%), and not wanting family (44.4% and 32.4%) or other people (46.9% and 32.4%) to know.

56. *Id.* at 23.

57. Sofi Sinozich & Lynn Langton, *Victimization Among College-Age Females*, 1995–2013, U.S. DEP'T. OF JUST. (Dec. 2014), www.bjs.gov/content/pub/pdf/rsavcaf9513.pdf/.

58. *Id.* at 11. "Rape is the unlawful penetration of a person against the will of the victim, with use or threatened use of force, or attempting such an act. Rape includes psychological coercion and physical force, and forced sexual intercourse means vaginal, anal, or oral penetration by the offender. Rape also includes incidents where penetration is from a foreign object … against males and females, and both heterosexual and homosexual rape. Attempted rape includes verbal threats of rape."

59. Nonresponse bias means "that those who participated in the survey may differ in important ways from those who did not participate, which could in turn impact the survey findings." *Id.* at 16.

60. *Id.* at 1.

61. *Id.* at 4.

62. *Id.* at 7.

63. *Id.* at 10.

64. *Id.* at 10.

65. *Id.* at 1.

66. *Id.* at 9.

67. *Id.* at 9.

68. *Id.* at 5.

69. *Id.* at 5.

70. Letter from Russlyn Ali, Assistant Sec'y for Civil Rights, Office for Civil Rights, U.S. Dep't. of Educ., to Title IX Coordinators 2 (Apr. 4, 2011), www2.ed.gov/about/offices/list/ocr/letters/colleague-201104.pdf.

71. CHRISTOPHER P. KREBS ET AL., THE CAMPUS SEXUAL ASSAULT (CSA) STUDY, FINAL REPORT TO THE NATIONAL INSTITUTE OF JUSTICE, NAT. INSTITUTE OF JUST. vii (2007), www.ojp.gov/pdffiles1/nij/grants/221153.pdf/.

72. *Id.* They also collected exploratory data on 1,375 males. *Id.* at x.

73. *Id.* at x.

74. Christopher Krebs & Christine Lindquist, *Setting the Record Straight on "1 in 5*,*"* TIME MAGAZINE (Dec. 15, 2014), https://time.com/3633903/campus-rape-1-in-5-sexual-assault-setting-record-straight/.

75. *Id.* at See Krebs et al. *supra* note 71 at 1–3–1–4 (2007). "Unwanted sexual contact occurring when a victim is unable to provide consent or stop what is happening because she is passed out, drugged, drunk, incapacitated, or asleep, regardless of whether the perpetrator was responsible for her substance use or whether substances were administered without her knowledge." *Id.* at ix.

76. *Id.* at 1–2.

77. *Id.* at 5–3.

78. *Id.* at 5–2.

79. *Id.* at 5–29.

80. *Id.* at 5–10.

81. *Id.* at 5–5.

82. *Id.* at 5–5.

83. *Id.* at 5–12.

84. *Id.* at 5–7.

85. Id. at 5–15. Just 23.3% of forced sexual assault and 11.5% of incapacitated sexual assault was perpetrated by someone the victim had never seen/talked to. 3.1% of forced sexual assault and 7.5% of incapacitated sexual assault was perpetrated by someone the victim had seen but not spoken with. The remaining assailants ranged from acquaintances (27.9% of forced sexual assault, 33.9% of incapacitated sexual assault) to a dating partner/spouse (17.8% forced sexual assault and 18.3% incapacitated sexual assault). *Id.* at 5–15.

86. *Id.* at 5–22.

87. *Id.* at 5–24.

88. *Id.* at 5–27. 0.6% of perpetrators of forced sexual assault and 0.8% of perpetrators of incapacitated sexual assault received disciplinary action from the university. 5.7% of perpetrators of forced sexual assault and 0.4% of perpetrators of incapacitated sexual assault were arrested, prosecuted, or convicted by the criminal justice system. *Id.* at 5–27.

89. *Id.* at 5–24.

90. David Cantor et al., Report on the AAU Campus Climate Survey on Sexual Assault and Sexual Misconduct, Assoc. of American Universities (Sept. 21, 2015) (revised 2017), www.aau.edu /sites/default/files/%40%20Files/Climate%20Survey/AAU_Campus_Cli mate_Survey_12_14_15.pdf/.

91. *See* Richard Pérez-Peña, *1 in 4 Women Experience Sex Assault on Campus*, N.Y. Times (Sept. 21, 2015), www.nytimes.com/2015/09/22/us/a-third-of-co llege-women-experience-unwanted-sexual-contact-study-finds.html; Teresa Watanabe, *One in Four Female Undergraduates Reports Sexual Misconduct, Survey Finds*, L.A. Times (Sept. 21, 2015 8:35 PM), www .latimes.com/local/lanow/la-me-ln-sexual-assault-survey-20150920-story.html; Michelle Gorman, *1 in 4 Women Experienced Sexual Assault While in College, Survey Finds*, Newsweek (Sept. 21, 2015 4:26 PM), www .newsweek.com/1-4-women-sexual-assault-college-374793.

92. Cantor et al., *supra* note 90, at iii–iv.

93. *Id.* at iii.

94. *Id.* at iii.

95. *Id.* at vi.

96. *Id.* at vi–vii.

97. *Id.* at viii. "Kissing, touching someone's breast, chest, crotch, groin, or buttocks; grabbing, groping, or rubbing against the other in a sexual way, even if the touching is over the other's clothes." *Id.* at viii.
98. *Id.* at viii. "When one person puts a penis, finger, or object inside someone else's vagina or anus; when someone's mouth or tongue makes contact with someone else's genitals."
99. *Id.* at viii. Physical force was defined as when someone was "holding you down with his or her body weight, pinning your arms, hitting or kicking you or using or threatening to use a weapon against you."
100. *Id.* at viii. Incapacitation was defined as a student being, "unable to consent or stop what was happening because you were passed out, asleep or incapacitated due to drugs or alcohol."
101. *Id.* at vii.
102. *Id.* at Table 3–20.
103. *Id.* at Table 3–20.
104. *Id.* at Table 3–20.
105. *Id.* at Table 3–20.
106. *Id.* at x.
107. *Id.* at xv.
108. *Id.* at 102.
109. *Id.* at 102.
110. *Id.* at 102.
111. *Id.* at 102.
112. *Id.* at ix.
113. *Id.* at Table 6–1.
114. *Id.* at Table 6–1.
115. Christopher Krebs et al., Campus Climate Survey Validation Study Final Technical Report, Bureau of Justice Statistics Research and Development Series (2016), www.ojp.gov/pdffiles1/bjs/grants/249545.pdf/, at xiii.
116. *Id.* at ES-2.
117. *Id.* at ES-3.
118. *Id.* at ES-3.
119. *Id.* at ES-5.
120. *Id.* at ES-5.
121. The number of unique victims who experienced one or more victimization during reference period.
122. *Id.* at ES-6.
123. *Id.* at ES-4 "Any unwanted and nonconsensual sexual contact that involved forced touching of a sexual nature, not involving penetration."
124. *Id.* at ES-6.

125. *Id.* at ES-4. "Any unwanted and nonconsensual penetrative act, including oral sex, anal sex, sexual intercourse, or sexual penetration with a finger or object."
126. *Id.* at ES-6.
127. *Id.* at 72–73.
128. *Id.* at 77.
129. *Id.* at 77.
130. *Id.* at 78.
131. *Id.* at 71.
132. *Id.* at 71.
133. *Id.* at 93.
134. *Id.* at 93.
135. *Id.* at 105–106.
136. *Id.* at 103.
137. *Id.* at 102–103.
138. *Id.* at 107.
139. *Id.* at 107.
140. *Id.* at 109.
141. *Id.* at 104.
142. *Campus Sexual Violence: Statistics*, RAINN, www.rainn.org/statistics/campus-sexual-violence/.
143. David Cantor et al., Report on the AAU Campus Climate Survey on Sexual Assault and Sexual Misconduct, Assoc. of American Universities (revised 2020), www.aau.edu/sites/default/files/AAU-Files/Key-Issues/Campus-Safety/Revised%20Aggregate%20report%20%20and%20appendices%201-7_(01–16–2020_FINAL).pdf/.
144. *Id.* at vii.
145. *Id.* at 5.
146. *Id.* at xi.
147. *Id.* at xi.
148. *Id.* at Table 14, page A7-14.
149. *Id.* at Table 15, page A7-15.
150. *Id.* at Table 15, page A7-15.
151. *Id.* at xi.
152. *Id.* at xi.
153. *See* Table 23, page A7-36.
154. *Id.* at xiii. 16.1% of freshman reported sexual contact by force or incapacitation, as compared with 11.3% of seniors.
155. *Id.* at xiii.
156. *Id.* at xiii.
157. *See* Krebs & Lindquist, *supra* note 74.
158. *Id.*

159. Black's Law Dictionary, *supra* note 1 (6th ed. 1990); Berger, *supra* note 1 (1977).
160. The Ohio definition that Koss et al. used in their 1987 study, for example, did not include voluntary intoxication.
161. *Id.* at 8.
162. I. Bennett Capers, *Real Women, Real Rape*, 60 Univ. of Cal. Los Angeles Law Rev. 826, 826–882 (2013).
163. Roger B. Dworkin, *The Resistance Standard in Rape Legislation*, 18 Stanford Law Rev. 680, 682 (1966).
164. Susan Schwartz, *An Argument for the Elimination of the Resistance Requirement from the Definition of Forcible Rape.* 16 Loy. Los Angeles Law Rev. 567, 570 (1983).
165. Baccio v. People, 41 N.Y. 265, 268 (1869).
166. State v. Neel, 21 Utah 151, 155–156 (1900).
167. Deborah W. Denno, *Why the Model Penal Code's Sexual Offense Provisions Should Be Pulled and Replaced*, 1 Ohio State J. Crim. Law 207, 214–215 (2003) (internal citations omitted).
168. *See* Kathryn M. Stanchi, *The Paradox of the Fresh Complaint Rule*, 37 B.C.L. Rev. 441–447 (1996), at 446.
169. *The Corroboration Rule and Crimes Accompanying a Rape*, 118 U. Penn. L. Rev. 458, 458–471 (1970), at 460.
170. Matthew Hale, *The History of the Pleas of the Crown*, 44 Fordham Urban L.J. 419, 410–430 (1976), https://ir.lawnet.fordham.edu/cgi/viewcontent.cgi?article=1477&context=ulj/.
171. *See generally* Jody Clay-Warner & Callie Harbin Burt, *Rape Reporting after Reforms: Have Times Really Changed?* 11 Violence against Women 150, 150–154 (2005); Stephen J. Schulhofer, *Reforming the Law of Rape*, 35 Law & Ineq. 335, 335–351 (2017).
172. Richard Klein, *An Analysis of Thirty-Five Years of Rape Reform: A Frustrating Search for Fundamental Fairness*, Akron Law Rev. 41 (4), 981, 981–1057 (2008).
173. Article 38.07 of the Texas Code of Criminal Procedure requires the victim to have informed any person of the sexual assault within one year of the date on which the offense is alleged to have occurred unless the victim was 17 or younger, 65 or older, 18 or older "who by reason of age or physical or mental disease, defect, or injury was substantially unable to satisfy the person's need for food, shelter, medical care, or protection from harm."
174. Michelle J. Anderson, *The Legacy of the Prompt Complaint Requirement, Corroboration Requirement, and Cautionary Instructions on Campus Sexual Assault*, 84 B.U.L. Rev. 945, 949 (2004). According to Anderson, by 2004, only California, Illinois, and South Carolina

continued to require prompt complaint and then only in cases of spousal sexual offenses.

175. A. Thomas Morris, *The Empirical, Historical and Legal Case against the Cautionary Instruction: A Call for Legislative Reform*, Duke L.J., 154, 154–155 (1988).

176. *See* Clay-Warner & Burt, *supra* note 171, at 167. See also Janice Du Mont, Karen-Lee Miller, & Terri L. Myhr, *The Role of "Real Rape" and "Real Victim" Stereotypes in the Police Reporting Practices of Sexually Assaulted Women*, 9 Violence against Women 466, 478–480 (2003) (finding that victims were more likely to report if their rape had elements of "real rape," specifically occurrence of physical injuries and use of physical force). *See also* Yingyu Chen & Sarah Ullman, *Women's Reporting of Sexual and Physical Assaults to Police in the National Violence against Women Survey*, 16 Violence against Women 262, 275 (2010) (finding that rape victims are still more likely to report incidents constituting stereotypical or "real rapes").

177. Clay-Warner & Burt, *supra* note 171, at 151 (internal citations omitted).

178. Melinda Tasca et al., *Police Decision Making in Sexual Assault Cases: Predictors of Suspect Identification and Arrest*, 28 Journal of Interpersonal Violence 1157, 1157–1177 (2012), at 1167.

179. Patrick A. Frazier & Beth Haney, *Sexual Assault Cases in the Legal System: Police, Prosecutor, and Victim Perspectives*, 20 Law and Human Behavior 607, 617–618 (1996).

180. Richard B. Felson & Paul-Philippe Pare, *Gender and the Victim's Experience with the Criminal Justice System* 37 Social Science Research 202, 202–219 (2008), at 214.

181. Morris Ploscowe, Sex and the Law, 164 (Ace Star Books, 1962) (Prentice-Hall, 1951).

182. Cassiah Spohn, Clair White, & Katherine Tellis, *Unfounding Sexual Assault: Examining the Decision to Unfound and Identifying False Reports*, 48 Law & Society Review, 161, 180 (2014).

183. Jan Jordan, *Beyond Belief: Police, Rape and Women's Credibility* 4 Criminal Justice 29, 36 (2004).

184. Meichun Mohler-Kuo et al., *Correlates of Rape While Intoxicated in a National Sample of College Women*, 9 J. of Stud. on Alcohol 37, 37–38 (2004) (discussing that one issue colleges should address is intoxication).

185. Teresa P. Scalzo, *Prosecuting Alcohol-Facilitated Sexual Assault*, American Prosecutors Research Institute, August 1, 7 (2007) (internal citations omitted).

186. Meichun Mohler-Kuo et al., *supra* note 184, at 37–38 (discussing that one issue colleges should address is intoxication).

187. Deborah Richardson & Jennifer L. Campbell, *Alcohol and Rape: The Effect of Alcohol on Attributions of Blame for Rape*, 8 PERSONALITY AND SOCIAL PSYCH. BULLETIN 468, 474 (1982).

188. William H. George, Susan J. Gournic, & Mary P. McAfee, *Perceptions of Postdrinking Female Sexuality: Effects of Gender, Beverage Choice, and Drink Payment*, 18 J. OF APPLIED SOCIAL PSYCH. 1295, 1309–1310 (1988).

189. Karla J. Stormo & Alan R. Lang, *Attributions about Acquaintance Rape: The Role of Alcohol and Individual Differences*, 27 J. OF APPLIED SOCIAL PSYCH. 279, 298–299 (1997).

190. *Id.* at 300–301.

191. *See* Jane E. Workman & Elizabeth W. Freeburg, *An Examination of Date Rape, Victim Dress, and Perceiver Variables within the Context of Attribution Theory*, 41 SEX ROLES 261, 272 (1999); *see also* Linda Cassidy & Rose Marie Hurrell, *The Influence of Victim's Attire on Adolescents' Judgment of Date Rape*, 30 ADOLESCENCE 319, 319–323 (1995).

192. Jane E. Workman & Robin L. Orr, *Clothing, Sex of Subject, and Rape Myth Acceptance as Factors Affecting Attributions About an Incident of Acquaintance Rape*, 14 CLOTHING & TEXTILE RES. J. 276 (1996).

2

The Fix?

No person in the United States shall, on the basis of sex, be excluded from participation in, be denied the benefits of, or be subjected to discrimination under any education program or activity receiving financial assistance.

The year 1964 marked a watershed moment for equality in the United States. On July 2, President Lyndon B. Johnson signed the 1964 Civil Rights Act into law. Although much of the Act was aimed at preventing discrimination on the basis of race, color, religion, or national origin, Title VII – which banned workplace discrimination – specifically included sex as a protected class. Eight years later, Congress extended the protection against sex discrimination to the classroom with Title IX. Enacted as part of the Educational Amendments of 1972, Title IX barred sex discrimination in any education program or activity receiving federal financial assistance.

There were notable exceptions to Title IX, however. It did not apply to the admissions policies of "any public institution of undergraduate higher education ... that traditionally and continually from its establishment has had a policy of admitting only students of one sex,"[1] religious schools where application of Title IX would be inconsistent with their religious beliefs, and military institutions. In 1974, the law was amended to exempt sororities, fraternities, and youth service organizations like the Boy Scouts.

Enactment of Title IX was momentous, but it was just a first step. It was now up to administrative agencies and courts to determine the contours of the law. Although Title IX was ostensibly about academics, the focus soon shifted to the law's impact on sports.[2] The controversy centered on how to make women's and men's sports equal. "Until the Obama administration launched its sexual harassment initiative in 2011," R. Shep Melnick writes, "no Title IX issue received nearly as much attention as college sports."[3] Indeed, it took almost ten years after the passage of Title IX for either the Department of

Education (DOE) or any federal court to formally recognize that Title IX covered sexual harassment, which included sexual assault. It would be another eighteen before the DOE issued any formal rules for how schools should handle sexual harassment.

This chapter describes how Title IX was expanded to include sexual harassment. I begin by moving in chronological order through actions by the DOE and the courts. I then turn to peer misconduct and explain why it was so difficult for advocates and institutions to even conceptualize this behavior as sexual harassment. I end by discussing the DOE's 1997 and 2001 Guidance documents.

2.1 THE EARLY YEARS, 1972–1988

2.1.1 *Department of Education, Office for Civil Rights*

Congress explicitly left enforcement of Title IX in the hands of the departments and agencies that allocated federal funds to education programs and/or activities. These agencies were "authorized and directed" to effectuate the prohibition against sexual discrimination.[4] They were supposed to do so "by issuing rules, regulations, or orders of general applicability."

Turning a law like Title IX from a promise on paper to change on the ground requires the work of an administrative agency, in this case, the DOE. The agency must first decide what the specifics of the law should be, and the next step is enforcement. The primary enforcement agency for Title IX is the Office for Civil Rights (OCR) at the DOE. The Office for Civil Rights was originally in the Department of Health, Education, and Welfare (HEW), but it moved to the DOE, which was created in 1979 and began operating in 1980.

The Office for Civil Rights spent two years preparing the proposed regulations to implement Title IX.[5] They were presented to the public in the Federal Register on June 20, 1974 and received over 9,700 comments. The final regulations became effective on July 21, 1975. They included the controversial requirement that men and women have equal opportunities in competitive athletics.[6]

In 1974, Congress established the National Advisory Council on Women's Educational Programs as part of the Women's Educational Equity Act.[7] The Council was tasked, in part, with advising federal officials on how to achieve gender equity in education. In 1978, the Council commissioned a study, which concluded that sexual harassment of students violated Title IX.[8] The Council, in conjunction with several advocacy groups, started pushing OCR to publish a major policy interpretation on sexual harassment and begin a dedicated enforcement campaign, but OCR did not respond to the recommendation.

In 1981, Antonio J. Califa, Director for Litigation, Enforcement and Policy Service at OCR, released a policy memorandum to all regional directors which stated for the first time that sexual harassment was prohibited by Title IX. "Sexual harassment consists of verbal or physical conduct of a sexual nature, imposed on the basis of sex, by an employee or agent of a recipient that denies, limits, provides different, or conditions the provision of aid, benefits, services or treatment protected under Title IX."[9] The memo also asserted OCR's jurisdiction over sexual harassment complaints.

Seven years later, OCR published a pamphlet called, *Sexual Harassment: It's not Academic.*[10] It called sexual harassment of students "a real and increasingly visible problem of serious consequence in higher education."[11] Schools, the pamphlet said, had to "adopt and publish grievance procedures that provide for the prompt and equitable resolution of sex discrimination complaints."[12] In addition, "[w]here there is evidence to substantiate a charge of sexual harassment, the institution must take immediate action to stop and prevent further harassment, as well as initiate appropriate remedial measures."[13]

Although the pamphlet was symbolically important, it didn't do much to advance Title IX on campus. The pamphlet did not go through any formal or informal rulemaking, and so it did not have any legal force. Instead it simply restated requirements that were already in existence. Asserting that schools had to adopt and publish grievance procedures that provided for prompt and equitable resolution was part of the rules OCR had enacted in 1975. So was saying that a school had to take remedial action.

The Office for Civil Rights should instead have been promulgating regulations that clarified what schools had to do to address sexual harassment; OCR did not tell schools what constituted a prompt or equitable resolution or what was an appropriate remedial action. Indeed, OCR seemed to go out of its way *not* to issue any firm guidance. It provided a list of considerations schools should contemplate, but it didn't advise which were best. For example, it asked, "Are there time frames in the grievance procedure by which a complaint should be investigated and resolved"[14] but it didn't say what those time frames should be. It also asked, "Can a student be accompanied by a friend or advisor throughout the complaint process?"[15] but it didn't advise schools on whether such an allowance should be made.

Without clarifying regulations, it is extremely difficult to formulate and evaluate a complaint. That makes it almost impossible to determine what Title IX compliance means nonetheless to achieve it.[16]

2.1.2 *Federal Courts*

During the first fifteen years after the passage of Title IX, there were only two federal court cases that claimed sexual harassment under Title IX.[17] The first case was *Alexander v. Yale University* (1977).[18] In *Alexander v. Yale*, a member of the Classics Department, a recent graduate, and three matriculating students sued Yale for violating Title IX. Although none of the plaintiffs ultimately prevailed (three had their cases dismissed, and one lost at trial), the case is still significant because it was the first time a federal judge had recognized sexual harassment as a cause of action under Title IX. The District Court wrote: ". . . it is perfectly reasonable to maintain that academic advancement conditioned upon submission to sexual demands constitutes sex discrimination in education, just as questions of job retention or promotion tied to sexual demands from supervisors have become increasingly recognized as potential violations of Title VII's ban against sex discrimination in employment."[19]

The second case occurred six years later in *Moire v. Temple University School of Medicine*.[20] Plaintiff Laura Klawitter Moire alleged that she had been subjected to sexual harassment by a faculty member. Although the Court found no credible evidence that the faculty member had made improper sexual advances toward her, it did accept that sexual harassment could violate Title IX. "Sexual harassment has been defined as 'the unwanted imposition of sexual requirements in the context of a relationship of unequal power' such as employer and employee or professor and student. Harassment of a student by tying academic advancement to submission to sexual pressures constitutes sex discrimination in education because such treatment demeans and degrades women."[21] The court then went on to demarcate two kinds of sexual harassment, quid pro quo "where specific academic or employment benefits are withheld as a means of coercing sexual favors" and "harassment from abusive environment ... where multiple incidents of offensive conduct lead to an environment violative of a victim's civil rights."[22]

2.1.3 *U.S. Supreme Court*

Although the Supreme Court didn't rule on any Title IX sexual harassment cases during this early period, it did decide related matters that would have a significant impact on future cases. For example, in 1979, the Court ruled definitively in *Cannon v. University of Chicago* that persons injured under Title IX did have a private right to action against the school.[23] This decision was important because it allowed aggrieved students to demand that schools comply with Title IX without having to rely on OCR for enforcement.

Another important case was *Grove City College v. Bell*,[24] in which the Supreme Court held that Title IX did not apply to an entire institution but just to the particular program receiving federal assistance. Thus, in *Grove*, the Court found that the receipt of federal tuition grants by students did not trigger Title IX coverage across the entire institution – but just of the school's financial aid program. Grove would have significantly limited the scope of Title IX, but Congress responded by enacting the Civil Rights Restoration Act of 1987 to clarify the "broad application of title IX."[25] It explicitly extended Title IX "to all of the operation[s] of … a college, university, or other postsecondary institution, or a public system of higher education … any part of which is extended Federal financial assistance."[26]

2.2 OCR ACTION AND PUSHBACK FROM THE COURTS, 1989–2001

2.2.1 *1997 Guidance Document*

In 1997, OCR finally published its first official guidance on Title IX in the Federal Register.[27] It did so in compliance with the requirements of the APA's notice and comment informal rulemaking. Before drafting the document, OCR met with representatives from interested parties, including students, teachers, school administrators, and researchers. It also twice publicly requested comments.

The 1997 Guidance Document applied to all students, and it "provide[d] information intended to enable school employees and officials to identify sexual harassment and take steps to prevent its occurrence."[28] The Office for Civil Rights distinguished between two major types of sexual harassment: *Quid pro quo* and hostile environment.[29] Quid pro quo harassment involved a "school employee explicitly or implicitly condition[ing] a student's partici-pation in an education program or activity or bas[ing] an educational decision on the student's submission to unwelcome sexual advances, requests for sexual favors, or other verbal, nonverbal, or physical conduct of a sexual nature."[30] One instance of quid pro quo behavior was enough to trigger Title IX liability. "A school will always be liable for even one instance of quid pro quo harass-ment by a school employee, such as a teacher or administrator, whether or not it knew, should have known, or approved of the harassment at issue."[31]

Hostile environment sexual harassment was more difficult to define, and liability depended on the school's response. Just because behavior had "sexual connotations," didn't mean it was sexual harassment under federal law.[32] "In order to give rise to a complaint under Title IX," OCR explained, "sexual harassment must be sufficiently severe, persistent, or pervasive that it adversely affects a student's education or creates a hostile educational environment or creates a hostile or abusive educational environment."[33] It was possible that one incident could constitute sexual harassment under the law, but for that to happen, "it must be severe."[34]

The 1997 Guidance Document then explained how a school was obligated to respond. A school that had "notice" of a sexually hostile environment and failed to take immediate and corrective action would be in violation of Title IX.[35] Actual knowledge was not required. "A school has notice if it actually 'knew, or in the exercise of reasonable care, should have known' about the harassment."[36] "Constructive notice exists," the 1997 Guidance Document explained, "if the school would have found out about the harassment through a 'reasonably diligent inquiry.'"[37] The 1997 Guidance Document made it difficult for a school to claim it wasn't aware of the misconduct. "[A]s long as an agent or responsible employee of the school received notice, the school has notice."[38]

Once a school had notice, "it should take immediate and appropriate steps to investigate or otherwise determine what occurred and take steps reasonably calculated to end any harassment, eliminate a hostile environment if one has been created, and prevent harassment from occurring again."[39] The Office for Civil Rights enumerated certain factors that grievance procedures should contain in order to be in compliance with Title IX. They included provisions providing for notice to students and other interested parties, such as "[a]dequate, reliable and impartial investigation of complaints, including the opportunity to present witnesses and other evidence"; "designated and reasonably prompt time frames for the major stages of the complaint process"; notice of the outcome to the parties; and "an assurance that the school will take steps to prevent reoccurrence of any harassment and to correct its discriminatory effects on the complainant and others, if appropriate."[40] It did not require that schools create a separate policy to deal with sexual harassment but instead explicitly permitted schools to use a general student disciplinary procedure.

The 1997 Guidance Document also discussed the due process rights of the accused. The Office for Civil Rights wrote: "[t]he rights established under Title IX must be interpreted consistently with any federally guaranteed rights involved in a complaint proceeding."[41] In addition to constitutional rights, OCR recognized that there could be additional rights created by state law, institutional regulations and policies, as well as collective bargaining. It emphasized that respecting the procedural rights of both parties was an important part of a just outcome. "Indeed, procedures that ensure the Title IX rights of the complainant while at the same time according due process to both parties involved will lead to sound and supportable decisions. Schools should ensure that steps to accord due process rights do not restrict or unnecessarily delay the protections provided by Title IX to the complainant."[42]

2.2.2 *Courts*

In 1992, the Supreme Court held for the first time that sexual harassment could violate Title IX. In doing so, it relied on Title VII's bar on gender discrimination in the workplace: "Unquestionably, Title IX placed on the Gwinnett County Public Schools the duty not to discriminate on the basis of sex, and 'when a supervisor sexually harasses a subordinate because of the subordinate's sex, that supervisor 'discriminates on the bases of sex.' We believe the same rule should apply when a teacher sexually harasses and abuses a student."[43] The Court also ruled that Title IX allowed a student who had experienced Title IX gender discrimination to ask for and receive monetary damages. The holding provided an important way of deterring noncompliance beyond OCR's ability to withhold federal funds. Such a right has proved especially important given the fact that OCR has rarely withheld federal funds from a school for violating Title IX's ban on sexual harassment.[44]

Six years later, in *Gebser v. Lago Vista*,[45] the Court set forth the threshold showing for recovery of monetary damages. Since the De Vos guidelines' definition of sexual harassment is based on the *Gebser* decision, it is worth spending some time on the case.

Frank Waldrop was a 52-year-old teacher and retired Marine Colonel when he started having a sexual relationship with Alida Star Gebser, his 14-year-old 9th grade student.[46] Waldrop eventually went to prison for sexual assault after a police officer found them naked together in the woods.[47] Gebser sued the Lago Vista School District under Title IX. She testified that she had been afraid to tell anyone about the relationship,[48] but she relied on the Department of Education, Office for Civil Rights 1997 "Policy Guidance" in arguing that the school district should be liable when "a teacher is 'aided in carrying out the sexual harassment of students by his or her position of authority with the institution,' irrespective of whether school district officials had any knowledge of the harassment and irrespective of their response upon becoming aware."[49]

In a 5–4 decision, the Supreme Court rejected Gebser's argument and thus OCR's standard for liability. "[W]e will not hold a school district liable in damages under Title IX for a teacher's sexual harassment of a student absent actual notice and deliberate indifference."[50] Instead, the Court held that the plaintiff had to prove that "an official who at a minimum has authority to address the alleged discrimination and to institute corrective measures on the recipient's behalf has actual knowledge of discrimination in the recipient's programs" and "refuses to take action to bring the recipient into compliance."[51]

The standard set a high standard for recovery. When the decision was announced, the founder and then co-president of the National Women's Law Center, Marcia D. Greenberger, said that it would "make the job of eliminating sexual harassment in schools far more difficult."[52] Greenberger was not being hyberbolic. Although OCR has the power to cut funding to recipients who discriminate, it almost never does, which leaves enforcement primarily in the hands of private parties. As Shep Melnick explains:

> Although the original purpose of Title VI and Title IX was to empower administrative agencies to act quickly to cut off funding to those who discriminate, that sanction proved too draconian and administratively cumbersome in practice to use in any but the most extreme situations. In fact, the federal government has *never* terminated funding to educational institutions for violating Title IX. Private suits seeking injunctions and damages have replaced the funding cutoff as the primary enforcement tool for Title VI and IX.[53]

The decision also created perverse incentives. In his dissenting opinion joined by the three other dissenting justices, Justice Stevens wrote: "As long as school boards can insulate themselves from knowledge about this sort of conduct, they can claim immunity from damages liability."[54]

Despite the high standard of proof for liability, universities face significant lawsuits. United Educator (UE), which provides insurance to 1,200 member universities, recently began offering insurance to cover sexual assault payouts. Between 2006 and 2010, UE paid out $36 million; 72 percent of the settlements were provided to parties suing the schools for incidents of sexual assault.[55] In 2014, the University of Connecticut settled a $1.28 million suit, and the University of Colorado at Boulder settled a suit for $825,000.[56]

2.2.3 *2001 Guidance Document*

In 2001, OCR published a revised guidance to sexual harassment under Title IX, principally in response to the Supreme Court's rulings in *Gebser* and *Davis v. Monroe City Board of Education*, which will be discussed in the next section.[57] As with the 1997 Guidance Document, the 2001 Guidance Document complied with APA rulemaking by going through notice and comment, albeit in a "truncated" fashion.[58] The purpose of the 2001 Guidance Document was to "[r]eaffirm ... the compliance standards that OCR applies in investigations and administrative enforcement of Title IX ... regarding sexual harassment."[59] It "re-grounds these standards in the Title IX regulations, distinguishing them from the standards applicable to private litigation for money damages...."[60] "In most other respects," OCR wrote, "the revised guidance is identical to the 1997 guidance."[61]

Although the Supreme Court rejected OCR's standard of liability in private lawsuits, OCR emphasized that it still had the power to "'promulgate and enforce requirements that effectuate [Title IX's] nondiscrimination mandate,' even in circumstances that would not give rise to a claim for money damages."[62] In keeping with that authority, OCR rejected the Supreme Court's requirement for civil liability that knowledge be actual. Instead, it kept the standard for Title IX liability that was put forth in the 1997 Guidance Document:

> A school has notice if a responsible employee "knew or in the exercise of reasonable care should have known" about the harassment ... For the purposes of compliance with the Title IX regulations, a school has a duty to respond to harassment about which it reasonably should have known, i.e., if it would have learned of the harassment if it had exercised reasonable care or made a "reasonably diligent inquiry."[63]

2.3 EVOLVING VIEWS ON PEER SEXUAL HARASSMENT

By 1992 there was no doubt that Title IX applied to sexual harassment perpetrated against students by teachers and staff, but the applicability of Title IX to peer sexual harassment took longer to establish. Even advocates initially conceived of sexual harassment in a narrow fashion. For instance, the National Council on Women's Educational Programs' 1980 report defined sexual harassment as, "... harassment in which the faculty member covertly or overtly uses the power inherent in the status of a professor to threaten, coerce or intimidate a student to accept sexual advances or risk reprisal in terms of a grade, a recommendation, or even a job."[64] Benson and Thomson's 1982 study of sexual harassment at U.C. Berkeley only asked questions about the conduct of male instructors against female undergraduates.[65] Similarly, Beauvais' 1986 study of the "Tell Someone" program at the University of Michigan didn't mention peer sexual harassment at all; nor did the myriad studies they discuss.[66] A 1987 article in the *Texas Law Review* entitled, "Sexual Harassment in Higher Education" acknowledged in a footnote that "the issue of sexual harassment of students by students recently has been raised."[67] It then referred to the fact that at Brown University, "the conduct of fraternities and their members toward female students has been the target of discussions, demonstrations, and possibly university sanctions."[68] Although the author wrote that Title IX might apply to this situation, "discussion of that issue is beyond the scope of this Article."[69]

The earliest OCR memorandum on sexual harassment focused on that perpetrated by employees or agents of the recipient. "Sexual harassment consists of verbal or physical conduct of a sexual nature, imposed on the basis of sex, *by an employee or agent of the recipient*, that denies, limits, provides different, or conditions the provision of aid, benefits, services or treatment protected under title IX."[70] Indeed, the memo *explicitly* declined to resolve whether peer harassment could violate Title IX. "The other unresolved issue relates to a recipient's responsibility for the sexual harassment acts of students against fellow students in the context of the situation in which neither student is in a position of authority, derived from the institution, over the other students."[71] By 1997, however, OCR had made its decision. The 1997 Guidance Document, which went through notice and comment, stated unequivocally that peer harassment could violate Title IX. "(A) school will be liable under Title IX if its students sexually harass other students if (i) a hostile environment exists in the school's programs or activities, (ii) the school knows or should have known of the harassment, and (iii) the school fails to take immediate and appropriate corrective action."[72]

Courts were initially split on the issue. The first federal case was decided in 1993, and most of the federal District Courts that considered the issue agreed that a student could indeed sue a school district under Title IX for failing to prevent hostile environment sexual harassment by another student.[73] Circuit courts were less receptive. In *Rowinsky v. Bryant Independent School District*, the mother of Jane and Janet Doe brought suit against the school district because of the repeated verbal and physical sexual harassment they suffered, primarily while riding the school bus.[74] The 8th grade girls were slapped, groped, and propositioned on multiple occasions and by more than one boy – sometimes in view of the driver. Although the girls and their mother complained to the driver, the assistant principal, and other school officials, the harassment continued. Despite these uncontested facts, the Fifth Circuit affirmed summary judgment in favor of the school district on the ground that Title IX did not impose liability for peer sexual harassment because it only covered acts perpetrated by recipients of federal grants. Unless Rowinsky could show that "the school responded to sexual harassment claims differently based on sex,"[75] she could not recover. The fact that school officials knew about the sexual misconduct and failed to act was not enough.

One year later, the Eleventh Circuit came to a similar decision. In *Davis v. Monroe City Board of Education*, Aurelia Davis sued on behalf of her daughter LaShonda who was repeatedly sexually harassed by one of her 5th grade classmates. The harassment included lewd comments, attempted touching of LaShonda's breasts and vagina, and rubbing against her in the hallway. LaShonda and her mother complained repeatedly to teachers and administrators, and yet the conduct continued for a six-month period. Although the Court of Appeals was sympathetic to what LaShonda had suffered, they didn't think it was actionable under Title IX:

> We condemn the harm that has befallen LaShonda, a harm for which Georgia tort law may indeed provide redress. Appellant's present complaint, however, fails to state a claim under Title IX because Congress gave no clear notice to schools and teachers that they, rather than society as a whole, would accept responsibility for remedying student-student sexual harassment when they chose to accept federal financial assistance under Title IX.[76]

Davis appealed to the Supreme Court, which held that Title IX did apply to peer-on-peer sexual harassment. In a 1999 opinion authored by Justice Kennedy, the Court wrote: "Having previously held that such harassment is 'discrimination' in the school context under Title IX, this court is constrained to conclude that student-on-student sexual harassment, if sufficiently severe, can likewise rise to the level of discrimination actionable under the statute."[77]

The Court determined further that a school could be held liable for monetary damages in a private lawsuit if one student sexually harasses another in the school's program.[78] To prevail, the complainant had to meet the conditions of notice and indifference set forth in *Gebser v. Lago Vista Independent School District*.[79] The Court then remanded the case to determine if these conditions could be met.

2.4 CONCLUSION

After almost thirty years of litigating and rulemaking, Title IX's reach was finally clear. Sexual harassment perpetrated by faculty and students was covered, and students were entitled to sue to get schools to enforce Title IX. They were also entitled to recover damages from the school, but to do so they had to meet the high threshold of knowledge and deliberate indifference. In addition, OCR had finally promulgated rules telling schools what they had to do in order to be in compliance with the law.

Despite all of this apparent progress, many students, especially women, were still being sexually assaulted on campus. And articles and exposes showed that schools weren't doing much to stop it. All of that set the stage for the 2011 Dear Colleague Letter, which will be the subject of Chapter 3.

NOTES

1. 20 U.S.C. § 1681(a)(1)(5) (1972).
2. R. SHEP MELNICK, THE TRANSFORMATION OF TITLE IX: REGULATING GENDER EQUALITY IN EDUCATION, Brookings University Press, 2018.
3. *Id.* at 77.
4. Education Amendments of 1972, Pub. L. No. 92–318, §§ 901–03, 86 Stat. 235, 373–375 (1972) (codified at 20 U.S.C. § 1681 (2012)).
5. *Implementing Title IX: The HEW Regulations*, 124 UNIV. PA LAW REV. 806–842 (1976), at 806.
6. 45 C.F.R. § 86.41 (1975).
7. Frank J. Till, SEXUAL HARASSMENT: A REPORT ON THE SEXUAL HARASSMENT OF STUDENTS, 4 (National Advisory Council on Women's Educational Programs, 1980).
8. PROJECT ON THE STATUS AND EDUCATION OF WOMEN, ASSOCIATION OF AMERICAN COLLEGES, *Sexual Harassment: A Hidden Issue* (ERIC Clearinghouse, 1978).
9. Policy Memorandum from Antonio J. Califa, Director of Litigation, Office for Civil Rights to Regional Civil Rights Directors (1981).
10. U.S. Department of Education, Office for Civil Rights, *Sexual Harassment: It's not Academic* (1988), https://files.eric.ed.gov/fulltext/E D330265.pdf.
11. *Id.* at 1.
12. *Id.* at 7.
13. *Id.* at 5.
14. *Id.* at 9.
15. *Id.*
16. Charles S. Bullock III & James L. Regens, *The Courts as a Source of Regulatory Revitalization: External Agenda Setting and Equal Education Programs*, 1 POLICY STUDIES REVIEW 565, 568 (1982).
17. Ronna Greff Schneider, *Sexual Harassment and Higher Education*, 65 TEX. L. REV. 525, 525–551 (1987).
18. *See* Alexander v. Yale University, 459 F. Supp. 1 (D. Conn. 1977).
19. *Id.* at 8.
20. Moire v. Temple University School of Medicine, 613 F. Supp. 1360 (ED Pa. 1985).

21. *Id.* at 1366 (internal citations omitted).
22. *Id.*
23. Grove City College v. Bell, 465 U.S. 555 (1984).
24. Civil Rights Restoration Act of 1987, Pub. L. No. 100–259, 102 Stat. 28 (1998).
25. *Id.* at § 908(2)(A).
26. The law actually reached more broadly, to extend for instance to "a department, agency, special purpose district, or other instrumentality of a State or of a local government." *See id.* At § 908(1)(A).
27. *Sexual Harassment Guidance: Harassment of Students by School Employees, Other Students, or Third Parties*, 62 Fed. Reg. 12034 (Mar. 13, 1997), www.govinfo.gov/content/pkg/FR-1997-03-13/pdf/97-6373 .pdf.
28. *Id.* at 12034.
29. *Id.* at 12038.
30. *Id.*
31. *Id.* at 12039.
32. *Id.* at 12034.
33. *Id.*
34. *Id.*
35. *Id.* at 12043.
36. *Id.*
37. *Id.*
38. *Id.*
39. *Id.*
40. *Id.* at 12044.
41. *Id.* at 12045.
42. *Id.* at 12045.
43. Franklin v. Gwinnett County Public Schools, 503 U.S. 60, 75 (1992) (internal citations omitted).
44. I know of only one case. In 2018, the Chicago school district did not receive a four-million-dollar federal grant that it would have otherwise received because it had failed to adequately address sexual violence complaints. Associated Press, *Chicago District Loses Federal Grant over Title IX Violations*, EDUCATION WEEK (Oct. 9, 2018).
45. Gebser v. Lago Vista Independent School District, 524 U.S. 274 (1998).
46. *Dawn Mackeen, Don't Stand So Close to Me*, SALON (Jun. 30, 1998), www .salon.com/1998/06/30/30hot_2/; David G. Savage, *Justices to Rule on Teacher-Student Sex*, L.A. TIMES (Dec. 6, 1997), www.latimes.com/arch ives/la-xpm-1997-dec-06-mn-61123-story.html (asserting that public schools and colleges could be exposed to costly lawsuits if they are held liable for instructors' sexual misconduct).

47. Associated Press, *Court Limits Harassment Liability* (1998), www
.washingtonpost.com/wp-srv/national/longterm/supcourt/stories/a
po62298.htm.
48. Linda Greenhouse, *School Districts Are Given a Shield in Sex
Harassment*, N.Y. TIMES (Jun. 23, 1998), www.nytimes.com/1998/06/23/
us/school-districts-are-given-a-shield-in-sex-harassment.html.
49. Gebser, 524 U.S. at 287.
50. *Id.* at 292–293.
51. *Id.* at 290.
52. Greenhouse *supra* note 48.
53. Melnick, *supra* note 2 at 35. Although Melnick writes that OCR has never
cut federal funding to schools that discriminate, as I mention in note 44,
the Chicago school district did not receive a four-million-dollar federal
grant that it would have otherwise received because it failed to adequately
address sexual violence complaints. Melnick could not have known about
this case because it occurred after he wrote his book.
54. Gebser, 524 U.S. at 300–301.
55. Gayle Nelson, *The High Cost of Sexual Assaults on Campuses*, NON
PROFIT QUARTERLY (June 23, 2015), https://nonprofitquarterly.org/the-
high-cost-of-sexual-assaults-on-college-campuses/.
56. LARGE LOSS REPORT 2015, UNITED EDUCATORS (2015), www.ue.org/
uploadedFiles/Large_loss_2015_Final.pdf.
57. U.S. Department of Education, Office for Civil Rights, *Revised Sexual
Harassment Guidance: Harassment of Students by School Employees,
Other Students or Third Parties* (Jan. 2001), www2.ed.gov/offices/OCR/ar
chives/pdf/shguide.pdf, [hereinafter OCR 2001]. *Revised Sexual
Harassment Guidance: Harassment of Students by School Employees,
Other Students, or Third Parties*, 66 Fed. Reg. 5512 (Jan. 19, 2001), www
.govinfo.gov/content/pkg/FR-2001-01-19/pdf/01-1606.pdf, [hereinafter 2001
Guidance Document].
58. Melnick describes how the Clinton Administration rushed to get the new
guidelines out before the inauguration of President George W. Bush.
"Once again, OCR employed a truncated form of rulemaking. On
November 2, 2000, less than a week before the presidential election, it
published a proposed 'Revision of Sexual Harassment Guidelines' in the
Federal Register. On January 19, 2001, the day before the inauguration of
George W. Bush, it published a short notice announcing that the
department had settled on a final set of guidelines that would soon be
made available to the public. Apparently, OCR was in such a rush to beat
the presidential clock that it could not get its thirty-seven pages of
guidelines into the Federal Register on time." (Melnick, *supra* note 2,
at 192.)
59. *Id.* at i.

60. *Id.*

61. *Id.*

62. *Id.* at ii.

63. *Id.*

64. Till, *supra* note 7, at 4.

65. Donna J. Benson & Gregg E. Thomson, *Sexual Harassment on a University Campus: The Confluence of Authority Relations, Sexual Interest and Gender Stratification*, 29 SOCIAL PROBLEMS 236, 236–251 (1982).

66. Kathleen Beauvais, *Workshops to Combat Sexual Harassment: A Case Study of Changing Attitudes*, 12 SIGNS: JOURNAL OF WOMEN IN CULTURE AND SOCIETY 130, 130–145 (1986).

67. Schneider, *supra* note 17, at 530.

68. *Id.*

69. *Id.*

70. Rowinsky v. Bryan Independent School District, 80 F.3d 1006, 1015 (5th Cir. 1996) (emphasis in original) (citing Califa, *supra* note 9).

71. *Id.*

72. *Sexual Harassment Guidance: Harassment of Students by School Employees, Other Students, or Third Parties*, 62 Fed. Reg. 12,034 (Mar. 13, 1997).

73. DANA L. LONG, PEER SEXUAL HARASSMENT, QUARTERLY REPORT (1997), www.doe.in.gov/sites/default/files/legal/1997octdec.pdf.

74. Rowinsky v. Bryan Independent School District, 80 F.3d 1006 (5th Cir. 1996).

75. *Id.* at 1016.

76. *Id.* at 1406.

77. Davis v. Monroe City Board of Education, 526 U.S. 629, 650 (1999).

78. *See* Franklin v. Gwinnet County Public Schools, *supra* note 43.

79. Gebser v. Lago Vista Independent School District, *supra* note 45.

3

Fixing the Fix*

Advocates were initially hopeful that Title IX would keep students safe from sexual violence. The National Women's Law Center called the Supreme Court's ruling in *Davis v. Monroe City School Board* (1999) a "tremendous advance." They applauded the Court's decision extending Title IX to peer sexual harassment because it "affirms schools' legal obligation to provide a safe, harassment-free environment to their students."[1]

Ten years later, however, it was clear that Title IX wasn't working. Women were still being raped on college campuses, and schools weren't doing enough to stop it.[2] An article published by the Center for Public Integrity described university proceedings cloaked in secrecy, with complainants given minimal opportunity to present evidence if they even got a hearing at all.[3] A twelve-month investigation found that "students deemed 'responsible' for alleged sexual assaults on college campuses can face little or no consequence for their acts."[4]

In April 2011, the Obama administration decided enough was enough. The Department of Education, Office for Civil Rights (OCR) issued its infamous Dear Colleague Letter (DCL), which was accompanied by a press release that declared:

> [T]he threat of violence continues for a new generation of women. Young women aged 16–24 experience the highest rates of rape and sexual assault, while 1 in 5 will be a victim of sexual assault during college. Today, with Secretary Duncan, the Vice President highlighted the Administration's commitment to raising awareness and promoting policies to prevent sexual violence against women of all ages.[5]

The DCL reminded universities that sexual violence constitutes a form of discrimination under Title IX.[6] It told universities that in order to be in compliance, they had to change disciplinary proceedings to hold rapists accountable more effectively. In no uncertain terms, OCR told universities that they had to reduce the standard of proof to a preponderance of the evidence, and it strongly discouraged them from allowing the parties to directly question one another. It also told universities that they should not allow the respondent to review the complainant's statement unless she was able to review his. It threatened to withhold federal funding to universities that did not adequately respond, and it later published a list that continued to grow of those under investigation.

Although no doubt well-intentioned, the Dear Colleague Letter was deeply problematic. It misrepresented existing data, violated federal law, and flouted existing norms. Most troublesome, it pressured schools into creating an adjudicatory process weighted heavily against the accused. This chapter will focus on the problems with how the DCL was created. The next will discuss the negative impact the DCL had on due process rights.

3.1 MISREPRESENTING DATA

The 2011 DCL was explicitly premised on the claim that we were facing a national crisis in the incidence of campus sexual assault. It called the statistics on sexual violence "deeply troubling and a call to action for the nation."[7] The DCL then cited a study by the National Institute of Justice (NIJ), which according to OCR had found "about 1 in 5 women are victims of completed or attempted sexual assault while in college."[8] But OCR's statement was misleading. As discussed in Chapter 1, the NIJ study looked only at two large public universities, and the findings were not nationally representative.[9] Indeed, the lead researchers were so troubled by the misuse of their findings that they "felt the need to set the record straight" and published a piece in *Time Magazine* in which they wrote:

> [T]he 1-in-5 statistic is not a nationally representative estimate of the prevalence of sexual assault, and we have never presented it as being representative of anything other than the population of senior undergraduate women at the two universities where data were collected – two large public universities, one in the South and one in the Midwest.[10]

Nor in subsequent communications did OCR ever even mention a 2014 nationally representative study conducted by the Department of Justice that found significantly lower rates of rape and sexual assault among college women.[11] As discussed in Chapter 1, Sinozich and Langton used data from the National Crime Victimization Survey (NCVS) and found that 6.1 per 1,000 women in post-secondary institutions were the victims of rape or sexual assault between 1995 and 2013. The NCVS is by no means perfect, and it has been criticized for likely underestimating the incidence of rape and sexual assault.[12] But it is a national study with a large sample size and a very high response rate; it should have been discussed.

Rape is a pressing problem, and OCR was right to take it seriously. However intentionally misrepresenting data to make the situation look worse than it is in order to justify lowering the bar for finding a student "guilty" of sexual assault is unforgivable. It is also counterproductive, as it allowed commentators like David French to proclaim in the *National Review*, "The campus-rape crisis is over. In fact, it never even existed."[13]

3.2 VIOLATING FEDERAL LAW

The Department of Education (DOE) was so eager to change the way that campuses adjudicated campus sexual misconduct that it was not just willing to misrepresent studies, but also to violate federal law. Trigger warning – this is a dense, highly technical argument, but it also provides an opportunity to provide a detailed account of the changes wrought by the DCL.

As mentioned in Chapter 2, the DOE is responsible for interpreting and enforcing Title IX. It can do so in a number of ways. First, it is "authorized and directed" to enforce Title IX by issuing legislative rules.[14] If substantively valid, legislative rules have "the force and effect of a statute on all those who are subject to [them] ... [and they] bind[] the agency, private parties, and the courts, and may preempt state statutes."[15] The DOE can also issue interpretive rules, but they do not bind agencies or the public. They instead signal how an agency will interpret a rule.[16] Agencies are also allowed to issue guidance documents – a broad category of nonlegislative rules, which includes "interpretive memoranda, policy statements, guidances, manuals, circulars, memoranda, bulletins, advisories, and the like." There is also a subset of guidance documents called "significant guidance documents," which is what the DCL purports to be.[17]

Because legislative rules are legally binding, the Administrative Procedure Act (APA) requires that they be promulgated in a way that allows for public input and participation. That means they must be created through formal rulemaking[18] or by informal rulemaking, also known as notice and comment.[19] Interpretive rules and guidance documents, on the other hand, do not have the force of law, and so they do not have to comply with these requirements.[20] Because significant guidance documents have a greater impact than usual guidance documents, the Office of Management and Budget (OMB) requires that they pass through additional procedural hoops.

"Not later than 180 days from the publication of this Bulletin, each agency shall establish and clearly advertise on its Web site a means for the public to submit electronically comments on significant guidance documents, and to request electronically that significant guidance documents be issued, reconsidered, modified or rescinded."[21]

Congress,[22] courts,[23] commentators,[24] and even the White House[25] have been concerned that agencies abuse guidance documents by promulgating new laws without going through notice and comment. In 2007, the Bush White House issued a Bulletin on Good Guidance Practices in an attempt to rein in these undemocratic processes.[26] Still, the problem remains. Part of the reason why agencies are able to abuse guidance documents is that it is difficult to distinguish between legislative and nonlegislative rules. David Franklin has called creating a workable distinction between the two perhaps the most "vexing conundrum in the field of administrative law"[27] – no surprise considering that courts have said the distinction is "fuzzy"[28] and "enshrouded in considerable smog."[29]

The OCR termed the DCL a "significant guidance document" and did not promulgate it through formal rulemaking or notice and comment. The test for whether the DCL was a legislative rule and thus should have gone through the APA's required rulemaking processes is whether it had a "legally binding" effect.[30]

3.3 DID THE DCL EFFECTIVELY AMEND A PRIOR LEGISLATIVE RULE?

In *American Mining Congress v. United States Department of Labor*,[31] the D.C. Circuit set out a "particularly influential" formulation of the legal effect test.[32] Determining "whether the purported interpretive rule has 'legal effect' ... is best ascertained by asking (1) whether in the absence of the rule there would not be an adequate legislative basis for enforcement action or other agency action to confer benefits or ensure the performance of duties, (2) whether the agency has published the rule in the Code of Federal Regulations, (3) whether the agency has explicitly invoked its general legislative authority, or (4) whether the rule affectively amends a prior legislative rule. If the answer to any of these questions is affirmative, we have a legislative, not an interpretive rule."[33] The last factor has been seen as the most important.[34] The D.C. Circuit Court of Appeals has used all or part of this same test to determine if each of the following were legislative rules: a Federal Aviation Association internal guidance document,[35] an EPA Guidance Document,[36] and Training and Employment Guidance Letters issued by the Department of Labor.[37]

In other words, if the 2001 Guidance Document was legislative and the DCL effectively amended it, then it was a legislative rule and not an interpretative rule, a policy document, or a guidance document. If it was a legislative rule, the DCL would have been invalid.

3.3.1 *Was the 2001 Guidance Document a Legislative Rule?*

Deciding whether the DCL amended a legislative rule requires first determining whether the 2001 Guidance Document, which the DCL amended and sometimes replaced, was itself a legislative rule. In issuing the 2001 Guidance Document, OCR explicitly invoked its general authority, and it used mandatory language. Although the agency did not actually claim in 2001 that it was engaged in rulemaking, it complied with all the requirements for rulemaking and probably needed to do so to make some of the pronouncements in that document legally valid.

The 2001 Guidance Document was issued in order to revise the 1997 Guidance Document in light of *Gebser v. Lago Vista Independent School District* and *Davis v. Monroe County Board of Education*, both discussed in Chapter 2. Although the legal status of the 1997 Guidance could be debated, a strong argument exists that it was in fact what it proclaimed to be. On the one hand, OCR complied with the requirements for rulemaking. and the 1997 Policy Guidance was published in the Federal Register. On the other hand, unlike the 2001 Guidance Document and the DCL, OCR did not specifically invoke its authority to issue the 1997 Guidance Document. Nor did it use the kind of mandatory language that appeared in both the 2001 Guidance Document and the DCL. Additionally, in its amicus brief in *Gebser*, OCR explicitly referred to the 1997 Guidance Document as guidance and not a legislative rule.

Notice of the availability of the 2001 Guidance Document was published in the Federal Register,[38] and OCR complied with the requirements for informal rulemaking by going through notice and comment. Unlike the 1997 Guidance, the 2001 Guidance Document contained the kind of mandatory language associated with legislative rules. For instance, it said: "Regardless of whether the student who was harassed, or his or her parent, decides to file a formal complaint or otherwise request action on the student's behalf . . . the school must promptly investigate to determine what occurred and then take appropriate steps to resolve the situation."[39] In contrast, the 1997 Guidance Document stated: "Once a school has notice of possible sexual harassment of students . . . it should take immediate and appropriate steps to investigate or otherwise determine what occurred and take steps reasonably calculated to end any harassment, eliminate a hostile environment if one has been created, and prevent harassment from occurring again."[40]

In light of the way that the 2001 Guidance Document was promulgated, the fact that OCR explicitly invoked its general legislative authority, and the fact that on at least one occasion it used mandatory language, a strong argument exists that it was a legislative rule.

3.3.2 *Did the DCL Effectively Amend the 2001 Guidance Document?*

If the 2001 Guidance Document was a legislative rule, the key question is whether the DCL "effectively amended" it. Changes were made in a number of areas, including how schools should handle police investigations, what the standard of proof should be, requirements regarding witnesses, the provision of information, lawyers, the right to appeal, how notice should be provided, the protocol for handling retaliation, mandates for providing remedies, and how OCR would enforce compliance. The question isn't whether the changes were good or bad but the extent to which they were made. Note that even if the 2001 Guidance Document was not a legislative rule, the test from *American Mining Congress* will still be used to see if the DCL was invalid on its own for having legal effect.

3.3.2.1 Grievance Procedures

The 2001 Guidance Document explicitly told schools they were allowed to use informal mechanisms for resolving sexual harassment, as long as both parties agreed. Later, it told schools that mediation was inappropriate for sexual assault, even if parties participated voluntarily:

> Grievance procedures may include informal mechanisms for resolving sexual harassment complaints to be used if the parties agree to do so. . . . In some cases, such as alleged sexual assaults, mediation will not be appropriate even on a voluntary basis.[41]

The DCL, however, limited the use of voluntary mechanisms to only some types of sexual harassment. The DCL also stated that mediation was inappropriate in cases of sexual assault:

> Grievance procedures generally may include voluntary informal mechanisms (e.g., mediation) for resolving some types of sexual harassment complaints. . . . [I]n cases involving allegations of sexual assault, mediation is not appropriate even on a voluntary basis.[42]

The difference between the 2001 Guidance Document and the DCL was subtle but significant. Although the 2001 Guidance Document limited the use of mediation, it did not limit the use of other types of informal mechanism. The DCL on the other hand seemed to equate all informal mechanisms with mediation and limited their use.

3.3.2.2 Police Investigation

The 2001 Guidance Document had discussed how schools should handle an ongoing police investigation regarding the underlying harassment. Although it reminded schools that they had an obligation to respond promptly and effectively on their own regardless of whether there was an ongoing police investigation, it did not provide specifics about what they should do. The 2001 Guidance Document stated:

> In some instances, a complainant may allege harassing conduct that constitutes both sex discrimination and possible criminal conduct. Police investigations or reports may be useful in terms of fact gathering. However, because legal standards for criminal investigations are different, police investigations or reports may not be determinative of whether harassment occurred under Title IX and do not relieve the school of its duty to respond promptly and effectively.[43]

The DCL, in contrast, provided much more elaborate instructions for what schools should do when there was a concurrent police investigation. As is evident from the text below, there was no flexibility in these instructions. The Office for Civil Rights told schools what they had to do to comply with their obligations under Title IX:

> Schools should not wait for the conclusion of a criminal investigation or criminal proceedings to begin their own Title IX investigation and, if needed, must take immediate steps to protect the student in the educational setting. For example a school should not delay conducting its own investigation or taking steps to protect the complainant because it wants to see whether the alleged perpetrator will be found guilty of a crime. Any agreement or Memorandum of Understanding (MOU) with a local police department must allow the school to meet its Title IX obligation to resolve complaints promptly and equitably. Although a school may need to delay temporarily the fact-finding portion of a Title IX investigation while the police are gathering evidence, once notified that the police department has completed its gathering of evidence (not the ultimate outcome of the investigation or the filing of any charges), the school must promptly resume and complete its fact-finding

for the Title IX investigation. Moreover, nothing in an MOU or the criminal investigation itself should prevent a school from notifying complainants of their Title XI rights and the school's grievance procedures, or from taking interim steps to ensure the safety and well-being of the complainant and the school community while the law enforcement agency's fact-gathering is in process. OCR also recommends that a school's MOU include clear policies on when a school will refer a matter to local law enforcement.[44]

The difference between the 2001 Guidance Document and the DCL is striking. The 2001 Guidance Document provided almost no direction regarding how schools should handle police investigations except to say that a police investigation may not be determinative of whether there was a Title IX violation and that schools still had an obligation to respond promptly and effectively. The DCL in contrast told schools that they could not wait for an investigation to end but had to take immediate steps to protect the complainant. It dictated the relationship between schools and the police, telling schools that any formal understanding between the police and schools had to allow the schools to meet their Title IX obligation of prompt investigation. It then told schools that even if they had to wait for the police to finish their investigation, they had to promptly resume after the police fact-finding portion was done. In effect, the DOE told schools what they had to do without knowing the needs of law enforcement or the local prosecutor's office, thus potentially undermining a criminal case.

3.3.2.3 The Standard of Proof

The 2001 Guidance Document contained a section on "Prompt and Equitable Grievance Procedures." It specifically told schools that they did not need to set up separate grievance procedures for handling sexual harassment cases. It did "identif[y] a number of elements in evaluating whether a school's grievance procedures were prompt and equitable."[45] These included: notice, "[a]dequate, reliable, and impartial investigation of complaints, including the opportunity to present witnesses and other evidence," and "[d]esignated and reasonably prompt timeframes for the major stages of the complaint process." At no point did it tell schools that the standard of proof needed to be set at a certain level.

The DCL, in contrast, told schools in unequivocal terms that the standard of proof had to be set at preponderance of the evidence. It stated: "in order for a school's grievance procedures to be consistent with Title IX standards, the school must use a preponderance of the evidence standard."[46] It also specifically acknowledged that in setting the standard of proof at preponderance, it would be forcing some schools to change their existing standard of proof. "The 'clear and convincing' standard ... currently used by some schools, is a higher standard of proof. Grievance procedures that use this higher standard are inconsistent with the standard of proof established for violations of the civil rights laws and are thus not equitable under Title IX."

3.3.2.4 Witnesses and Information

As mentioned earlier, the 2001 Guidance Document identified a number of elements that the DOE looked for in evaluating whether the school's grievance procedures were prompt and equitable. Among others, it told schools that there must be "[a]dequate, reliable, and impartial investigation of complaints, including the opportunity to present witnesses and other evidence."[47]

The DCL, in contrast, set out new rules for how schools should institute this element. It stated: "Throughout a school's Title IX investigation, including at any hearing, the parties must have an equal opportunity to present witnesses and other evidence. The complainant and the alleged perpetrator must be afforded similar and timely access to any information that will be used at the hearing."[48]

The DCL changed the student disciplinary procedure in fundamental ways. A school might have concluded that since the accused faced a disciplinary sanction he should know the information that would be presented against him at the hearing and have the right to present evidence on his own behalf. The DCL effectively altered the proceedings so that there were three people putting on evidence: the school, the accused, and the complainant. By mandating the complainant's equal right to call witnesses and put on evidence it extended the length of the hearings, and it removed from schools the right to decide what evidence was relevant and should be admitted. Further, by requiring that both parties had similar and timely access to information, it forced schools to adjust their processes and shift resources so that they could meet these time requirements for two parties when before there was just one.

3.3.2.5 Lawyers

The 2001 Guidance Document did not mention lawyers at all, thus taking no view as to whether the accused could or should have legal representation in university disciplinary proceedings. The DCL, in contrast, mandated that schools give parties equal access to attorneys and that both attorneys have the same restrictions on their ability to speak or put on evidence. It stated:

> While OCR does not require schools to permit parties to have lawyers at any stage of the proceedings, if a school chooses to allow the parties to have the lawyers participate in the proceedings, it must so do equally for both sides. Additionally, any school-imposed restrictions on the ability of lawyers to speak or otherwise participate in the proceeding should apply equally.[49]

In effect, OCR limited a university's right to decide how it wanted to handle counsel.

3.3.2.6 Appeals

The 2001 Guidance Document acknowledged that some schools would provide a right to appeal, but it did not provide any particulars about the way the right should work, saying only "[m]any schools also provide an opportunity to appeal the findings or remedy, or both."[50] The DCL, in contrast, added specific requirements for the appeals process, if a school chooses to have one: "OCR also recommends that schools provide an appeals process. If a school provides for appeal of the findings or remedy, it must do so for both parties."[51]

Once again, OCR made the disciplinary process more resource expensive and time consuming since universities that once provided only the accused with the right to appeal had to provide that right to the complainant as well.

3.3.2.7 Notice of Outcome

The 2001 Guidance Document told schools that one of the elements it would consider in evaluating its grievance procedures was whether it provided notice to the parties of the outcome. The document did not specify what form that notice should take. The DCL in contrast, told schools that notice was required, and that it had to be in writing: "Both parties must be notified, in writing, about the outcome of both the complaint and any appeal."[52]

3.3.2.8 Retaliation

The 2001 Guidance Document told schools that they "should take steps to prevent any further harassment and to prevent retaliation against the student who made the complaint (or was the subject of the harassment), against the person who filed a complaint on behalf of a student, or against those who provided information as witnesses."[53] At a minimum, it said, schools should make sure that harassed students and their parents know how to report these problems and that the school should make follow-up inquiries to see if there have been any additional incidents of retaliation. It then said that counseling may be appropriate for the offender and that depending on how widespread the harassment was, they may need to provide training to the larger community for recognizing harassment and knowing how to respond. Later it stated: "In addition, because retaliation is prohibited by Title IX, schools may want to include a provision in their procedures prohibiting retaliation against any individual who files a complaint or participates in a harassment inquiry."[54]

The DCL, in contrast told schools that they "must have policies and procedures in place to protect against retaliatory harassment."[55] It then mandated how it should be done. "At a minimum, schools must ensure that complainants and their parents, if appropriate, know how to report any subsequent problems, and should follow-up with complainants to determine whether any retaliation or new incidents of harassment have occurred."[56]

3.3.2.9 Remedies

The 2001 Guidance Document told schools that they must respond immediately once they had notice of a student harassing another student. If they responded immediately, the 2001 Guidance Document stated that they would not be responsible for taking additional steps:

> As long as the school, upon notice of the harassment, responds by taking prompt and effective action to end the harassment and prevent its recurrence, the school has carried out its responsibility under the Title IX regulations. On the other hand, if, upon notice, the school fails to take prompt, effective action, the school's own inaction has permitted the student to be subjected to a hostile environment that denies or limits the student's ability to participate in or benefit from the school's program on the basis of sex. In this case, the school is responsible for taking effective corrective actions to stop the harassment, prevent its recurrence, and remedy the effects on the victim that could reasonably have been prevented had it responded promptly and effectively.[57]

The DCL, in contrast, told schools that they were responsible for remedying the effects on the victim regardless of whether they responded in a timely fashion:

> As discussed above, if a school determines that sexual harassment that creates a hostile environment has occurred, it must take immediate action to eliminate the hostile environment, prevent its recurrence, and address its effects.

In addition to counseling or taking disciplinary action against the harasser, effective corrective action may require remedies for the complainant, as well as changes to the school's overall services or policies.... Depending on the specific nature of the problem, remedies for the complainant might include, but are not limited to: providing an escort to ensure that the complainant can move safely between classes and activities; ensuring that the complainant and alleged perpetrator do not attend the same classes; moving the complainant or alleged perpetrator to a different residence hall ... ; providing counseling services; providing medical services; providing academic support services, such as tutoring; arranging for the complainant to re-take a course or withdraw from a class without penalty, including ensuring that any changes do not adversely affect the complainant's academic record; and reviewing any disciplinary action taken against the complainant to see if there is a causal connection between the harassment and the misconduct that may have resulted in the complainant being disciplined.[58]

These changes were significant. The 2001 Guidance Document told schools that if, upon notice of harassment, they took prompt and effective action to end the harassment and prevent its recurrence they would have carried out their responsibility under Title IX. It was only if they did not take prompt and effective action that they would be responsible for remedying the effects of the harassment on the victim. In contrast, the DCL made schools responsible for remedying the effects on the victim regardless of how quickly or effectively they responded. This change significantly increased the financial burden on schools, as they had to provide for extensive services that they would not have had to otherwise.

3.3.2.10 Enforcement

The DCL was also much more heavy-handed than the 2001 Guidance Document on enforcement. The 2001 Guidance Document made it clear that if a school took certain steps it would be found to be in compliance with Title IX, even if actual harassment occurred. The 2001 Guidance Document stated in relevant part:

If the school has taken, or agrees to take, each of these steps, OCR will consider the case against the school resolved and will take no further action, other than monitoring compliance with an agreement, if any, between the school and OCR. This is true in cases in which the school was in violation of the Title IX regulations ... as well as those in which there had been no violation of the regulations ... . This is because, even if OCR identifies a violation, Title IX requires OCR to attempt to secure voluntary compliance.

Thus, because a school will have the opportunity to take reasonable correct-ive action before OCR issues a formal finding of violation a school does not risk losing its Federal funding solely because discrimination occurred.[59]

The DCL, in contrast, took a markedly more punitive tone. Although it acknowledged that it sought voluntary compliance, it emphasized the conse-quences of not complying instead of the positive effects of complying. The DCL stated:

> When OCR finds that a school has not taken prompt and effective steps to respond to sexual harassment or violence, OCR will seek appropriate remed-ies for both the complainant and the broader student population. When conducting Title IX enforcement activities, OCR seeks to obtain voluntary compliance from recipients. When a recipient does not come into compli-ance voluntarily, OCR may initiate proceedings to withdraw Federal funding by the Department or refer the case to the U.S. Department of Justice for litigation.[60]

3.3.2.11 General Tone

One striking part of the 2001 Guidance Document was its emphasis on the rights of the accused student. Just as with the 1997 Guidance Document, the 2001 Guidance Document discussed the due process rights of the accused. In the 1997 Guidance Document, OCR wrote: "the rights established under title IX must be interpreted consistently with any federally guaranteed rights involved in a complaint proceeding."[61] In addition to constitutional rights, OCR recognized in the 1997 Guidance Document that state law, institutional regulations and policies and collective bargaining could create additional rights for accused students. In the 1997 Guidance Document OCR empha-sized that respecting the procedural rights of both parties was an important part of a just outcome. "Indeed, procedures that ensure the Title IX rights of the complainant while at the same time according due process to both parties involved will lead to sound and supportable decisions. . . . Schools should ensure that steps to accord due process rights do not restrict or unnecessarily delay the protections provided by Title IX to the complainant."[62]

In comparison with the 1997 Guidance Document, the 2001 Guidance Document actually stressed the importance of the rights of the accused to an even greater degree. The 2001 Guidance Document included a new section entitled "Due Process Rights of the Accused."[63] This newly appointed section contained all of the language discussed earlier from the 1997 Guidance Document, but it also told schools that "the Family Rights and Privacy Act

(FERPA) does not override federally protected due process rights of Persons accused of sexual harassment." The 2001 Guidance Document concluded by saying: "[s]chools should be aware of these rights and their legal responsibilities to individuals accused of harassment." Thus it was understandable, based on both the 1997 and 2001 Guidance Documents, that an institution would think it could set a standard of proof at clear and convincing evidence or even beyond a reasonable doubt.

In a significant about-face, the DCL deemphasized the due process rights of respondents. The section entitled "Due Process of the Accused" was deleted. Missing was any explicit mention of the Constitution's due process guarantee and that rights under Title IX must be interpreted consistently with any federally guaranteed due process rights. Absent was any acknowledgement of additional rights that might have been granted by a state or the particular institution. Instead, in marked contrast to its prior guidelines, the DCL almost begrudgingly stated that schools had to provide alleged perpetrators with due process. It devoted just one sentence to the rights of the accused: "Public and state-supported schools must provide due process to the alleged perpetrator."[64] Tellingly, it followed that sentence by once again emphasizing the rights of alleged victims: "However, schools should ensure that steps taken to accord due process rights to the alleged perpetrator do not restrict or unnecessarily delay the Title IX protections for the complainant."

3.3.3 *Summary*

Under the "legal effect" test as articulated by *American Mining Congress*, a "purported interpretive rule" has legal affect if it effectively amends a legislative rule. Although *American Mining Congress* concerned Program Policy Letters, courts have used the same test to evaluate purported guidance documents, like the DCL. The 2001 Guidance Document was probably a legislative rule. It met the procedural requirements of a legislative rule because it went through notice and comment. It also met two of the substantive parts of a legislative rule in that OCR explicitly invoked its general legislative authority, and on at least one occasion it used mandatory language. Whatever the 2001 Guidance Document was, there can be little doubt that the DCL effectively amended it. As detailed earlier, the DCL adds many requirements that are not part of the 2001 Guidance Document. In addition, the general tone of these changes is to downplay the procedural due process rights of the accused, which is a repudiation of the 2001 Guidance Document's emphasis on these rights. If a court finds that the DCL effectively amended a legislative rule then it will be deemed procedurally invalid. What is more, even if a court were to find that the 2001 Guidance Document was not a legislative rule, the DCL might still be held invalid if it has the force of law, that is, impermissibly imposes legal obligations that require legislative rulemaking.[65]

3.4 DOES THE DCL HAVE THE FORCE OF LAW?

In *General Electric Co. v. Environmental Protection Agency*, in an opinion authored by then Chief Judge and later Supreme Court Justice Ruth Bader Ginsburg, the United States Court of Appeals for the District of Columbia was asked to decide whether an Environmental Protection Agency (EPA) Guidance Document was actually a legislative rule. The Court wrote that in deciding how to draw the line between legislative rules and statements of policy, "we have considered whether the agency action (1) 'imposes any rights and obligations' or (2) 'genuinely leaves the agency and its decisionmakers free to exercise discretion.'"[66] It went on further: "'if a statement denies the decisionmaker discretion in the area of its coverage, so that [the agency] will automatically decline to entertain challenges to the statement's position, then the statement is binding, and creates rights or obligations.'"[67]

At issue in *General Electric* was whether the guidelines for how to conduct a risk assessment on sampling, cleaning up, or disposing of PCB remediation waste was legislative or merely advisory. General Electric had argued that the Guidance Document was a legislative rule "because it gives substance to the vague language" of the statute at issue and it "does so in an obligatory fashion."[68] The EPA countered that the Guidance Document did not have the force of law "because it does not purport to be binding and because it has not been applied as though it were binding."[69] In finding that the Guidelines were legislative, the Court emphasized the language of the Guidance Document at issue. It noted that the Document twice used the word "must", and it explained: "To the applicant reading the Guidance Document the message is clear: in reviewing applications the Agency will not be open to considering approaches other than those prescribed in the Document."[70]

Like the Guidance Document in *General Electric*, the DCL purports to be a non-binding statement that "does not add requirements to applicable law, but provides information and examples to inform recipients about how OCR evaluates whether covered entities are complying with their legal obligations."[71] As *General Electric* and other cases show, however, even if an agency purports to be issuing an interpretive rule, courts may still find that it exercises power that can only be invoked in a legislative rule.[72] "It is well-established that an agency may not escape the notice and comment requirements ... by labeling a major substantive legal addition to a rule a mere interpretation."[73] A court must "still look to whether the interpretation itself carries the force and effect of law, ... or rather whether it spells out a duty fairly encompassed within the regulation that the interpretation purports to construe."[74]

Using the legal effect test as articulated in *General Electric*, it is clear that the DCL was a legislative rule on its own terms even if the earlier 2001 Guidance Document was not. As previously explained, on multiple occasions, OCR tells schools that they must take certain steps to be in compliance with Title IX. Specifically, DCL tells schools:

(1) They may only use informal mechanisms to address some forms of sexual harassment.[75]

(2) "Any agreement or Memorandum of Understanding (MOU) with a police department must allow the school to meet its Title IX obligation to resolve complaints promptly and equitably."[76]

(3) "Although a school may need to delay temporarily the fact-finding portion of a Title IX investigation while the police are gathering evidence, once notified that the police department has completed its gathering of evidence (not the ultimate outcome of the investigation or the filing of any charges), the school must promptly resume and complete its fact-finding for the Title IX investigation."[77]

(4) "[I]n order for a school's grievance procedures to be consistent with Title IX standards, the school must use a preponderance of the evidence standard."[78]

(5) "[T]he parties must have an equal opportunity to present witnesses and other evidence."[79]

(6) "The complainant and the alleged perpetrator must be afforded similar and timely access to any information that will be used at the hearing."[80]

(7) "If a school chooses to allow the parties to have their lawyers participate in the proceedings, it must do so equally for both sides."[81]

(8) "If a school provides for appeal of the findings or remedy, it must do so for both parties."[82]

(9) "Both parties must be notified, in writing, about the outcome of both the complaint and any appeal."[83]

(10) Schools must have policies and procedures to protect against retaliatory harassment,[84] and they must ensure that both complainants and their parents know how to report problems.[85]

(11) "[I]f a school determines that sexual harassment that creates a hostile environment occurred, it must take immediate action to eliminate the hostile environment, prevent its recurrence, and address its effects."[86]

"On its face" the DCL "imposes binding obligations" upon schools.[87] It does not leave "the agency and its decisionmakers free to exercise discretion."[88] Just as in *Appalachian Power Co. v. Environmental Protection Agency*, "[t]he entire Guidance, from beginning to end . . . reads like a ukase. It commands, it requires, it orders, it dictates."[89] In other words, the DCL has "the force of law."[90] Such language also specifically violates OMB's Final Bulletin for Agency Good Guidance Practices, which states:

> Each significant guidance document shall ... [n]ot include mandatory language such as "shall," "must," "required" or "requirement," unless the agency is using these words to describe a statutory or regulatory requirement, or the language is addressed to agency staff and will not foreclose agency consideration of positions advanced by affected private parties.[91]

Since the DCL is a procedural rule and did not go through either formal or informal rulemaking, it is procedurally invalid, and universities have no legal obligation to adhere to it.

3.5 DID THE DCL EFFECTIVELY LEAVE SCHOOLS NO OTHER CHOICE?

Even if the DCL did not have the force and effect of law, the DCL made the consequences for not abiding by it so significant that it was effectively legally binding. In *Chamber of Commerce v. U.S. Department of Labor*,[92] the Occupational Safety and Health Administration (OSHA) engaged in similar conduct. At issue was an OSHA directive telling agencies that they would not inspect workplaces as frequently or thoroughly if the employer abided by certain safety standards, which were being set forth for the first time.[93] The D.C. Circuit struck this directive down as being procedurally invalid on the ground that the burden of inspections was so great that employers had no real choice except to avoid them, which in effect made the directive binding.[94]

Similarly, in the DCL, OCR told academic institutions that if they didn't take certain measures (like lowering the burden of proof) they would be found in violation of Title IX. In an unprecedented move, OCR began publishing a list of universities under investigation for violating Title IX, which put tremendous financial and social pressure on schools to comply with the DCL. Even universities that might have found the DCL to be procedurally or substantively invalid were rolling over and complying because the cost of not doing so was simply too high. In essence, OCR's actions transformed what could have been a legitimate guidance document (if it had not had language that gave it the force of law) into something that was legally binding.

3.6 SUMMARY

The DCL effectively amended a legislative rule, which made it invalid. Alternately, even if the DCL did not amend a legislative rule it had the force of law, and so could only be promulgated as a legislative rule. In addition, by making the consequences of not complying so deleterious for schools, OCR effectively made the DCL legally binding. The consequence of each of these arguments is that the DCL was invalid and should not have been enforced.

3.7 CONCLUSION

Misrepresenting data and violating federal law were done to push through changes in how campus rape was handled, but such naked instrumentalism would prove to be a mistake. The existing studies, investigations, and court cases were enough on their own to justify OCR stepping in; misrepresenting what the studies showed was unnecessary. The mendacity was also counterproductive because it fomented distrust and undermined OCR's legitimacy.

The actions of OCR also raised the ire of a Republican-controlled Congress. In January 2016, Senator James Lankford, Chairman of the Subcommittee on Regulatory Affairs and Federal Management, U.S. Senate Committee on Government Affairs and Homeland Security, wrote a letter to the Acting Secretary for the DOE demanding that DOE provide statutory authority for the DCL.[95] Although Catherine E. Lhamon, the Assistant Secretary for Civil Rights, wrote a response,[96] Lankford was not satisfied:

> I again call on you personally to clarify that these policies are not required by Title IX, but reflect only one of various ways schools may choose to develop and implement policies for the prevention and remedy of sexual harassment and sexual violence that best meet the needs of their students and are compliant with federal law. I further ask that you immediately rein in the regulatory abuses within the Department of Education and take measures to ensure that all existing and future guidance documents issued by your agency are clearly and firmly rooted in statutory authority.[97]

Not complying with federal law ultimately doomed the DCL. It made it easy for the new Trump administration to undo. Indeed, on September 22, 2017, Secretary of Education Betsy DeVos formally rescinded the DCL.[98]

But the lesson to be learned here is not just a procedural one. Rejecting the notice and comment process deprived OCR of the opportunity to make the

Title IX guidelines better. As one administrator explained to me in a 2014 interview, "I'm not sure if all of the mandates have been thought through for all universities in all universities' context, it feels like stuff is missing or there would have been benefit to talking to campus administrators who are already doing this."[99] The next chapter takes a substantive look at the impact the Dear Colleague Letter had on the fairness of campus sexual misconduct adjudication.

REFERENCES

Letter from Russlyn Ali, Assistant Sec'y for Civil Rights, Office for Civil Rights, U.S. Dep't of Educ., to Title IX Coordinators 2 (Apr. 4, 2011), www2.ed.gov /about/offices/list/ocr/letters/colleague-201104.pdf/.

Cantalupo, Nancy Chi, *Burying Our Heads in the Sand: Lack of Knowledge, Knowledge Avoidance, and the Persistent Problem of Campus Peer Sexual Violence*, 43 LOY. U. CHI. L.J., 205, 205–266 (2011).

CANTOR, DAVID ET AL., AUU CLIMATE SURVEY ON SEXUAL ASSAULT AND SEXUAL MISCONDUCT (2015), ASSOC. OF AMERICAN UNIVERSITIES (Sept. 21, 2015), www.aau.edu/uploadedFiles/AAU_Publications/AAU_Re ports/Sexual_Assault_Campus_Survey/AAU_Campus_Climate_Surve y_12_14_15.pdf/.

Franklin, David L., *Legislative Rules, Nonlegislative Rules, and the Perils of the Short Cut*, 120 YALE L.J. 276, 282 (2010).

French, David, The Campus-Rape Lie, NAT'L REV. (July 6, 2015, 5:00 AM), www.nationalreview.com/magazine/2015/07/06/campus-rape-lie/.

Funk, William, A Primer on Nonlegislative Rules, 53 (4) ADMIN. L.J. 1321, 1321–1352 (2001).

Krebs, Christopher P. et al., *The Campus Sexual Assault Study*, NAT'L INST. OF JUST. (Dec. 2017), www.ojp.gov/pdffiles1/nij/grants/221153.pdf/.

Krebs, Christopher & Christine Lindquist, Setting the Record Straight on "1 in 5," TIME (Dec. 15, 2014, 1:53 PM EST), https://time.com/3633903/campus-rape-1-in-5-sexual-assault-setting-record-straight/.

Kruttschnitt, Candace et al., Estimating the Incidence of Rape and Sexual Assault, THE NAT'L ACAD. PRESS (Dec. 15, 2014, 1:53 PM EST), https://doi .org/10.17226/18605/.

Mendelson, Nina A., *Regulatory Beneficiaries and Informal Agency Policymaking*, 92 (3) CORNELL L. REV. 397–452 (2007).

Office of Management and Budget, Executive Office of the President, *Final Bulletin for Agency Good Guidance Practices*, 72 Fed. Reg., 3432, 3434 (Jan. 25, 2007).

Press Office, *Vice President Biden Announces New Administration Effort to Help Nation's Schools Address Sexual Violence*, U.S. DEP'T OF EDUC.

(Apr. 4, 2011), www.ed.gov/news/press-releases/vice-president-biden-announces-new-administration-effort-help-nations-schools-ad/.

Raso, Connor N., *Note, Strategic or Sincere? Analyzing Agency Use of Guidance Documents*, 119 YALE L.J. 782, 785 (2010).

SINOZICH, SOFI & LYNN LANGTON, SPECIAL REPORT: RAPE AND SEXUAL ASSAULT VICTIMIZATION AMONG COLLEGE AGE FEMALES, 1995–2013, U.S. DEP'T OF JUST., 1 (Dec. 2014), www.bjs.gov/content/pub/pdf/rsav caf9513.pdf/.

Strauss, Peter L., *Comments, The Rulemaking Continuum*, 41 DUKE L.J., 1463–1489, at 1463 (1992).

STRAUSS, PETER L. ET AL., *Administrative Law: Cases and Comments*, Foundation Press, 11th ed. 194 (2011).

NOTES

* First published by University of Kansas Law Review, Volume 64, Issue 4.

1. David G. Savage, *Schools Ruled Liable for Sex Harassment*, L.A. TIMES (May 25, 1999, 12 AM PT), www.latimes.com/archives/la-xpm-1999-may-25-mn-40816-story.html/.

2. Nancy Chi Cantalupo, *Burying Our Heads in the Sand: Lack of Knowledge, Knowledge Avoidance, and the Persistent Problem of Campus Peer Sexual Violence*, 43 (1) LOY. U. CHI. L.J. 205, 205–266 (2011).

3. Kristen Lombardi, Sexual Assault on Campus Shrouded in Secrecy, THE CENTER FOR PUBLIC INTEGRITY (Mar. 26, 2015, 5:21 PM ET), https://publicintegrity.org/education/sexual-assault-on-campus-shrouded-in-secrecy/.

4. Kristen Lombardi, A Lack of Consequences for Sexual Assault, THE CENTER FOR PUBLIC INTEGRITY (Jul. 14, 2014, 4:50 PM ET), https://publicintegrity.org/education/a-lack-of-consequences-for-sexual-assault/.

5. Press Office, *Vice President Biden Announces New Administration Effort to Help Nation's Schools Address Sexual Violence*, U.S. DEP'T OF EDUC. (Apr. 4, 2011), www.ed.gov/news/press-releases/vice-president-biden-announces-new-administration-effort-help-nations-schools-ad/.

6. Letter from Russlyn Ali, Assistant Sec'y for Civil Rights, Office for Civil Rights, U.S. Dep't of Educ., to Title IX Coordinators 2 (Apr. 4, 2011), www2.ed.gov/about/offices/list/ocr/letters/colleague-201104.pdf/.

7. *Id.* at 2.

8. *Id.*

9. Christopher P. Krebs et al., *The Campus Sexual Assault Study*, NAT'L INST. OF JUST. (Dec. 2017), www.ojp.gov/pdffiles1/nij/grants/221153.pdf/.

10. Christopher Krebs & Christine Lindquist, *Setting the Record Straight on "1 in 5,"* TIME (Dec. 15, 2014, 1:53 PM EST), https://time

.com/3633903/campus-rape-1-in-5-sexual-assault-setting-record-straight/.

11. SOFI SINOZICH & LYNN LANGTON, SPECIAL REPORT: RAPE AND SEXUAL ASSAULT VICTIMIZATION AMONG COLLEGE AGE FEMALES, 1995–2013, U.S. DEP'T OF JUST. (Dec. 2014), www.bjs.gov/content/pub/pdf/rsavcaf9513.pdf/.

12. Candace Kruttschnitt et al., *Estimating the Incidence of Rape and Sexual Assault*, THE NAT'L ACAD. PRESS (Dec. 15, 2014, 1:53 PM EST), https://doi.org/10.17226/18605/.

13. David French, *The Campus-Rape Lie*, NAT'L REV. (July 6, 2015, 5:00 AM), www.nationalreview.com/magazine/2015/07/06/campus-rape-lie/.

14. 20 U.S.C. § 1682 (2012).

15. Peter L. Strauss, Comments, *The Rulemaking Continuum*, 41 DUKE L.J. 1463, 1463 (1992).

16. Nina A. Mendelson, *Regulatory Beneficiaries and Informal Agency Policymaking*, 92 (3) CORNELL L. REV. 397–452 (2007).

17. Dear Colleague Letter, *supra* note 6, at 1 n.1.

> The Office of Management and Budget (OMB) has defined a significant guidance document as a guidance document which may reasonably be anticipated to: (i) Lead to an annual effect on the economy of $100 million or more or adversely affect in a material way the economy, a sector of the economy, productivity, competition, jobs, the environment, public health or safety, or State, local, or tribal governments or communities; or (ii) Create a serious inconsistency or otherwise interfere with an action taken or planned by another agency; or (iii) Materially alter the budgetary impact of entitlements, grants, user fees, or loan programs or the rights and obligations of recipients thereof; or (iv) Raise novel legal or policy issues arising out of legal mandates, the President's priorities, or the principles set forth in Executive Order 12866, as further amended.

Office of Management and Budget, Executive Office of the President, *Final Bulletin for Agency Good Guidance Practices*, 72 Fed. Reg., 3432, 3434 (Jan. 25, 2007).

18. 5 U.S.C. § 553(c), 556, 557 (2012). This process is more demanding and less common than notice and comment. David L. Franklin, *Legislative Rules, Nonlegislative Rules, and the Perils of the Short Cut*, 120 YALE L.J. 276, 282 (2010).

19. 5 U.S.C. § 553(b)(3), (c) (2012); Franklin, *supra* note 18, at 282.

20. 5 U.S.C. § 553(b)(A) (2012).

21. Final Bulletin, *supra* note 17, at 3437; *Cf.* Sean Croston, *The Petition Is Mightier than the Sword: Rediscovering an Old Weapon in the Battles Over "Regulation Through Guidance,"* 63 ADMIN. L. REV. 381, 382–383 (2011).

22. H.R. REP. NO. 106–1009, at 1 (2000) ("Regrettably, the committee's investigation found that some guidance documents were intended to bypass the rulemaking process and expanded an agency's power beyond the point at which Congress said it should stop. Such 'backdoor' regulation is an abuse of power and a corruption of our Constitutional system.").

23. *See* Appalachian Power Co. v. Envtl. Prot. Agency, 208 F.3d 1015, 1020 (D. C. Cir. 2000). The D.C. Circuit noted:

> The phenomenon we see in this case is familiar. Congress passes a broadly worded statute. The agency follows with regulations containing broad language, open-ended phrases, ambiguous standards and the like. Then as years pass, the agency issues circulars or guidance or memoranda, explaining, interpreting, defining and often expanding the commands in regulations. One guidance document may yield another and then another and so on. Several words in a regulation may spawn hundreds of pages of text as the agency offers more and more detail regarding what its regulations demand of regulated entities. Law is made, without notice and comment, without public participation, and without publication in the Federal Register or the Code of Federal Regulations. *Id.*

24. *See* Mark Seidenfeld, *Substituting Substantive for Procedural Review of Guidance Documents*, 90 TEX. L. REV. 331, 352 (2011); Robert A. Anthony, *Interpretive Rules, Policy Statements, Guidances, Manuals and the Like – Should Federal Agencies Use Them to Bind the Public?*, 41 DUKE L.J. 1311, 1327 (1992). *But see* Connor N. Raso, Note, *Strategic or Sincere? Analyzing Agency Use of Guidance Documents*, 119 YALE L.J. 782, 785 (2010).

25. Final Bulletin, *supra* note 17, at 3432 ("OMB has been concerned about the proper development and use of agency guidance documents.").

26. *See Id.*

27. *See* Franklin *supra* note 18, at 278.

28. Am. Hosp. Ass'n v. Bowen, 834 F.2d 1037, 1046 (D.C. Cir. 1987) (citing Cmty. Nutrition Inst. v. Young, 818 F.2d 943, 946 (D.C. Cir. 1987)).

29. Gen. Motors Corp. v. Ruckelshaus, 742 F.2d 1561, 1565 (D.C. Cir. 1984); Richard J. Pierce, Jr., *Distinguishing Legislative Rules from Interpretive Rules*, 52 ADMIN. L. REV. 547, 547–548 (2000).

30. William Funk, *A Primer on Nonlegislative Rules*, 53 (4) ADMIN. L.J. 1321, 1321–1352 (2001).

31. Am. Mining Cong. v. United States Dep't of Labor, 995 F.2d 1106 (D.C. Cir. 1993).

32. PETER L. STRAUSS ET AL., ADMINISTRATIVE LAW: CASES AND COMMENTS, FOUNDATION PRESS, 11th ed. 194 (2011).

33. Am. Meeting Cong., 995 F.2d at 1112.

34. See Raso, *supra* note 24 at 789.

35. *See* Ass'n of Flight Attendants-CWA v. Huerta, 785 F.3d 710, 716 (D.C. Cir. 2015).

36. *See* Nat'l Res. Def. Council v. Envtl. Prot. Agency, 643 F.3d 311, 321 (D.C. Cir. 2011).

37. *See* Mendoza v. Perez, 754 F.3d 1002, 1020–1021 (D.C. Cir. 2014).

38. www.govinfo.gov/content/pkg/FR-2001-01-19/pdf/01-1606.pdf.

39. U.S. Department of Education, Office for Civil Rights, *Revised Sexual Harassment Guidance: Harassment of Students by School Employees, Other Students or Third Parties*, U.S. DEP'T OF EDUC. 1, 1–39 (Jan. 19, 2001), www2.ed.gov/offices/OCR/archives/pdf/shguide.pdf/.

40. U.S. Department of Education, Office for Civil Rights, *Sexual Harassment Guidance 1997: Harassment of Students by School Employees, Other Students, or Third Parties*, U.S. DEP'T OF EDUC. 12042 (Mar. 13, 1997), www2.ed.gov/about/offices/list/ocr/docs/sexhar01.html/.

41. *Revised Sexual Harassment Guidance*, at 21.

42. *See* Dear Colleague Letter *supra* note 6, at 8.

43. Revised Sexual Harassment Guidance (Jan. 2001), at 21.

44. *Id.* at 10.

45. *Id.* at 20.

46. *See* Dear Colleague Letter, *supra* note 6, at 11.

47. Revised Sexual Harassment Guidance (Jan. 2001), at 20.

48. *See* Dear Colleague Letter, *supra* note 6, at 11.

49. *See* Dear Colleague Letter, *supra* note 6, at 12.

50. Revised Sexual Harassment Guidance (Jan. 2001), at 20.

51. *See* Dear Colleague Letter, *supra* note 6, at 12.

52. *See* Dear Colleague Letter, *supra* note 6, at 13.

53. Revised Sexual Harassment Guidance (Jan. 2001), at 17.

54. *Id.* at 20.

55. *See* Dear Colleague Letter, *supra* note 6, at 16.

56. *Id.* at 16.

57. Revised Sexual Harassment Guidance (Jan. 2001), at 21.

58. *See* Dear Colleague Letter, *supra* note 6, at 15–17.

59. Revised Sexual Harassment Guidance (Jan. 2001), at 14–15.

60. *See* Dear Colleague Letter, *supra* note 6, at 16.

61. Sexual Harassment Guidance (Mar. 1997).

62. Revised Sexual Harassment Guidance (Jan. 2001), at 31.

63. *Id.*

64. *See* Dear Colleague Letter, *supra* note 6, at 12.
65. Gen. Elec. Co. v. Envtl. Prot. Agency, 290 F.3d 377, 382 (D.C. Cir. 2002).
66. *Id.* (quoting Cmty. Nutrition Inst. v. Young, 818 F.2d 943, 946 (D.C. Cir. 1987); Chamber of Commerce v. Dep't of Labor, 174 F.3d 206, 212 (D.C. Cir. 1999)).
67. *Id.* (quoting McLouth Steel Prod. Corp. v. Thomas, 838 F.2d 1317, 1320 (D.C. Cir. 1988)); *see also* Miller v. Cal. Speedway Corp., 536 F.3d 1020, 1033 (9th Cir. 2008). In Miller, the Ninth Circuit articulated a similar test:

> "Interpretive rules merely explain, but do not add to, the substantive law that already exists in the form of a 'statute or legislative rule,' whereas legislative rules 'create rights, impose obligations or affect a change in existing law pursuant to authority delegated by Congress.'"

Id. (quoting Hemp Indus. Ass'n v. DEA, 333 F.3d 1082, 1087 (9th Cir. 2003)).
68. *Id.*
69. *Id.* at 383.
70. *Id.* at 384.
71. *See* Dear Colleague Letter, *supra* note 6, at 1 n.1.
72. *See* Appalachian Power Co. v. Envtl. Prot. Agency, 208 F.3d 1015, 1023, 1028 (D.C. Cir. 2000) (holding in a unanimous decision that the guidance document was a legislative rule despite issuing a disclaimer at the beginning of the document saying: "The policies set forth in this paper are intended solely as guidance, do not represent final Agency action, and cannot be relied upon to create any rights enforceable by any party."); *see also* McLouth Steel Prod. Corp. v. Thomas, 838 F.2d 1317, 1324 (D.C. Cir. 1988) (holding that the EPA's vertical and horizontal spread model is a rule and not a policy).
73. *Appalachian Power Co.*, 208 F.3d at 1024. *But see* SBC Inc. v. FCC, 414 F.3d 486, 495 (3d Cir. 2005) (quoting Viacom Int'l, Inc. v. FCC, 672 F.2d 1034, 1042 (2d Cir. 1982)) ("An agency's determination that 'its order is interpretive,' and therefore not subject to notice and comment requirements, 'in itself is entitled to a significant degree of deference.'").
74. Appalachian Power Co., 208 F.3d at 1024 (internal citations omitted).
75. Dear Colleague Letter, *supra* note 6, at 8.
76. *Id.* at 10.
77. *Id.*
78. *Id.* at 11.
79. *Id.*
80. *Id.*
81. *Id.* at 12.

82. *Id.*
83. *Id.* at 13.
84. *Id.* at 16.
85. *Id.*
86. *Id.* at 15.
87. Gen. Elec. Co. v. Envtl. Prot. Agency, 390 F.3d 377, 385 (D.C. Cir. 2002).
88. *Id.* at 382 (internal citations omitted).
89. Appalachian Power Co. v. Envtl. Prot. Agency, 208 F.3d 1015, 1023 (D.C. Cir. 2000).
90. Gen. Elec. Co., 390 F.3d at 385.
91. Final Bulletin, *supra* note 17, at 3440.
92. Chamber of Commerce of the U.S. v. U.S. Dep't of Labor, 174 F.3d 206 (D.C. Cir. 1999).
93. *Id.* at 208.
94. *Id.* at 213.
95. James Lankford, Sen. Lankford Letter to Education Department, SCRIBD (Jan. 7, 2016), www.scribd.com/doc/294821262/Sen-Lankford-letter-to-Education-Department/.
96. Catherine E. Lhamon, Letter from Catherine Lhamon to Sen. Lankford, CHRONICLE (Feb. 17, 2016), http://chronicle.com/items/biz/pdf/DEPT.%20of%20EDUCATION%20RESPONSE%20TO%20LANKFORD%20LETTER%202-17-16.pdf/.
97. James Lankford, Sen. Lankford Letter to the Honorable John B. King, Jr., JAMES LANKFORD (Mar. 4, 2016), www.lankford.senate.gov/imo/media/doc/3.4.16%20Lankford%20letter%20to%20Dept.%20of%20Education.pdf/.
98. Valerie Strauss, *DeVos Withdraws Obama-era Guidance on Campus Sexual Assault. Read the Letter*, WASHINGTON POST (Sept. 22, 2017), www.washingtonpost.com/news/answer-sheet/wp/2017/09/22/devos-withdraws-obama-era-guidance-on-campus-sexual-assault-read-the-letter/.
99. Telephone Interview with Univ. Adm'r (Nov. 14, 2014).

4

The Rubber Meets the Road[*]

The 2011 Dear Colleague Letter (DCL) constituted a sea change in Title IX enforcement. For the first time, the federal government gave extensive, detailed requirements on what schools needed to do. Five months after the DCL was published, "[a]t least 25 schools, ranging from Stanford University to the University of Virginia, had already changed some policies in response to the letter."[1] Those that resisted were aggressively pushed to comply. High profile investigations into top universities were conducted by OCR, and it found a number of schools in violation of Title IX, including Princeton University[2] and Harvard Law School.[3] Although OCR has rarely taken away federal funding for Title IX violations,[4] it has reached settlements in which schools agreed to change the way they handled sexual assault so as to meet the protocol set forth in the DCL.[5]

Under pressure from survivors, OCR also resorted to publicly naming schools under investigation.[6] Advocates claimed that doing so provided "information crucial for survivors seeking help and change when their schools violate their rights."[7] They also contended that it improved government enforcement and increased government accountability. On May 1, 2014, OCR released a list of forty-four colleges and universities under investigation.[8] By the last day of the Obama administration, there were 305 sexual harassment cases under investigation at 224 postsecondary institutions.[9]

Many were critical of the list. They argued that because "... colleges and universities are placed on the list merely because they are under Title IX investigation, the list unfairly casts institutions in a negative light ... ."[10] Publishing such information also marked a notable departure from government policy. The information was released even though the Equal Employment Opportunity Commission (EEOC) is statutorily barred from releasing the names of those under investigation in Title VII cases,[11] and "[a]ny person who makes public information in violation of this subsection shall be fined not more than \$1,000 or imprisoned for not more than one year, or both."[12] Similarly, the Department of Justice has an explicit policy against releasing information on current investigations except in unusual circumstances.[13] The reason for this non-disclosure policy is in part because "Justice Department guidelines, rules of professional conduct, and rules of court, as well as considerations of fairness to defendants, require that we not make comments that could prejudice a defendant's right to a fair trial."[14]

Whether or not these lists were ethical, they certainly had an impact. People paid attention, and they negatively influenced the schools' financial bottom line. Schools under suspicion for violating Title IX received fewer applications from prospective students and fewer donations from alumnae.[15]

In this chapter, I provide an overview to how schools were adjudicating campus sexual misconduct in the wake of the DCL. I present data gathered over a twenty-seven-month period, from October 2014 to January 2017. That means it was compiled while the DCL was fully in effect.

4.1 METHODOLOGY

In October 2014, fifty flagship state universities were contacted by email and asked a series of questions about the procedural protections afforded to students alleged to have committed sexual assault.[16] Nine months later, in June 2015, the highest-ranked twenty universities, the top ten liberal arts colleges, and the top five historically black colleges, as determined by the 2014 U.S. News and World Reports higher education rankings,[17] were contacted by email and asked the same series of questions. Although a few colleges and universities responded to the initial inquiries, many did so only after additional emails and phone calls. Some administrators were extremely reluctant to share information,[18] and most who agreed to talk more generally about their feelings toward the climate at the time did so only with the promise that neither they nor their institution would be identified. Online policies were used to fill in the gaps, but even if the written policy answered most or even all the questions, follow-up emails and/or phone calls were attempted to confirm results. These findings should be regarded with some caution since online information may be incorrect and/or schools may have changed their policies soon after.

All of the schools were asked about protections considered fundamental to those accused of a crime by the state: the standard of proof, the right to an adjudicatory hearing, the right to confront and cross-examine witnesses, the right to counsel, the right to silence, and the right to appeal. Other than the right to appeal, all are part of the Bill of Rights, which through the incorporation clause of the Fourteenth Amendment have been deemed to apply to the states.[19] Although no school, whether public or private, is "required to adhere to the standards of due process guaranteed to criminal defendants ... courts may refer to those rules in evaluating the fairness of a particular hearing."[20]

4.2 FINDINGS

The Table 4.1 shows the findings of this investigation.

TABLE 4.1 *Standard of Proof*

Standard of proof	98% Preponderance of the evidence (83)		1% Beyond reasonable doubt (1)		1% Unknown (1)	
	40% Private (33)	60% Public (50)	100% Private (1)	0% Public (0)	100% Private (1)	0% Public (0)

Different standard for non-sex offenses?	18% Yes (15)		73% No (62)		9% Unknown (8)	
	53% Private (8)	46% Public (7)	35% Private (22)	65% Public (40)	63% Private (5)	37% Public (3)

The most controversial part of the DCL was requiring schools to set the standard of proof at preponderance of the evidence. The Office for Civil Rights justified its decision on the grounds that preponderance is the standard used in Title VII hearings,[21] but it did not adopt Title VII protections that would have benefited the accused. For instance, the Civil Rights Act of 1991 gives both parties in a Title VII case the right to a jury trial if one party requests compensatory or punitive damages.[22] The right to trial means that both parties enjoy a panoply of other protections including the right to counsel and the right to confront and cross-examine witnesses. Not only did OCR not mandate or even recommend that these Title VII rights be provided, it actually recommended against some of them in the DCL. For instance, OCR strongly discouraged schools from allowing the parties to directly question one another.[23]

Prior to the DCL, many schools used a higher burden of proof. A 2011 study by the Foundation for Individual Rights in Education (FIRE) found that seventeen of the top 100 colleges used the higher standard of clear and convincing evidence or beyond a reasonable doubt.[24] However one school of the top 100, Brown University, clearly used a lower standard – "reasonable basis."[25] By 2017, all but one school (the U.S. Naval Academy, which is exempt from Title IX)[26] had changed their standard to preponderance of the evidence. Fourteen schools (18%) set a higher standard of proof for at least some non-sex allegations. Of the fourteen schools with a higher standard for non sex allegations, one used proof beyond a reasonable doubt and the others used clear and convincing evidence.

TABLE 4.2 *Right to an Adjudicatory Hearing*

Adjudicatory or Investigatory	72% Adjudicatory (61)		28% Investigatory (24)		0% Unknown	
	33% Private (20)	67% Public (41)	63% Private (15)	37% Public (9)	0% Private (0)	0% Public (0)

As shown in Table 4.2, all schools used either an adjudicatory or an investigatory model for determining whether a violation occurred. For the sixty-one schools (72%) that used the adjudicatory model, the first step was almost always an initial investigation, but the determination of whether a violation occurred could be made at an adjudicatory hearing. An adjudicatory hearing is similar to a trial in the sense that evidence is presented in front of a fact finder with the accused present. Witnesses testify at the hearing, although schools usually allow hearsay evidence, which means the fact finder may consider a written witness statement or the Title IX Investigator's report summarizing a witness interview.

Twenty-four schools (28%) used an investigatory model. The investigatory model is one in which a single investigator (or sometimes two) prepares a report after having met with the parties and any witnesses. The accused student does not have the right to be present for these interviews. Sometimes that same investigator determines whether a violation occurred, and sometimes the report is turned over to a third party (or parties) who determine(s) whether a violation occurred based on the contents of the investigation report. That person may request additional information, but there will never be a live hearing in which all of the evidence is presented in one place, with the accused present.

TABLE 4.3 *Schools that Provide Right to Adjudicatory Hearing*

	Adjudicatory Model Detail (% of 61 schools)		
Right to an Adjudicatory Hearing	89% – Yes (54)	26% Private (14)	74% Public (40)
	10% – Yes, Limited–school decides (6)	83% Private (5)	17% Public (1)
	1% – Yes, Limited–evidence (1)	100% Private (1)	0% Public (0)
Panel Composition	15% – 1 staff / faculty / admin / outsider (8)	25% Private (2)	75% Public (6)
	1% – 1–2 faculty / staff / admin (1)	0% Private (0)	100% Public (1)
	24% – 3 or more faculty / staff / admin (14)	57% Private (8)	43% Public (6)
	47% – 3 or more faculty / staff / student (28)	18% Private (5)	82% Public (23)
	1% – 3 or more student only (1)	0% Private (0)	100% Public (1)
	3% – 3 or more unspecified (2)	50% Private (1)	50% Public (1)
	8% Unknown (7)	57% Private (4)	43% Public (3)
Right to Challenge Panelist	77% – Yes (47)	26% Private (12)	74% Public (35)
	3% – No (2)	0% Private (0)	100% Public (2)
	20% Unknown (12)	67% Private (8)	33% Public (4)
Panel vote	62% – majority (38)	32% Private (12)	68% Public (26)
	11% – 1 decider (7)	29% Private (2)	71% Public (5)
	2% – 1 or 2 deciders (1)	0% Private (0)	100% Public (1)
	5% – consensus (3)	0% Private (0)	100% Public (3)
	7% – unanimous (4)	75% Private (3)	25% Public (1)
	13% Unknown (8)	38% Private (3)	62% Public (5)

For the sixty-one schools that used the adjudicatory model, as depicted in Table 4.3, fifty-four (89%) gave the accused an absolute right to an adjudicatory hearing. That meant that if he requested a hearing to resolve guilt, he would get one. Six schools (10%) allowed for an adjudicatory hearing but only if the school decided it was the appropriate way to determine guilt.

For those schools that used an adjudicatory model, eight (15%) allowed a single person to determine responsibility. One school (1%) had one or two decide. Fourteen schools (24%) had a panel of three or more faculty, staff, or administrators. Twenty-eight (47%) had a panel of three or more, but it included students. One (1%) had a panel of three or more students determine responsibility, and two (3%) had three or more decide, but the exact composition was unknown.

Thirty-eight schools (62%) used a majority vote to determine guilt. The minimum size of the adjudicatory body using a majority vote was three. Seven schools (11%) had one person make the decision, and one school (2%) required that one or two make the decision. Three schools (5%) required that the decision be made by consensus, and four schools (7%) mandated that the decision be unanimous.

TABLE 4.4 *Schools that Use Investigatory Model*

Investigatory Model Detail (% of 24 schools)			
Who Decides Responsibility	42% – Single Model-Investigator & Decision-Maker Are the Same (10)	60% Private (6)	40% Public (4)
	21% – Split Model-Investigator Reports & Separate Single Individual Decides (5)	20% Private (1)	80% Public (4)
	33% – Split Model-Investigator Reports & 2 or More Individuals Decide (8)	88% Private (7)	12% Public (1)
	4% Unknown (1)	100% Private (1)	0% Public (0)

All of the schools that used the investigatory model (Table 4.4) had an investigator prepare a report into what occurred, but they differed regarding who determined responsibility. Ten schools (42%) used the single investigator model. That meant that the person who investigated the case was also responsible for determining whether a violation had occurred. Five schools (21%) used a split model in which one person investigated, and a separate person determined whether a violation had occurred. Eight schools (33%) had two or more people (all separate from the investigator) determine whether a violation had occurred.

TABLE 4.5 *Right to Confront and Cross-Examine*

Right to Confront			
	Yes – 8% (6)	33% Private (2)	67% Public (4)
	Limited through Investigator – 7% (6)	50% Private (3)	50% Public (3)
	Limited through Panel – 60% (51)	35% Private (18)	65% Public (33)
	No – 20% (18)	56% Private (10)	44% Public (8)
	Unknown – 5% (4)	50% Private (2)	50% Public (2)

As Table 4.5 shows, only six schools gave the accused the right to directly question the complainant. Fifty-seven schools (67%) provided for a limited right to question the complainant. Six of these schools (7%) required that the question be asked through the investigator, who could decide whether to ask it. If the investigator did ask, the accused would not be there to hear the answer. The other fifty-one (60%) that allowed a limited right to question required the respondent to submit a question orally or in writing to the hearing officer, who decided whether to ask.

Some of these schools explicitly stated that the complainant need not be present or respond, but I believe this policy applied to all schools – even those that gave the accused the right to question the complainant. In *Doe v. Cincinnati*, for example, Doe had the right, per the written policy at the University of Cincinnati, to question his accuser. However, his accuser did not show up for the hearing, and the school still admitted her statement even though she never testified before the hearing panel, and Doe never had an opportunity to question her. Cincinnati insisted that his accuser's nonappearance did not impact the fairness of the proceedings "because Doe still had an opportunity to be heard ... Because plaintiff was able to draw attention to alleged inconsistencies in Roe's statement, defendants argue that cross-examination would have been futile."[27] As will be discussed in more detail in the next chapter, the Sixth Circuit disagreed.

Eighteen schools (20%) did not allow any questioning of the other side, either direct or indirect. Four schools (5%) were unknown.

TABLE 4.6 *Additional Procedural Rights*

Procedural Right	Yes			No		Unknown	
Right to Counsel	Yes, robust 11% (9)	Yes, as advisor but silent in hearing 80% (68)	Yes, but limited role 3% (3)	No % (4)		Unknown 0% (1)	
	11% Private (1) / 88% Public (8)	44% Private (30) / 56% Public (38)	33% Private (1) / 67% Public (2)	50% Private (2) / 50% Public (2)		0% Private (1) / 0% Public (0)	
Right to Remain Silent	Yes, no adverse inference 73% (61)	Yes, but adverse inference may be drawn 4% (3)		No 1% (1)		Unknown % (20)	
	41% Private (19) / 69% Public (42)	0% Private (0) / 100% Public (3)		100% Private (1) / 0% Public (0)		75% Private (15) / 25% Public (5)	
Right to Appeal	Yes 99% (84)			No 1% (1)		Unknown 0% (0)	
	42% Private (35) / 58% Public (49)			0% Private (0) / 100% Public (1)		0% Private (0) / 0% Public (0)	

As Table 4.6 shows, the vast majority of universities (80 or 94%) gave accused students the right to counsel, but it was almost always an abridged right. Just nine schools (11%) gave a robust right to counsel. That meant the attorney would be allowed to participate fully in the hearing by questioning witnesses and addressing the panel directly. Sixty-eight (80%) allowed counsel but only in an advisory role, and three (4%) allowed counsel but only in a limited role. Four schools (5%) denied the right to counsel completely. One school was unknown.

Sixty-one schools (73%) gave respondents the right to remain silent. Three schools (4%) allowed the respondent to remain silent but explicitly allowed an adverse inference to be drawn. One school (1%) did not give respondents the right to remain silent. The results were unknown for twenty schools (24%).

Finally, all schools but one (1%) provided the right to appeal.

4.3 CONCLUSION

Many applauded OCR's efforts to improve campus sexual assault adjudication,[28] but others contended that universities had gone too far in sacrificing the rights of the accused.[29] In this chapter, I have discussed how schools adjudicated campus sexual assault in the wake of the DCL. In the next chapter, I evaluate the fairness of these proceedings.

NOTES

* The date on the public schools was originally published by Arizona State Law Journal, Volume 48, Issue 3. The data on the private schools was originally published by University of Miami Law Review, Volume 71, Issue 2.

1. Stacy Teicher, *Feds Warn Colleges: Handle Sexual Assault Reports Properly*, THE CHRISTIAN SCIENCE MONITOR (Sept. 2, 2011), www .csmonitor.com/USA/Education/2011/0902/Feds-warn-colleges-handle-se xual-assault-reports-properly.

2. Press Office, *Princeton University Found in Violation of Title IX, Reaches Agreement with U.S. Education Department to Address, Prevent Sexual Assault and Harassment of Students*, U.S. DEP'T. OF EDUC. (Nov. 5, 2014), www.ed.gov/news/press-releases/princeton-university-found-violation-title-ix-reaches-agreement-us-education-department-address-prevent-sexual-assault-and-harassment-students [hereinafter *Princeton Violation*].

3. Press Office, *Harvard Law School Found in Violation of Title IX, Agrees to Remedy Sexual Harassment, Including Sexual Assault of Students*, U.S. DEP'T. OF EDUC. (Dec. 30, 2014), www.ed.gov/news/press-releases/har vard-law-school-found-violation-title-ix-agrees-remedy-sexual-harassment-including-sexual-assault-students [hereinafter *Harvard Violation*].

4. In 2018, the Chicago school district did not receive a four-million-dollar federal grant that it would have otherwise received because it had failed to adequately address sexual violence complaints. Associated Press, *Chicago District Loses Federal Grant over Title IX Violations*, EDUCATION WEEK (Oct. 9, 2018), www.edweek.org/leadership/chicago-district-loses-federal-grant-over-title-ix-violations/2018/10.

5. *See Princeton Violation, supra* note 2; *Harvard Violation, supra* note 3.

6. Dana Bolger & Alexandra Brodsky, Trump's *Administration Wants to Hide Colleges That Have Problems with Sexual Assault*, THE WASHINGTON POST (June 30, 2017), www.washingtonpost.com/news/posteverything/wp/2017/06/30/trumps-administration-wants-to-hide-colleges-that-have-problems-with-sexual-assault/.

7. *Id.*

8. Press Office, *U.S. Department of Education Releases List of Higher Education Institutions with Open Title IX Sexual Violence Investigations*, DEP'T. OF EDUC. (May 1, 2014), www.ed.gov/news/press-releases/us-department-education-releases-list-higher-education-institutions-open-title-i/.

9. U.S. Department of Education, Office for Civil Rights, *List of Sexual Violence Investigations Open at the Postsecondary Level, Including the Dates the Specific Investigations Were Initiated* (Mar. 22, 2017), https://static1.squarespace.com/static/5722daf11d07c02f9c1739cc/t/58e579ddff7c500aec554c96/1491433949950/Ed_titleIX-investigations-27March2017.pdf/.

10. Benjamin Wermund, *Title IX List Going out of Print?* (June 29, 2017), www.politico.com/tipsheets/morning-education/2017/06/29/title-ix-list-going-out-of-print-221112/.

11. 42 U.S.C. § 2000e-5(b) (2012) ("Charges shall not be made public by the Commission.").

12. *Id.*

13. *Frequently Asked Questions*, U.S. DEP'T. OF JUST. (June 23, 2015), www.justice.gov/usao-ri/frequently-asked-questions-0/.

14. *Id.*

15. Gayle Nelson, *The High Cost of Sexual Assaults on College Campuses*, NON PROFIT QUARTERLY (June 23, 2015), https://nonprofitquarterly.org/2015/06/23/the-high-cost-of-sexual-assaults-on-college-campuses/; Tyler Kingkade, *Alumni Are Creating a Network to Put Pressure on Universities over Sexual Assault*, HUFFINGTON POST (May 28, 2014), www.huffingtonpost.com/2014/05/28/alumni-network-sexual-assaultcollege_n_5401194.html.

16. The author used a table from the *Journal of Blacks in Higher Education* to determine the flagship universities. Since State University of New York (SUNY) was not on the list, the author chose SUNY Albany because it is the capital of New York. *See Ranking the Nation's Flagship State Universities and Historically Black Colleges on Their Success in Enrolling Low-Income Students*, J. BLACKS IN HIGHER EDUC. (Sept. 2, 2016), www.jbhe.com/news_views/60lowincomeenrolls.html.

17. The author referred to the list compiled by the 2014 U.S. News and World Reports. NATIONAL UNIVERSITY RANKINGS, U.S. NEWS & WORLD REPORT (Sept. 10, 2013), http://colleges.usnews.rankingsandreviews.com/b est-colleges/rankings/national-universities/spp+25[https://web.archive.org/we b/20140707054623/http://colleges.usnews.rankingsandreviews.com/best-col leges/rankings/national-universities/spp+25]; *National Liberal Arts College Rankings*, U.S. NEWS & WORLD REPORT (Sept. 10, 2013), http://col leges.usnews.rankingsandreviews.com/best-colleges/rankings/national-lib eral-arts-colleges/spp+25[https://web.archive.org/web/20140401054309/http:// colleges.usnews.rankingsandreviews.com/best-colleges/rankings/national-lib eral-arts-colleges/spp+25]; *Historically Black College and Universities Ranking*, U.S. NEWS & WORLD REPORT (Sept. 10, 2013), http://colleges .usnews.rankingsandreviews.com/best-colleges/rankings/hbcu/.

18. For instance, one Title IX official stated that he would not answer any questions. Information from that school was obtained from someone in the Dean's office. At another school, the person working as the Title IX Officer hung up the phone, but, fortunately, another person at that institution was willing to answer questions.

19. U.S. CONST. amend. XIV, § 1. (The Fourteenth Amendment of the U.S. Constitution prohibits states from depriving "any person of life, liberty, or property, without due process of law."). In determining what that means, the Supreme Court turned to the first ten Amendments of the Constitution, otherwise known as the Bill of Rights. U.S. CONST. amends. I-X. Over time, in piecemeal fashion, the Court held that almost all of these rights were protected against state action through the Due Process Clause of the Fourteenth Amendment. *See generally* Duncan v. Louisiana, 391 U.S. 145 (1968).

20. Doe v. Brandeis Univ., 177 F. Supp. 3d 561, 602 (D. Mass. 2016) (internal citations omitted).

21. *Id.* at 10–11.

22. 42 U.S.C. § 1981a(c) (2012).

23. Dear Colleague Letter, *supra* note 19, at 12.

24. *Standard of Evidence Survey: Colleges and Universities Respond to OCR's New Mandate*, FIRE (Oct. 28, 2011), www.thefire.org/standard-of-evidence-survey-colleges-and-universities-respond-to-ocrs-new-mandate/.

25. *Id.*

26. Title IX "does not apply to an educational institution whose primary purpose is the training of individuals for the military service of the United States, or the merchant marine." 20 U.S.C. § 1681(a)(4); 34 C.F. R. § 106.13.

27. Doe v. Univ. of Cincinnati, 872 F.3d 393, 401 (6th Cir. 2017).

28. *See* Michelle J. Anderson, *Campus Sexual Assault Adjudication and Resistance to Reform*, 125 YALE L.J. 1940, 1940–2005 (2016); Lavinia

M. Weizel, Note, *The Process That Is Due: Preponderance of the Evidence as the Standard of Proof for University Adjudications of Student-on-Student Sexual Assault Complaints*, 53 B.C. L. Rev. 1613, 1642–1655 (2012); Amy Chmielewski, Note, *Defending The Preponderance of the Evidence Standard in College Adjudications of Sexual Assault*, 2013 BYU Educ. & L.J. 143, 149–174 (2013).

29. *See* William A. Jacobsen, *Accused on Campus: Charges Dropped, but the Infamy Remains*, Legal Insurrection (May 16, 2015, 8:30 PM), http://legalinsurrection.com/2015/05/accused-on-campus-charges-dropped-but-the-infamy-remains/; *see also* Ryan D. Ellis, Note, *Mandating Injustice: The Preponderance of the Evidence Mandate Creates a New Threat to Due Process on Campus*, 32 Rev. Litig. 65, 80–81 (2013); Barclay Sutton Hendrix, Note, *A Feather on One Side, a Brick on the Other: Tilting the Scale Against Males Accused of Sexual Assault in Campus Disciplinary Proceedings*, 47 Ga. L. Rev. 591, 599 (2013); Stephen Henrick, Note, *A Hostile Environment for Student Defendants: Title IX and Sexual Assault on College Campuses*, 40 N. Ky. L. Rev. 49 (2013); Naomi Shatz, *Feminists, We Are Not Winning the War on Campus Sexual Assault*, Huffington Post (Oct. 29, 2014, 6:44 PM), www.huffingtonpost.com/naomi-shatz/feminists-we-are-not-winn_b_6071500.html/.

5

Ready, Fire, Aim*

The Dear Colleague Letter was extremely controversial. Some approved of OCR's changes to campus sexual assault adjudication,[1] including at least ninety professors who signed a White Paper in support of the DCL.[2] In addition, many university officials voiced confidence that students' rights were being respected. One administrator told me: "A student can always be disappointed with an outcome, but did they think they were treated fairly? I've had letters from students that were expelled but thanked me for the support they were given."[3]

Others were deeply critical.[4] Members of the law faculty at both Harvard[5] and the University of Pennsylvania[6] publicly called for greater procedural rights for the accused, and a Senior Fellow at Stanford University's Hoover Institute decried OCR's Dear Colleague Letter for "institutionalizing a presumption of guilt in sexual assault cases."[7] The popular press also started to call attention to the experiences of men who claimed their universities never gave them a meaningful chance to defend themselves before finding them responsible for rape and expelling them.[8] A few college administrators were also concerned by the current climate. As one official framed it to me:

> The pendulum has shifted so far that it's "ready, fire, aim" when it comes to the rights of respondents. Whether truly innocent, the reality is that OCR wants you to take action against them because underreporting is such a huge problem so that even if we get it wrong ... This system is offensive to legal minds ... We are the people breaking the casks of whiskey during prohibition. This is the law, but it doesn't feel quite right. To be in the trenches doesn't feel quite right.[9]

More and more students started challenging Title IX proceedings in court. They advanced many theories under both state and federal law, including negligent infliction of emotional distress, violation of equal protection, and reverse gender discrimination.[10] In this chapter, I focus on two such theories in evaluating the fairness of DCL-influenced proceedings: violation of procedural due process and breach of contract for failure to comport with basic procedural fairness. The first provides a stronger basis for recovery, but it requires state action, which means it is probably only available to public school students.[11]

5.1 DO THESE PROCEDURES SATISFY PROCEDURAL DUE PROCESS?

The Fourteenth Amendment to the U.S. Constitution states in relevant part: "no state shall make or enforce any law which shall … deprive any person of life, liberty or property without due process of law."[12] Since the disciplinary proceedings of public universities clearly constitute state action,[13] two questions must be answered: Does the punishment constitute a deprivation of liberty or property, and if so, what procedural protections does due process require?[14]

5.1.1 *Does the Punishment Constitute a Deprivation of Liberty or Property?*

In *Goss v. Lopez*, the U.S. Supreme Court held that public high school students facing suspension had a property interest in their education as guaranteed by Ohio law as well as a liberty interest in their good name.[15] In support of its decision, the Court noted that since the "landmark" case of *Dixon v. Alabama State Board of Education*,[16] "lower federal courts have uniformly held the Due Process Clause applicable to decisions made by tax-supported educational institutions to remove a student from the institution long enough for the removal to be classified as an expulsion."[17] Although the Court has never held that university students are entitled to procedural due process, it explicitly assumed it in the cases of *Bd. of Curators of the Univ. of Mo. v. Horowitz*[18] and *Regents of the Univ. of Mich. v. Ewing*.[19] In addition, other than the Seventh Circuit,[20] all lower federal courts across the country have held,[21] or at least presumed,[22] that students at public colleges and universities are entitled to procedural due process.

Since the Supreme Court has never explicitly held that students at public institutions are entitled to procedural due process, this question will be explored. Although suspension or expulsion certainly constitutes a "grievous loss"[23] for the accused, the Court has rejected the notion that the importance of the benefit (here a college degree) determines whether it is property for the purposes of the Fourteenth Amendment.[24] Similarly, although the

reputational stigma associated with an allegation of sexual assault is significant, the Court has made it clear that due process claims cannot rest on harm
to "reputation alone."[25] Regardless, university students still have a strong
argument that they are entitled to procedural due process when facing suspension or expulsion.

To begin with, the Court has made it abundantly clear that "the property
interests protected by procedural due process extend well beyond actual
ownership of real estate, chattels, or money."[26] In the companion cases of
Board of Regents v. Roth and *Perry v. Sindermann*, the Court considered when
the deprivation of a benefit falls under the protection of the Fourteenth
Amendment. In both cases, the benefit at stake was employment, and the
specific issue was when a teacher had the right to a hearing after his contract
was not renewed.[27]

The Court began its analysis in *Roth* by discussing previous cases in which it
had found that the contested benefit constituted property under the
Fourteenth Amendment. It explained at a general level what motivated the
decision in these cases:

> To have a property interest in a benefit, a person clearly must have more than
> an abstract need or desire for it. He must have more than a unilateral
> expectation of it. He must, instead, have a legitimate claim of entitlement
> to it. It is a purpose of the ancient institution of property to protect those
> claims upon which people rely in their daily lives, reliance that must not be
> arbitrarily undermined. It is a purpose of the constitutional right to a hearing
> to provide an opportunity for a person to vindicate those claims.[28]

The Court also discussed how a benefit became a property interest. The
Court wrote:

> [P]roperty interests ... are not created by the Constitution [but instead] ...
> are created and their dimensions are defined by existing rules or understand-
> ings that stem from an independent source such as state law – rules or
> understandings that secure certain benefits and that support claims of entitle-
> ment to those benefits.[29]

The Court then determined that Roth did not have a property interest in his
employment because his rights were created by his contract, and that contract
specifically stated that it would terminate on a certain date.[30] Under no
condition did it provide for renewal.[31]

In *Sindermann*, the Court acknowledged a less formal ground for the
creation of a property interest. Although a written contract could provide
a clear property interest, so could one that was implied. The Court wrote: "A

person's interest in a benefit is a 'property' interest for due process purposes if there are such rules or mutually explicit understandings that support his claim of entitlement to the benefit and that he may invoke at a hearing."[32]

Based on that definition, the Court ruled that Sindermann had the right to a hearing on the grounds that someone like him, "who has held his position for a number of years, might be able to show from the circumstances of this service – and from other relevant facts – that he has a legitimate claim of entitlement to job tenure."[33]

Applying the reasoning from *Roth* and *Sindermann*, students facing suspension or expulsion have a strong claim of entitlement to their education. Although students get secondary benefits from attending college like learning and making friends, the principal reason people attend university is to obtain a degree, and schools explicitly refer to the benefits of a diploma from their institution in recruiting students. For example, this author visited the website of one of her alma maters, the University of California, Berkeley. On the Admissions page was the following:

> Come to UC Berkeley, the world's premier public university. Study with Nobel laureate faculty at top research facilities. Meet the best students from the United States and around the globe. And graduate with a diploma that introduces you to a family of more than 450,000 alumni.[34]

Should a student decide they want to attend a certain school, they must go through significant hurdles in applying. These include paying a fee to have their application considered, taking standardized tests, requesting and obtaining letters of recommendation, being interviewed, and writing essays explaining why they should be admitted.

Once an offer of admission is made and accepted, the university and student have entered into a contract. The consideration for the contract is as follows. The student will pay substantial fees to matriculate, and he promises to take a minimum number of credits, maintain a certain grade point average, and comply with specified rules of conduct. In return, he will be awarded a degree. As Berger and Berger explained, "[t]he contract, formed when an accepted student registers, arises from the mutual understanding that the student who satisfactorily completes a program's academic requirements will receive the appropriate degree."[35]

5.1.2 *What Procedural Protections Does Due Process Require?*

Now that I have made the case for why students at public universities are entitled to procedural due process before they can be suspended or expelled, the next question is how much process is due. At a minimum, the Court held in *Goss* that "the student be given oral or written notice of the charges against him and, if he denies them, an explanation of the evidence the authorities have and an opportunity to present his side of the story."[36] Although the Court stopped short of requiring a school to provide the accused with counsel, the right to confront and cross-examine witnesses, and the right to call his own witnesses,[37] it emphasized the fact that it was only addressing short suspensions, not exceeding ten days; "[l]onger suspensions or expulsions for the remainder of the school term, or permanently, may require more formal procedures."[38] Three years later, in *Board of Curators of the University of Missouri v. Horowitz*, the Court made it clear that students facing disciplinary action are entitled to more stringent procedural protections than those charged with academic misconduct.[39]

In determining whether the protections schools used in the wake of the DCL are constitutionally sufficient to protect students facing expulsion for sexual assault, I will use the balancing test from *Mathews v. Eldridge*.[40] It is the test used by courts across the country in deciding whether campus proceedings at public schools meet procedural due process. Two important caveats: First, I acknowledge that students are not entitled to the same procedural protections as criminal defendants.[41] As the Sixth Circuit put it in *Doe v. University of Cincinnati* (2017), "[r]eview under *Matthews* asks only whether John Doe 'had an opportunity to "respond, explain, and defend,"' not whether a jury could constitutionally convict him using the same procedures."[42]

Second, I recognize the many shortcomings of the *Eldridge* test. Jerry Mashaw famously criticized *Eldridge* because it views "the sole purpose of procedural protections as enhancing accuracy, and thus limits its calculus to the benefits or costs that flow from correct or incorrect decisions."[43] As a result, it undervalues bedrock constitutional interests like dignity and equality.[44] Furthermore, *Eldridge* requires courts to use a balancing test to reconcile the different factors, a methodology that has been roundly criticized. As Edward Rubin aptly put it, "This reliance upon 'weight,' which is a useful approach for dealing with bananas, leaves something to be desired where factors such as those in *Mathews* are concerned."[45] The cost-benefit apparatus has a way of "dwarf[ing] soft variables" and "ignor[ing] complexities and ambiguities,"[46] which makes it difficult for individuals to prevail.

More recently, however, the Court has applied a less parched version of *Matthews v. Eldridge*, one that shows greater concern for the individual interests at stake. In *Hamdi v. Rumsfeld* (2004)[47] and subsequent cases involving immigration and national security, application of the *Matthews v. Eldridge* factors has "produced surprisingly rights-affirming outcomes."[48]

As Joseph Landau explained, "The Court's recent rulings involving national security and immigration ... reveal a Court that is increasingly concerned with the individual interests at stake and especially willing to intervene to ensure that executive and legislative action not go unchecked."[49]

5.1.3 *Applying the* Mathews v. Eldridge *Balancing Test*

Mathews v. Eldridge dictates that in determining the requirements of due process in a particular circumstance, three factors must be considered:

> [T]he private interest that will be affected by the official action; ... the risk of an erroneous deprivation of such interest through the procedures used, and the probable value, if any, of additional or substitute procedural safeguards; and finally, the Government's interest, including the function involved and the fiscal and administrative burdens that the additional or substitute proced-ural requirement would entail.[50]

5.1.3.1 Factor One: Private Interest at Stake

Without question, the private interest at stake is significant. Being suspended or expelled from university has profound consequences on a person's well-being. As the Fifth Circuit explained back in 1961:

> It requires no argument to demonstrate that education is vital and, indeed, basic to civilized society. Without sufficient education the plaintiffs would not be able to earn an adequate livelihood, to enjoy life to the fullest, or to fulfill as completely as possible the duties and responsibilities of good citizens.... It is most unlikely that a public college would accept a student expelled from another public college of the same state. Indeed, expulsion may well prejudice the student in completing his education at any other institution. Surely no one can question that the right to remain at the college in which the plaintiffs were students in good standing is an interest of extremely great value.[51]

Studies have shown that earning a college degree has been positively linked to a multitude of benefits including better health, longer life, a more fulfilling workplace, and higher lifetime earnings.[52] Graduating from college is particu-larly important for those coming from disadvantaged backgrounds. A 2011 study found that "the chances of achieving economic success are independent of social background among those who attain a BA."[53] In other words, being denied a college degree constitutes a serious loss.

Furthermore, the reputational harm from being found to have committed sexual assault is significant.[54] Sex offenders are modern-day bogeymen; being adjudicated (or even accused) of being a rapist can destroy friendships and eviscerate the kind of connections that lead to jobs and satisfying long-term relationships, both romantic and fraternal.[55] As the Sixth Circuit explained in *Doe v. Baum*:

> Being labeled a sex offender by a university has both an immediate and lasting impact on a student's life. The student may be forced to withdraw from his classes and move out of his university housing. His personal relationships might suffer. And he could face difficulty obtaining educational and employment opportunities down the road, especially if he is expelled.[56]

John Doe experienced first-hand what happens when a person is found responsible for sexual misconduct. In 2014, Doe received a "Disciplinary Warning" from Brandeis University, which left a permanent mark on his educational record for "serious sexual transgressions."[57] Brandeis students "publicly taunted and accused [him] of rape."[58] His internship employer explained that he had been "made aware" of John's situation from "several sources" and fired him.[59] Doe also stopped receiving calls from an employer who had promised to hire him only months before.[60]

5.1.3.2 Factor Two: The Risk of Erroneous Deprivation of Liberty and the Value of Additional Safeguards

Next, courts must assess the risk of an erroneous deprivation of liberty due to the procedures used, and the probable value of additional safeguards.

NO RIGHT TO AN ADJUDICATORY HEARING. The most concerning trend in university disciplinary proceedings after the DCL was universities moving from a formal, adjudicatory hearing to an investigatory model in which a single person gathers and reviews evidence and then on their own determines whether an assault occurred. The Obama White House publicly applauded this approach because "[p]reliminary reports from the field suggest that these innovative models, in which college judicial boards play a much more limited role, encourage reporting and bolster trust in the process, while at the same time safeguarding an alleged perpetrator's right to notice and to be heard."[61] One administrator indicated that training conducted by the Association of Title IX Administrators (ATIXA) recommended against using hearing panels. Since ATIXA is "the main source of national training and legal interpretation for Title IX,"[62] left unchallenged, this recommendation would have likely influenced many schools to switch to the single investigatory model.

Universities that moved to the investigatory model insisted that they were providing students with a hearing. As another administrator explained to me:

> The term hearing can mean different things. Some people would think of a hearing as a single time where all of the parties and witnesses show up and formally present evidence and each side has an opportunity to present its case to a decision maker. We don't have that. Our process involves an investigation in which the investigator meets with both parties and witnesses at separate times, and often times multiple times, and collects all of the relevant evidence and makes a determination based on the evidence. Our view is that this is a hearing.[63]

Providing accused students with an opportunity to present their case to an Investigator may constitute a hearing in some technical sense, but it misses important procedural protections including the right to an impartial fact-finder. As the Court acknowledged in *Withrow v. Larkin* (1975), a "fair trial in a fair tribunal is a basic requirement of due process"[64] and it applies to both court cases and hearings before administrative agencies.[65] "Not only is a biased decisionmaker constitutionally unacceptable," the Court wrote, "but 'our system of law has always endeavored to prevent even the probability of unfairness.'"[66]

Congress recognized the importance of role separation when it unanimously passed the Administrative Procedure Act (APA) in 1946.[67] The APA *specifically* bars an individual from performing both an investigatory and an adjudicatory role.[68] Section 554(d)(2) states that a hearing officer "may not be responsible to or subject to the supervision or direction of an employee or agent engaged in the performance or investigative or prosecution functions for an agency."[69] The firewall was strengthened in 1976 with the passage of Section 557(d),[70] and so now the law states:

> An employee or agent engaged in the performance of investigative or prosecuting functions for an agency in a case may not, in that or a factually related case, participate or advise in the decision, recommended decision, or agency review pursuant to section 557 of this title, except as witness or counsel in public proceedings.[71]

The APA's separation of roles was not mere happenstance. When President Roosevelt appointed a committee in 1939 to study "existing (administrative) practices and procedures,"[72] one of the "most intense" attacks was on the combining of roles at formal adjudication.[73] Then state judge and future

Supreme Court Justice William Brennan eloquently expressed the concern in a concurring opinion to a 1952 case:

> Concern with the problem of merger of the powers of prosecutor and judge in the same agency springs from the fear that the agency official adjudicating upon private rights cannot wholly free himself from the influences toward partiality inherent in his identification with the investigative and prosecuting aspects of the case; in other words, that the atmosphere in which he must make his judgments is not conducive to the critical detachment toward the case expected of the judge. In a sense the combination of functions violates the ancient tenet of Anglo-American justice that "No man shall be a judge in his own cause." "The litigant often feels that, in this combination of functions within a single tribunal or agency, he has lost all opportunity to argue his case to an unbiased official and that he has been deprived of safeguards that he has been taught to revere."[74]

Although the Court has held that combining investigatory and adjudicatory functions does not necessarily violate due process, the cases in which it upheld the combination of functions differ in important ways from the university proceedings at issue here. In *FTC v. Cement Institute* (1948), the Court held that it did not violate due process to have FTC Commission Members who had investigated cases later adjudicate them.[75] Central to the Court's holding, however, was the fact that the adjudicatory nature of the hearing helped to prevent Members from being biased:

> [T]he fact that the Commission had entertained such views as the result of its prior ex parte investigations did not necessarily mean that the minds of its members were irrevocably closed on the subject of the respondents' basing point practices. Here, in contrast to the Commission's investigations, members of the cement industry were legally authorized participants in the hearings. They produced evidence – volumes of it. They were free to point out to the Commission by testimony, by cross-examination of witnesses, and by arguments, conditions of the trade practices under attack which they thought kept these practices within the range of legally permissible business activities.[76]

In *Withrow*, the Court held that it did not violate due process to have a hearing board investigate allegations of wrongdoing and then decide to suspend the person's medical license.[77] The Court emphasized that the standard of proof was low (probable cause), and that the suspension was only temporary.[78] Most importantly, the accused would have the right to a full adjudicatory hearing before his license could be suspended permanently.[79]

The level of process that helps to protect against bias in both *FTC v. Cement Institute* and *Withrow* is nonexistent in the investigatory model. The accused student does not have the right to be present for witness testimony, and he is explicitly prohibited from asking direct questions. Furthermore, the standard of proof is preponderance of the evidence, and the investigator is often making the final determination as to whether a violation occurred. In addition, we know a lot more than we did in 1975 about the way that bias affects judgment and decision-making. As will be discussed in what follows, implicit bias and confirmation bias pose profound fairness problems for the investigatory model of adjudication.

Implicit Bias Part of the problem with putting everything in the hands of one person is that even an administrator with the best of intentions is almost certainly biased in some way.[80] This poses a concern not just for accused students but the complainant as well. Implicit biases (or unconscious stereotypes) have been shown to affect judgment and produce discriminatory behavior.[81] These include biases based on race, gender, ethnicity, nationality, social status, and weight. Although I am not aware of any studies on implicit bias in campus disciplinary proceedings, numerous studies have shown its effect in the criminal setting. For instance, unconscious racial discrimination has been shown to affect prosecutors' charging decisions in homicide cases (black people were more likely than whites to face the death penalty for similar conduct)[82] and jurors' willingness to convict black defendants.[83] Researchers have also found that judges hold implicit racial biases, and that it can influence their rulings.[84]

So how should these biases be countered? Specialized training has been shown to reduce bias[85] as has a longstanding and deep personal commitment to eradicating personal bias.[86] Ironically, the commitment to be objective may just exacerbate the problem. Studies have shown that subjects who profess to be objective are more likely to make biased decisions.[87]

Changing the context in which people are rendering decisions, however, may be the most effective way of promoting objectivity. Specifically, a larger and more diverse hearing body has been shown to increase the quality of deliberation and reduce bias. One study looked at the effects of having a racially homogeneous versus a heterogeneous jury.[88] It found that on every relevant measure, racially heterogeneous groups outperformed homogeneous ones. Not only did racially mixed groups spend more time deliberating, but they discussed a wider range of case facts and personal perspectives. They also made fewer factual errors than all-white juries.[89] This finding means that universities should be increasing and diversifying the number of decision-makers not reducing them down to one person.

Confirmation Bias Confirmation bias – the tendency for people to seek or interpret evidence in a manner that is partial to existing beliefs, expectations, or an existing hypothesis[90] – poses a particular challenge to the fairness of the investigatory model. Confirmation bias has "proven strikingly robust across diverse domains of human thinking, including logical problem solving, social interaction and medical reasoning."[91] Nickerson described the phenomenon in his oft-cited 1998 article:

> A great deal of empirical evidence supports the idea that the confirmation bias is extensive and strong and that it appears in many guises. The evidence also supports the view that once one has taken a position on an issue, one's primary purpose becomes that of defending or justifying that position. This is to say that regardless of whether one's treatment of evidence was evenhanded before the stand was taken, it can become highly biased afterward.[92]

Researchers have also shown how confirmation bias can infect criminal investigations. Kassin, Goldstein, and Savitsky (2003) demonstrated that interrogators who had been cued to believe that most suspects were guilty chose more guilt-presumptive questions, used more interrogation techniques (including the presentation of false evidence), were more aggressive in questioning innocent suspects, and more likely to view a suspect as guilty. They also found that an interrogator's presumption of guilt affected the behavior of those being questioned and made impartial observers more likely to judge them guilty.[93] Ask and Granhag (2007) found that experienced Investigators judged witness statements differently depending on whether the statement was consistent or inconsistent with their initial theory.[94] Although Ask, Rebelius, and Granhag showed that Investigators will be more receptive to certain kinds of evidence (such as DNA), the kind of evidence that is most likely to be proffered at college adjudicatory hearings, witness testimony, is the most subject to confirmation bias.[95]

A former Title IX Investigator whom I spoke with provided more detail about why the single investigatory model was "the absolute worst" for student investigations and hearings:

> I don't see how they could not be biased ... You have students who are very polite, you have students who are always late ... you'll be interviewing friends who will tell you things that are totally irrelevant. There is so much information that comes through the investigation that is potentially inadmissible, and I do think it creates a problem when that same investigator is also determining responsibility. I don't think you can get through a thorough investigation process;

it's very difficult if not impossible to get through without a taint of bias. I think it is more objective when you have fresh eyes, they won't have information to fill the facts; they will only have to work with the information provided. A student blows off a meeting because they say they have a test and then you see them at the (campus bar). Should that impact your opinion of the case? It's just messy.

Confirmation bias hurts both the accused and the complainant. Having the same person conduct the investigation and render final judgment undermines the fairness of the proceedings for both parties. As the court explained in *Doe v. Brandeis University*:

> The dangers of combining in a single individual the power to investigate, prosecute, and convict, with little effective power of review, are obvious. No matter how well-intentioned, such a person may have preconceptions and biases, may make mistakes, and may reach premature conclusions.[96]

Although Investigators may begin their analysis with an impartial perspective, once they believe that the accused either did or didn't commit the act in question, they may be unable to fully consider conflicting evidence. Admittedly, confirmation bias poses a problem for the fairness and accuracy of all investigations and adjudications, but at least in an adversarial hearing with an independent fact-finder, both sides have the chance to tell their story before a person or persons who have not already considered the evidence and come to a judgment.

NO RIGHT TO EVIDENCE. The DCL ordered universities not to let a respondent review the complainant's statement unless she could read his.[97] The *Francisco Sousa* case, which I discussed in the Introduction, demonstrates the way that this policy worked in some universities. San Diego State University refused to turn over the complainant's statement (indeed any evidence in the case) because Sousa had not given a formal enough account about what happened.[98] Apparently the professions of innocence that he made in person and through his attorney were insufficient. Making notice contingent on first meeting some nebulous standard[99] significantly interferes with the accused knowing what he is alleged to have done, and without this information, he cannot decide which evidence/witnesses to introduce, and thus he cannot fully defend himself.

NO RIGHT TO QUESTION THE COMPLAINANT. Not giving the accused the right to question his accuser seriously impairs his right to a fair and accurate determination of responsibility. In *Goldberg v. Kelley* (1970), the Supreme Court wrote that in almost every proceeding "where important decisions turn on questions of fact, due process requires an opportunity to confront and cross-examine

adverse witnesses."[100] The right to ask questions is not a mere formality; the Court
has called cross-examination "the 'greatest legal engine ever invented for the
discovery of truth'."[101] As the court in *Doe v. Brandeis University* explained, cross-
examination is particularly important in credibility contests where there are no
witnesses or other extrinsic evidence.[102]

In *Doe v. Cincinnati* (2017), John Doe and Jane Roe had sex. Doe said it was
consensual, but Roe claimed it was not. There was no physical evidence
supporting either side, which meant the case required the factfinder to decide
who they believed. The Sixth Circuit explained why cross-examination is so
critical in these sorts of cases:

> A cross-examiner may "delve into the witness' story to test the witness'
> perceptions and memory." He may "expose testimonial infirmities such as
> forgetfulness, confusion, or evasion ... thereby calling to the attention of the
> factfinder the reasons for giving scant weight to the witness' testimony." He
> may "reveal possible biases, prejudices, or ulterior motives" that color the
> witness' testimony. His strategy may also backfire, provoking the kind of
> confident response that makes the witness appear more believable to the
> fact finder than he intended ... Whatever the outcome, "the greatest legal
> engine ever invented for the discovery of truth" will do what it is meant to:
> "permit the [factfinder] that is to decide the [litigant]'s fate to observe the
> demeanor of the witness in making his statement, thus aiding the [factfinder]
> in assessing his credibility."[103]

Social science supports the importance courts place on cross-examination.
Although researchers have shown people are not very good at judging
a person's veracity based on his demeanor,[104] cross-examination is still an
important vehicle for discerning truth.[105] This is because a witness's cognitive
limitations make it demonstrably more difficult for him to consistently answer
spontaneous questions under live cross-examination if he is being insincere.[106]
In addition, there is certain observable behavior that has been linked to
deception, such as vocal tension and pitch.[107] At least one study has shown
that subjects are more than twice as effective at detecting deception when they
are able to observe a speaker's body and hear his voice as opposed to simply
reviewing a written transcript.[108]

Yet, as I have shown, after the DCL the vast majority of universities studied
did not give the respondent the right to question his accuser. Under almost all
the procedures studied, the accused had to direct his questions through the
panel, which could decide whether to ask. Even if they did ask, the complainant didn't need to answer. Nor was the complainant even required to be
present; schools allowed her account to the Title IX Investigator to be

presented to the hearing panel, assuming there was even an independent person deciding the case.

LIMITED RIGHT TO COUNSEL. The vast majority of universities gave students the right to retain counsel, but it was almost always an abridged right.[109] Counsel was required to play a silent role, meaning that she was not allowed to question witnesses or address the hearing in any way. Denying students the right to active representation creates a real danger that innocent people will be found responsible.

When a university is deciding whether to allow more robust representation, which the new Title IX regulations allow but do not require,[110] it should consider why the right to counsel is enshrined in the Sixth Amendment of the U.S. Constitution. I am not contending that what is at stake in a college disciplinary proceeding is anywhere akin to that of a criminal trial, but it still helps to remember why counsel is a fundamental right. As the Supreme Court wrote in *Argersinger v. Hamlin* (1972), "[t]he assistance of counsel is often a requisite to the very existence of a fair trial."[111] This because of the "obvious truth that the average defendant does not have the professional legal skill to protect himself when brought before a tribunal with power to take his life or liberty ..."[112] In *Powell v. Alabama*, Justice Sutherland explained why even innocent people need a lawyer: "Without [the guiding hand of counsel], though he be not guilty, he faces the danger of conviction because he does not know how to establish his innocence."[113]

Of course, university grievance procedures are not as complicated as jury trials; for instance, university tribunals do not require participants to know the federal or state rules of evidence. But helping students navigate complicated proceedings is not the only purpose of an attorney. Lawyers also aid those who are uncomfortable speaking in public because they may be shy, have difficult thinking on their feet, or lack proficiency in English. For these students, not having an attorney creates a Hobson's choice. Remain silent but forsake the opportunity for vigorous self-defense or speak but run the risk that they be judged a liar. This conundrum is especially ironic because the stress of public speaking is likely to exacerbate classic symptoms of nervousness like gaze aversion and fidgeting, which many wrongly believe are indicative of deception.[114]

Lawyers may be especially important for students who are in categories of accused more likely to be found responsible based solely on what they look like. Studies show that unattractive defendants receive significantly longer sentences for the same crime as compared with attractive defendants, and African Americans are given longer sentences than whites.[115] Research suggests that if a defendant has a face considered to be more consistent with the charged offense, he is more likely to be convicted of that crime than a person with a face that does not match.[116] This has been found to be true regardless of the strength of the evidence.[117] A good lawyer can help to offset these biases through effective advocacy, such as by bringing out important facts or pointing out possible credibility issues.

STANDARD OF PROOF – PREPONDERANCE OF THE EVIDENCE. As one university administrator explained, "preponderance of the evidence is 50% plus a feather."[118] In determining whether a feather should be enough to tip the scales in a campus disciplinary proceeding for rape, it helps to remember the purpose of the standard of proof. In *Addington v. Texas* (1979), the Court said that the function of the standard of proof is to "instruct the factfinder concerning the degree of confidence our society thinks he should have in the correctness of factual conclusions for a particular type of adjudication."[119] Setting a high or low standard is a way "to allocate the risk of error between the litigants and to indicate the relative importance attached to the ultimate decision."[120]

The Court then differentiated between types of cases across the spectrum. At one end lies the archetypal civil case involving a pecuniary dispute between private parties. "Since society has a minimal concern with the outcome of such private suits, plaintiff's burden of proof is a mere preponderance of the evidence. The litigants thus share the risk of error in roughly equal fashion."[121] This is to be contrasted with criminal cases in which "the interests of the defendant are of such magnitude that historically and without any explicit constitutional requirement they have been protected by standards of proof designed to exclude as nearly as possible the likelihood of an erroneous judgment."[122] Because so much is at stake, the state has the burden of proving guilt beyond a reasonable doubt, which is a way of guaranteeing that "our society imposes almost the entire risk of error on itself."[123]

In the middle are cases that use the intermediate standard of clear and convincing evidence. This standard is typically used in civil cases involving "quasi-criminal wrongdoing" like fraud.[124] The rationale for this intermediate standard is that the interests at stake are "more substantial than mere loss of money."[125] For that reason, "some jurisdictions accordingly reduce the risk to the defendant of having his reputation tarnished erroneously by increasing the plaintiff's burden of proof."[126] The Court noted that it also used this higher standard in certain civil proceedings as a way of "protect[ing] particularly important individual interests."[127] The Court mentioned deportation and denaturalization, and in *Addington* it held that civil commitment also requires this higher standard of proof.[128]

The question then is where a university adjudication of sexual assault falls on this spectrum. Many have argued that the standard of proof should be preponderance of the evidence.[129] They contend that this lower standard adequately protects the accused,[130] while at the same time making it easier for victims whose only evidence is their word to lodge complaints.[131] Finally, some maintain that preponderance is the correct standard because it treats the interests of the accused student, the victimized student, and the entire student body as equally important.[132]

A person will not go to jail if he is found to have violated the code of conduct, but his life is still likely to be gravely affected. Although the Family Educational Rights and Privacy Act (FERPA) generally prohibits the improper disclosure of personally identifiable information obtained from education records, exceptions exist for crimes of violence.[133] Universities may notify the victim of the outcome of the proceedings,[134] and they are allowed to disclose to third parties when they find a student has committed rape or sexual assault.[135] Some universities mark official transcripts to indicate that the person committed non-academic misconduct.[136] Although some students have the savvy and resources to transfer to another school after being expelled, many do not. Without an undergraduate degree, a person's earning potential and career opportunities are significantly curtailed.

Furthermore, requiring that the standard of proof be set at preponderance means that some schools may have a lower standard of proof for allegations of sexual harassment or assault than for other offenses. As the Massachusetts District Court observed in *Doe v. Brandeis University*, intentionally making it easier to find men responsible for sexual assault compared to other misconduct is particularly problematic in light of the elimination of other basic procedural rights of the accused.[137]

5.1.3.3 Factor Three: Government Interest and Burdens of Additional Protections

Under the final *Eldridge* factor, courts must consider the governmental interest at stake and the burdens of additional protections.

PREVENTING SEXUAL ASSAULT. The primary function of universities is to provide an education,[138] and Title IX law recognizes that this end cannot be achieved unless women are free from sexual discrimination and assault. The consequences of sexual assault endure long beyond the physical injury;

victims report feeling the psychological and emotional consequences many years after the attack occurred. Studies show that between 32 percent and 70 percent of rape survivors develop PTSD, and 38–43 percent meet the criteria for major depression.[139]

In addition, at least one study found that being the victim of sexual assault had a negative impact on academic success.[140] Researchers found that women who were sexually assaulted during their first semester of university tended to have a lower grade point average (GPA) by the end of the semester as compared with women who had not experienced sexual assault during that first semester.[141] Importantly, however, it appears that the negative impact did not last long; researchers found that these same women did not have a lower GPA at the end of their second semester as compared with those who had not been sexually assaulted.[142] Finally, the study found that the more traumatic the sexual assault, the more dramatic the impact on academic performance.[143]

It is clear that universities have an interest and a responsibility in preventing sexual assault, but it is important not to misrepresent the extent of the problem. The procedural changes in the DCL were justified by the OCR in part on the notion that female college students were at particular risk of being sexually assaulted. Although a study by the Bureau of Justice Statistics found that these women were in the highest risk age group,[144] they were actually *less* likely to be raped or sexually assaulted than their peers who were not in college.[145]

The Office for Civil Rights also cited a study by NIJ in support of its claim that "[t]he statistics on sexual violence are both deeply troubling and a call to action for the nation."[146] Yet, as I explained in Chapter 1, the 1 in 5 study only reported the findings from a sample size of two universities, and they were not nationally representative. The 2015 AAU Campus Climate Survey, though often cited,[147] has similar limitations, as does the 2019 Survey. Neither are nationally representative, and both have a low response rate. However, there was a 2014 nationally representative study that the Obama Administration's OCR never discussed. The National Crime Victimization Survey found that between 1995 and 2013, 6.1 per 1,000 women in postsecondary institutions were the victims of rape or sexual assault.[148] Granted, the NCVS has its own problems. Although it has a large sample size and very high response rate (historically between 86% and 91%),[149] it has been criticized for likely underestimating the incidence of rape and sexual assault.[150]

But there is another issue the Obama OCR should have considered: the fact that many of these assaults *don't* take place on campus and/or the assailant is *not* associated with the college or university. The 2015 Bureau of Justice Statistics Campus Climate Survey Validation Study measured campus sexual assault at nine schools. Researchers found only 33 percent of rape incidents and 28 percent of sexual battery incidents took place on campus.[151] They also found that a little more than half of the offenders in rape (55%) and sexual battery (56%) were affiliated with the school as students, professors, or other employees.[152] That means the incidence of *campus* sexual assault has been significantly exaggerated.

Furthermore, whatever the rate of sexual assault, it is an open question whether lowering procedural protections for the accused actually furthers the government's interest in protecting women. It is true that some universities have an appalling record of punishing rape and sexual assault,[153] but as the *Erika Kinsman* case showed, lowering the standard of proof does not necessarily solve the problem. More to the point, states across the country were able to increase reporting and prosecution of rape without lowering procedural protections.[154] They did it by instituting reforms that included: changing evidentiary standards (many states had previously required a witness to corroborate the allegation), redefining the crime of rape to include more than just vaginal/penile penetration, eliminating the resistance requirement, and creating rape shield statutes, which barred evidence about the victim's dress or prior sexual history unless a judge found that it was particularly relevant to the facts of the case.[155] Importantly, however, researchers found that although reporting of aggravated rape (defined as stranger rape, use of a weapon, or resulting in injury)[156] went up, there was no change to reporting of simple rape.[157] Since a college campus is more likely to involve rape between people who know each other, the reforms described here may not increase reporting. Instead, colleges may have to take other measures like combatting intoxication since most campus rapes take place while one or both of the parties are intoxicated.[158]

FAIR PROCEEDINGS. The university also has a "vital interest" in fair proceedings because they "serve[] the goals of both students and schools alike."[159] As the Sixth Circuit explained, "if a university's procedures are insufficient to make 'issues of credibility and truthfulness ... clear to the decision makers,' that institution risks removing the wrong students, while overlooking those it should be removing."[160] Finding an innocent person responsible for rape means the university will unnecessarily lose that person's tuition as well as any contribution they would otherwise make to the community, such as through participation in sports or student government. If the case was one of mistaken identification, then a wrongful finding means that there will still be a dangerous person at large on campus.

On a more general level, ensuring that disciplinary proceedings are fair may actually promote community safety by increasing respect for campus rules. Although many believe that it is the threat or use of punishment that shapes compliance with the law,[161] social psychologists like Tom Tyler contend that legitimacy is a more powerful force. "Legitimacy is a feeling of obligation to obey the law and to defer to the decisions made by legal authorities."[162] In his 1990 book *Why People Obey the Law*, Tyler argued that the basis of legitimacy is procedural justice.[163] Subsequent research laid out the six components of procedural justice: representation (the extent to which parties believe they had the opportunity to take part in the decision-making process); consistency (similarity of treatment over time and as compared with like parties); impartiality (when the legal authority is unbiased); accuracy (ability to make competent, high-quality decisions, which includes the public airing of the problem); correctability (whether the legal system has a mechanism for correcting mistakes); and ethicality (when the authorities treat parties with dignity and respect).[164] Importantly, Tyler found that it was perceived fairness and not case outcome that most influenced people's attitude toward the legal system.[165]

In addition, increasing perceived fairness may be the best way to achieve bystander intervention, which many advocates believe is critical for lowering sexual assault on campuses.[166] Bystander intervention (which includes "a full range of options and levels of action, from speaking to a resident assistant about an encounter in a residence hall to calling the police")[167] requires "a paradigm shift in the thinking of the campus community."[168] Tyler and Fagan found that people were more likely to view police as legitimate when they believed they were using fair procedures in the way they interacted with the public.[169] They also found that members of the public who viewed police as legitimate were more likely to report crime and criminals and more likely to work with others in their community to fight crime.[170] Assuming Tyler and Fagan's findings hold in the university context – students may be more likely to intervene when they see someone being assaulted if they feel confident that the perceived attacker will be treated fairly.

From a procedural justice standpoint, OCR's justification for setting the standard of proof at preponderance of the evidence was particularly problematic; OCR argued that the standard of proof should be preponderance because that was what the government used in Title VII hearings. If OCR wanted to base its procedural protections on Title VII, however, then it should have required all of the same rights afforded at Title VII hearings. Under Title VII, the Equal Employment Opportunity Commission (EEOC) is barred from releasing the names of those under investigation,[171] and if someone does release a name, they can be fined, jailed, or both.[172] If OCR wanted to pattern its proceedings on those under Title VII, then it should have also penalized releasing the names of schools under investigation.

In addition, the Civil Rights Act of 1991 gives both parties in a Title VII case the right to a jury trial if one party requests compensatory or punitive damages.[173] Having the right to trial under Title VII means that employers enjoy a panoply of other protections including: the right to counsel; the right to a jury[174] comprised of jurors who have not been excluded on account of race or gender;[175] the right to strike jurors for cause;[176] the right to three peremptory challenges;[177] the right to confront and cross-examine witnesses (including the complainant); the right to depose witnesses;[178] and the right to the rules of evidence[179] (thus barring hearsay evidence, unless it is subject to a recognized exception). Finally, an employer cannot be found responsible for violating Title VII unless the jurors are unanimous.[180]

Not only did the 2011 DCL not mandate that these Title VII rights be provided, it actually recommended against some of them. For instance, the DCL strongly discouraged schools from allowing the parties to directly question one another,[181] and it told schools that they "should not allow the alleged perpetrator to review the complainant's statement without also allowing the complainant to review the alleged perpetrator's statement."[182] Cherry-picking the provisions of Title VII that lower a student's procedural rights while ignoring the provisions that strengthen them undermines the legitimacy of a school's disciplinary proceedings because accused students understandably feel like they are not being treated fairly.

COST. Finally, *Eldridge* requires courts to consider what the additional procedural requirements will cost because they "entail the expenditure of limited resources, [and] . . . at some point the benefit to individuals from an additional safeguard is substantially outweighed by the cost of providing such protection."[183] Fortunately, the direct costs of the additional protections described earlier are not unduly burdensome. Providing an advocate will not require substantial additional resources unless the person is a paid attorney, and elevating the standard of proof, allowing direct questioning, providing full notice of the evidence against a person, and granting an adjudicatory hearing need not cost any extra money. A hearing will take more time than the single investigatory method, which creates an opportunity cost for the panelists and hearing personnel. An additional cost may be the impact these procedures have on the complainant. As the Sixth Circuit explained, "Strengthening those procedures is not without consequence for victims. 'Allowing an alleged perpetrator to question an alleged victim directly may be traumatic or intimidating, thereby possibly escalating or perpetuating' the same hostile environment Title IX charges universities with eliminating."[184]

5.1.3.4 Balancing All the Factors

The last step under *Eldridge* is balancing the different factors. I concede that courts are not going to require the appointment of counsel in campus disciplinary proceedings as a matter of procedural due process,[185] although they may find that students have the right to the assistance of an attorney of their choice.[186] In *Lassiter v. Department of Social Services* (1981), the Court stated that there is a presumption against the right to counsel where there is no threat of incarceration,[187] and although students face serious consequences at university disciplinary proceedings, jail time is not one of them. Illustrating just how reluctant the Court is to require counsel in non-criminal cases, it held in *Lassiter* that a parent was not entitled to counsel when they were facing permanent loss of their children even though it agreed that assistance of counsel would likely increase the accuracy of the proceedings,[188] and in *Turner v. Rogers*, the Court held that there was no categorical right to counsel in proceedings that involved possible civil contempt and incarceration for non-payment of child support.[189] Thus, the best that a student can hope for is that a court will decide that due process calls for the appointment of counsel in his particular case,[190] for instance if he has a cognitive, emotional, or physical disability that prevents him from adequately representing himself.

I also acknowledge that preponderance of the evidence is likely to be deemed constitutionally sufficient[191] even though the stakes are considerable, and raising the standard would not directly cost universities any money.[192] Some courts have actually upheld the lower standard of "substantial evidence" in university disciplinary proceedings.[193] Others have found substantial evidence too low and have required preponderance of the evidence.[194] I am aware of no court that has required the standard be set at clear and convincing evidence, although at least one has stated that such a higher standard may be appropriate. In *Smyth v. Lubbers*, the U.S. District Court for the Western District of Michigan stated in dicta that the standard could not be lower than preponderance of the evidence in a case in which a student was charged with conduct that also constituted a crime.[195] In fact the Court wrote: "given the nature of the charges and the serious consequences of conviction, the court believes the higher standard of 'clear and convincing evidence' may be required."[196]

With regard to the right to have a copy of the complainant's statement, however, the Supreme Court has arguably already settled the issue of whether an accused student has the right to know the evidence against him. *Goss* carefully distinguished between the initial notice requirement and what a school has to provide once a student has denied the charges against him.[197] The initial notice requirement is not that high, it requires only that a student be told what he is accused of doing and what the basis of the accusation is.[198] As the Second Circuit put it, "[n]otice must be 'reasonably calculated, under all the circumstances, to apprise interested parties of the pendency of the action and afford them an opportunity to present their objections.'"[199] Once the student denies the charges, however, the university has a higher burden. It must provide "an explanation of the evidence the authorities have" against him.[200] Although a university could argue that it is complying with its due process obligations by providing the accused with a synopsis of the accusations through its Title IX coordinator, the accused student has a good argument that the university is only meeting its notice obligation, not its weightier obligations under the "explanation of evidence" portion of *Goss*.

Students should also have the right to question their accuser as well as other witnesses in sexual assault hearings. Although some courts do not think students are entitled to cross-examine witnesses in disciplinary hearings,[201] many do. They have found that an accused student should be allowed to question a witness "whose testimony was critical"[202] or when they faced possible expulsion.[203] Even an early Second Circuit opinion court that was otherwise hostile to the right to cross-examine in campus disciplinary hearings acknowledged that it might be necessary if the case hinged on a credibility determination.[204]

Although the First and Sixth Circuits agree that accused students must have the right to question their accuser, they disagree on the way it should be done. The Sixth Circuit has held unequivocally that the accused has an absolute right to question his accuser where credibility is at issue. In 2018, the court reaffirmed its holding in *Doe v. Cincinnati*: "... if a public university has to choose between competing narratives to resolve a case, the university must give the accused student or his agent an opportunity to cross-examine the accuser and adverse witnesses in the presence of a neutral fact finder."[205] The First Circuit, on the other hand, is "simply not convinced that the person doing the confronting must be the accused student or that student's representative."[206] Instead, they agree that "due process in the university disciplinary setting requires 'some opportunity for real-time cross-examination, even if only through a hearing panel.'"[207]

The right to directly question the accuser doesn't equate to a right of physical confrontation. In *Doe v. Cincinnati*, the Sixth Circuit acknowledged the difficulties schools might face in arranging for witness questioning "given a victim's potential reluctance to interact with the accused student."[208] For that reason, the Court emphasized "that UC's obligations here are narrow: it must provide a means for the ARC panel to evaluate an alleged victim's credibility, not for the accused to physically confront his accuser."[209] The Court then noted that the university already had procedures that could accommodate this requirement: Skype. "What matters for credibility purposes is the ARC panel's ability to assess the demeanor of both the accused and his accuser. Indisputably, demeanor can be assessed by the trier of fact without physical presence, especially when facilitated by modern technology. This fact mitigates UC's administrative burden."[210]

Importantly, an accused student should only be allowed to question a witness who is providing evidence against him. In *Plummer v. Univ. of Houston*, the Fifth Circuit rightfully held that confrontation and cross-examination were not required when "... it is undisputed that Female UH Student remembered little about the incident, and no one testified to the substance of any conversations with her about her memory that night."[211] Instead the primary evidence presented to the adjudicatory panel was the "degrading and humiliating" videos and photo taken and distributed by one of the accused students.[212]

Finally, students should have the right to an adjudicatory hearing. Although I recognize that the investigatory model is informal and may demand fewer resources (two values articulated by *Goss*), it is inadequate for what is at stake. Although most agree that students facing expulsion have the right to a hearing of some sort, several courts have held that when a student is facing expulsion for a disciplinary matter, they have the right to a more formal hearing in which they have the opportunity to hear the evidence against them, ask questions and present evidence on their own behalf.[213] In *Dixon v. Alabama State Board of Education*,[214] the Fifth Circuit explained why such a formal hearing was necessary:

> By its nature, a charge of misconduct, as opposed to a failure to meet the scholastic standards of the college, depends upon a collection of the facts concerning the charged misconduct, easily colored by the point of view of the witnesses. In such circumstances, a hearing which gives the Board or the administrative authorities of the college an opportunity to hear both sides in considerable detail is best suited to protect the rights of all involved.[215]

For all of these reasons, procedural due process at a minimum should give students the right to a live hearing, the right to read an accuser's written statement about what happened before that hearing, and the right to question their accuser in real time.

5.2 DO THESE PROCEDURES SATISFY BASIC PROCEDURAL FAIRNESS?

Students who are not entitled to procedural due process can challenge their university's disciplinary procedures for failing to comply with basic procedural fairness. Such a failure would constitute a breach of contract. Since this is not a federal constitutional claim, there is no Supreme Court case that governs. Instead, these cases are adjudicated under applicable state law. Without the Constitution acting as a constraint, courts can be miserly in their interpretation of basic fairness. As the widely cited *Doe v. Brandeis* shows, however, many courts have had a surprisingly robust notion of what minimal protections are required.

In *Doe v. Brandeis*, the Massachusetts District Court considered the fairness of Brandeis' Title IX disciplinary proceedings. John Doe had been involved in a two-year romantic and sexual relationship with another Brandeis student, J. C. After they broke up, J.C. alleged that Doe had engaged in sexual misconduct during their relationship, and Doe was ultimately found responsible. Doe sued Brandeis, and Brandeis filed a motion to dismiss. In ruling on the motion, the Court considered whether Doe had plausibly alleged a violation of "the basic fairness" to which he was due.

"Basic fairness," the Court explained "is an uncertain and elastic concept, and there is little case law to serve as guideposts in conducting the fairness inquiry."[216] It is a requirement that goes above and above and beyond the rules set forth in the student conduct handbook.[217] Determining the processes that satisfy "basic fairness" depends on the competing interests involved, including the seriousness of the alleged violation, the severity of the possible sanction, and the university's experience and proficiency in resolving such disputes.[218] Sound familiar? That's because these competing interests are similar to those in the *Mathews v. Eldridge* test. Here, though, courts must also "recognize and respect the strong interest of a private university in managing its own affairs."[219]

In assessing whether Doe had been treated with "basic fairness," the Massachusetts District Court voiced concern with Brandeis' failure to provide a variety of procedural protections. These included not providing meaningful notice of the charges, a practice the DCL appeared to endorse at least some of the time. Brandeis never gave a detailed account of the allegations against Doe, which forced him to defend himself against "vague and open-ended" charges.[220] This withholding was particularly problematic since the dispute was not about "a single isolated event ... [but] a lengthy and apparently tangled relationship that went on for nearly two years."[221] Brandeis' refusal to let Doe have an attorney who could actively participate or at least offer passive advice – a practice that was approved by the DCL – also troubled the Court. The Court noted that Brandeis had retained an outside attorney, but "it expected a student, approximately 21 years old, with no legal training or background, to defend himself, alone, against those same charges."[222]

The Court was also disturbed by the restrictions on Doe's ability to challenge the evidence against him, especially his inability to question J.C. – a ban explicitly encouraged by the DCL. "The entire investigation . . . turned on the credibility of the accuser and the accused," the Court wrote. "Under the circumstances, the lack of an opportunity for cross-examination may have had a very substantial effect on the fairness of the proceeding."[223] Also problematic was the fact that Brandeis did not give Doe witness statements or allow him to ask them any questions. Nor did Brandeis interview Doe's witnesses or include his affidavit or his additional facts.

The Court was also critical of Brandeis combining investigation, prosecution, and adjudication in one person – a practice encouraged by the White House in 2014. It explained:

> The dangers of combining in a single individual the power to investigate, prosecute, and convict, with little effective power of review, are obvious. No matter how well-intentioned, such a person may have preconceptions and biases, may make mistakes, and may reach premature conclusions.[224]

Because Brandeis also followed the practice of most schools in precluding an appeal based on insufficiency of facts or new evidence, "[t]he Special Examiner, for all practical purposes, had the first and only say in determining John's guilt."[225]

Although the Court didn't have a problem with the standard of proof per se, it did question the fairness of having a lower standard for sexual misconduct as opposed to other kinds of cases. As discussed earlier, the DCL mandated a preponderance of the evidence standard no matter what the standard was in other kinds of violations. The Court was extremely concerned by this unequal treatment, especially in light of the elimination of other basic procedural rights in sexual misconduct cases:

> The standard of proof in sexual misconduct cases at Brandeis is proof by a "preponderance of the evidence." For virtually all other forms of alleged misconduct at Brandeis, the more demanding standard of proof by "clear and convincing evidence" is employed. The selection of a lower standard (presumably, at the insistence of the United States Department of Education) is not problematic, standing alone; that standard is commonly used in civil proceedings, even to decide matters of great importance. Here, however, the lowering of the standard appears to have been a deliberate choice by the

university to make cases of sexual misconduct easier to prove – and thus more difficult to defend, both for guilty and innocent students alike. It retained the higher standard for virtually all other forms of student misconduct. The lower standard may thus be seen, in context, as part of an effort to tilt the playing field against accused students, which is particularly troublesome in light of the elimination of other basic rights of the accused.[226]

Looking at the entirety of the proceedings, the charges, and the circumstances of the case, the Court found that Doe's complaint plausibly alleges that Brandeis' procedures did not give him the "basic fairness" he was due. "[John] was required to defend himself in what was essentially an inquisitorial proceeding that plausibly failed to provide him with a fair and reasonable opportunity to be informed of the charges and to present an adequate defense."[227] However, the Court emphasized that it was not making a determination about what combination of proceedings would have passed muster. "It is not necessary for the Court to decide what the bare minimum might be – that is, how many procedural protections Brandeis could have removed and still provided 'basic fairness' to the accused – or whether any particular procedural protection was required under the circumstances of the case."[228]

5.3 CONCLUSION

Although courts across the country recognized the "critical importance" of "ensuring that allegations of sexual assault on college campuses are taken seriously,"[229] many were critical of the DCL influenced misconduct proceedings. More and more started finding that campus sexual misconduct disciplinary proceedings offended procedural due process or basis fairness.[230] In July 2015, a judge ordered the University of California, San Diego to reverse the suspension of a male student because the disciplinary proceedings violated his due process rights,[231] and nine months later, a different judge overturned the suspension of a University of Southern California student on the ground that he was denied a fair hearing and the substantive evidence did not support the Appeal Panel's findings.[232] On March 31, 2016, the Massachusetts District Court ruled in favor of a Brandeis University student who had been found responsible for "serious sexual transgressions."[233] The Court wrote: "Brandeis appears to have substantially impaired, if not eliminated, an accused student's right to a fair and impartial process."[234]

In 2016, the Republican National Committee (RNC) made reforming campus sexual assault adjudication part of its official party platform. It condemned sexual assault as a "terrible crime" but criticized the Obama Administration's "distortion of Title IX to micromanage the way colleges and universities deal with allegations of abuse." In so doing, it "contravenes our country's legal traditions and must be halted."[235] The RNC called for sexual assault, whenever reported, to be "promptly investigated by civil authorities and prosecuted in a courtroom, not a faculty lounge."

On November 8, Donald Trump was elected the 45th President of the United States. Within the first nine months of his presidency, the DCL had been rescinded. Soon after, OCR began the arduous process of meeting with stakeholders and drafting new Title IX guidelines. They will be the subject of the next two chapters.

NOTES

* First published by Arizona State Law Journal, Volume 48, Issue 3.
1. *See* Michelle J. Anderson, *Campus Sexual Assault Adjudication and Resistance to Reform*, 125 YALE L.J. 1940 (2016); Lavinia M. Weizel, *The Process that is Due: Preponderance of the Evidence as the Standard of Proof for University Adjudications of Student-on-Student Sexual Assault Complaints*, 53 B.C. L. REV. 1613, 1642–1655 (2012); Amy Chmielewski, *Defending the Preponderance of the Evidence Standard in College Adjudications of Sexual Assault*, 2013 BYU EDUC. & L.J. 143, 149–174 (2013).
2. *See* Katherine K. Baker, Deborah L. Blake, & Nancy Chi Cantalupo, *Title IX and the Preponderance of the Evidence: A White Paper* (2nd ed. 2016).
3. Telephone conversation with university administrator on Jan. 29, 2015.
4. *See* William A. Jacobsen, *Accused on Campus: Charges Dropped, but the Infamy Remains*, LEGAL INSURRECTION (May 16, 2015, 8:30 PM), http://legalinsurrection.com/2015/05/accused-on-campus-charges-dropped-but-the-infamy-remains/; *see also* Ryan D. Ellis, *Mandating Injustice: The Preponderance of the Evidence Mandate Creates a New Threat to Due Process on Campus*, 32 REV. LITIG. 65, 80–81 (2013); Barclay Sutton Hendrix, *A Feather on One Side, a Brick on the Other: Tilting the Scale Against Males Accused of Sexual Assault in Campus Disciplinary Proceedings*, 47 GA. L. REV. 591, 599 (2013); Stephen Henrick, *A Hostile Environment for Student Defendants: Title IX and Sexual Assault on College Campuses*, 40 N. KY. L. REV. 49 (2013); Naomi Shatz, *Feminists, We Are Not Winning the War on Campus Sexual Assault*, HUFFINGTON POST (Oct. 29, 2014, 6:44 PM), www.huffingtonpost.com/naomi-shatz/feminists-we-are-not-winn_b_6071500.html.

5. Elizabeth Bartholet et al., *Rethink Harvard's Sexual Harassment Policy*, BOSTON GLOBE (Oct. 15, 2014), www.bostonglobe.com/opinion/2014/10/14/rethink-harvard-sexual-harassment-policy/HFDDiZN7nU2Uwu UuWMnqbM/story.html.

6. David Rudovsky et al., *Open Letter from Members of the Penn Law School Faculty, Sexual Assault Complaints: Protecting Complainants and the Accused Students at Universities*, PHILLY.COM (Feb. 18, 2015), http://media.philly.com/documents/OpenLetter.pdf.

7. Peter Berkowitz, *College Rape Accusations and the Presumption of Male Guilt*, WALL ST. J. (Aug. 20, 2011), www.wsj.com/articles/SB10001424053111903596904576516232905230642.

8. Tovia Smith, *Some Accused of Sexual Assault on Campus Say System Works Against Them*, NPR (Sept. 3, 2014, 1:12 PM), www.npr.org/2014/09/03/345312997/some-accused-of-campus-assault-say-the-system-works-against-them; Teresa Watanabe, *More College Men Are Fighting Back Against Sexual Misconduct Cases*, L.A. TIMES (June 7, 2014, 6:15 PM), www.latimes.com/local/la-me-sexual-assault-legal-20140608-story.html; Emily Yoffe, *The College Rape Overcorrection*, SLATE (Dec. 7, 2014, 11:53 PM), www.slate.com/articles/double_x/doublex/2014/12/college_rape_campus_sexual_assault_is_a_serious_problem_but_the_efforts.html.

9. Telephone conversation with university administrator on Oct. 17, 2014.

10. *See e.g.*, School's or School Official's Liability for Unfair Disciplinary Action against Student Accused of Sexual Harassment or Assault, 34 A.L. R. 7th 1.

11. I have elsewhere argued that a private university's decision to lower procedural protections in response to the Dear Colleague Letter and the actions of the Department of Education constituted state action. *See* Tamara Rice Lave, *A Critical Look at How Top Colleges Are Adjudicating Sexual Assault*, 71 U. MIAMI L. REV. 376 (2017).

12. U.S. CONST. amend. XIV, § 1.

13. *See* Duke v. N. Tex. State Univ., 469 F.2d 829, 837 (5th Cir. 1972).

14. *See* Tonya Robinson, *Property Interests and Due Process in Public University and Community College Student Disciplinary Proceedings*, 30 SCH. L. BULL. 10, 10 (1999).

15. 419 U.S. 565, 574 (1975).

16. 294. F.2d 150 (5th Cir. 1961), *cert denied*, 368 U.S. 930 (1961).

17. *See* Goss, 419 U.S. at 576 n.8.

18. 435 U.S. 78, 84–85 (1978) ("Assuming the existence of a liberty or property interest, respondent has been awarded at least as much due process as the Fourteenth Amendment requires.").

19. 474 U.S. 214, 222–23 (1985) (Writing for the majority, Justice Stevens penned: "But remembering Justice Brandeis' admonition not to

'formulate a rule of constitutional law broader than is required by the precise facts to which it is to be applied,'. . . we again conclude, as we did in *Horowitz*, that the precise facts disclosed by the record afford the most appropriate basis for decision. We therefore accept the University's invitation to 'assume the existence of a constitutionally protectible property right in [Ewing's] continued enrollment,' and hold that even if Ewing's assumed property interest gave rise to a substantive right under the Due Process Clause to continued enrollment free from arbitrary state action, the facts of record disclose no such action.").

20. *See* Charleston v. Bd. of Trs. of the Univ. of Ill. at Chi., 741 F.3d 769, 772 (7th Cir. 2013) ("However, our circuit has rejected the proposition that an individual has a stand-alone property interest in an education at a state university, including a graduate education.").

21. Wells v. Columbus Tech. Coll., 510 F. App'x 893, 896 (11th Cir. 2013) ("As for procedural due process, a student generally should be afforded notice and an opportunity to be heard before being suspended from a state school."); Phat Van Le v. Univ. of Med. & Dentistry of N.J., No. 08–991, 2009 U.S. Dist. LEXIS 37672 at *23 (3d Cir. 2010) ("It is well-established that the requirements of the Fourteenth Amendment's Due Process Clause apply to student disciplinary proceedings at public institutions."); Flaim v. Med. Coll. of Ohio, 418 F.3d 629, 633 (6th Cir. 2005) ("In this Circuit we have held that the Due Process Clause is implicated by higher education disciplinary decisions."); Woodis v. Westark Cmty. Coll., 160 F.3d 435, 440 (8th Cir. 1998) (internal citations omitted) ("We have indicated that procedural due process must be afforded a student on the college campus 'by way of adequate notice, definite charge, and a hearing with opportunity to present one's own side of the case and with all necessary protective measures.'"); Tellefsen v. Univ. of N.C. at Greensboro, No. 89–2665, 1989 U.S. App. LEXIS 21332, at *3 (4th Cir. 1989) ("[A] student facing expulsion or suspension from a public educational institution is entitled to the protections of due process."); Gorman v. Univ. of R.I., 837 F.2d 7, 12 (1st Cir. 1988) ("It is also not questioned that a student's interest in pursuing an education is included within the fourteenth amendment's protection of liberty and property."); Gaspar v. Bruton, 513 F.2d 843, 850 (10th Cir. 1975) (Court had "no difficulty" in concluding that a nursing student had a property right in her education "and the more prominently so in that she paid a specific, separate fee for enrollment and attendance at the Gordon Cooper School."); Dixon v. Ala. State Bd. of Educ., 294 F.2d 150, 158 (5th Cir. 1961) (holding that due process requires notice and some opportunity for hearing before a student at a tax-supported college is expelled for misconduct); Bradley v. Oklahoma *ex rel.* Bd. of Regents of Se. Okla. State Univ., No. CIV-13–293-KEW, 2014 U.S. Dist. LEXIS

58576, at *7, (E.D. Okla. Apr. 28, 2014) ("[A] student facing expulsion or suspension from a public educational institution is entitled to the protections of due process."); Oladokun v. Ryan, No. 06 cv 2330 (KMW), 2010 U.S. Dist. LEXIS 103381, at *14 (S.D.N.Y. Sept. 30, 2010) ("It is well-settled that due process concerns are implicated by the disciplinary decisions of public institutions of higher education."); Gomes v. Univ. of Me. Sys., 365 F. Supp. 2d 6, 15 (D. Me. 2005) ("Here, the Plaintiffs were students at a public university and potentially subject to expulsion or suspension. They are, therefore, entitled to the protections of due process.").

22. Lucey v. Nevada ex rel. Bd. of Regents of the Nev. Sys. of Higher Educ., 380 F. App'x 608, 610 (9th Cir. 2010) (internal citations omitted) ("On the facts alleged, Lucey's right to procedural due process at the December 4 Hearing was satisfied because Lucey was subject to sanctions less than suspension or expulsion and received 'some kind of notice and [was] afforded some kind of hearing.'").

23. *See* Goldberg v. Kelly, 397 U.S. 254, 263 (1970).

24. *See* Bd. of Regents v. Roth, 408 U.S. 564, 571 (1972); *see also* Perry v. Sindermann, 408 U.S. 593, 601 (1972). *See generally* Peter N. Simon, *Liberty and Property in the Supreme Court: A Defense of Roth and Perry*, 71 CAL. L. REV. 146 (1983).

25. *See* Paul v. Davis, 424 U.S. 693, 701 (1976). Some courts refer to this standard as "stigma plus." *See e.g.,* Pendleton v. City of Haverhill, 156 F.3d 57, 63 (1st Cir. 1998).

26. Roth, 408 U.S. at 571–572 (internal citations omitted).

27. Roth concerned a teaching assistant who was hired for a fixed one-year contract, and the contract was not renewed. Sindermann involved a teacher in the state college system of the State of Texas under a system of one-year contracts for a ten-year period, from 1959 to 1969. After Sindermann became involved in some public disputes with the Board of Regents, his contract was not renewed.

28. Roth, 408 U.S. at 577.

29. *Id.*

30. *Id.* at 578.

31. *Id.*

32. Sindermann, 408 U.S. at 601.

33. *Id.* at 602.

34. *See* UNIVERSITY OF CALIFORNIA BERKELEY OFFICE OF UNDERGRADUATE ADMISSIONS, http://admissions.berkeley.edu/beberkeley.

35. Curtis J. Berger & Vivian Berger, *Academic Discipline: A Guide to Fair Process for the University Student*, 99 COLUM. L. REV. 289, 292 (1999).

36. Goss v. Lopez, 419 U.S. 565, 581 (1975).

37. *Id.* at 583.

38. *Id.* at 584.
39. 435 U.S. 78, 86 (1978).
40. 424 U.S. 319, 335 (1976).
41. *See* Henson v. Honor Comm. of Univ. of Va., 719 F.2d 69, 74 (4th Cir. 1983) ("Labeling a school proceeding disciplinary in nature, however, does not mean that complete adherence to the judicial model of decision-making is required."); Yench v. Stockmar, 483 F.2d 820, 823 (10th Cir. 1973) ("Student disciplinary proceedings are not comparable to criminal proceedings.").
42. Doe v. Univ. of Cincinnati, 872 F.3d 393, 400 (6th Cir. 2017).
43. Jerry L. Mashaw, *The Supreme Court's Due Process Calculus for Administrative Adjudication in Mathews v. Eldridge: Three Factors in Search of a Theory of Value*, 44 U. Chi. L. Rev. 28, 48 (1976).
44. *See id.* at 49.
45. Edward L. Rubin, *Due Process and the Administrative State*, 72 Calif. L. Rev. 1044, 1138 (1984).
46. Mashaw, *supra* note 43, at 48.
47. 542 U.S. 507 (2004) (plurality opinion).
48. Joseph Landau, *Due Process and the Non-Citizen: A Revolution Reconsidered*, 47 Conn. L. Rev. 879, 882 (2015). More recently, in Nelson v. Colorado, 137 S. Ct. 1249 (2017) the Court applied the Matthews' factors to a Colorado law, which had allowed the state to keep conviction-related assessments from a defendant whose conviction had been invalidated by a reviewing court and no retrial could occur. "Absent conviction of a crime," the Court wrote, "one is presumed innocent." (*Id.* at 1252.) Thus it violated the Fourteenth Amendment guarantee of due process for the state to retain these assessments, "unless and until the prevailing defendant institute[d] a discrete civil proceeding and prove[d] her innocence by clear and convincing evidence." (*Id.*)
49. *Id.* at 925–926.
50. Mathews v. Eldridge, 424 U.S. 319, 335 (1976).
51. Dixon v. Ala. State Bd. of Educ., 294 F.2d 150, 157 (5th Cir. 1961).
52. Sandy Baum, Jennifer Ma, & Kathleen Payea, Education Pays 2013: The Benefits of Higher Education for Individuals and Society 5–6 (College Board, 2013), https://trends.collegeboard.org/pdf/education-pays-2013-full-report.pdf; Howard R. Bowen, Investment in Learning: The Individual and Social Value of American Higher Education 45–50 (Johns Hopkins Press, 1977); Larry L. Leslie & Paul T. Brinkman, The Economic Value of Higher Education 37 (American Council on Education, 1988).
53. Florencia Torche, *Is a College Degree Still the Great Equalizer? Intergenerational Mobility Across Levels of Schooling in the United States*

117 Am. J. Soc. 763, 798 (2011) ("The finding is largely consistent across all indicators of socioeconomic standing: social class, occupational status, individual earnings, and total family income.").

54. Ariel Kaminer, *Accusers and the Accused, Crossing Paths at Columbia University*, N.Y. Times (Dec. 21, 2014), www.nytimes.com/2014/12/22/n yregion/accusers-and-the-accused-crossing-paths-at-columbia.html? _r=0.

55. *Consequences of Registration and Community Notification Laws for Registrants and their Loved Ones*, Human rights watch (Sept. 11, 2007), www.hrw.org/reports/2007/us0907/8.htm.

56. Doe v. Baum, 903 F.3d 575, 582 (6th Cir. 2018) (internal citations omitted).

57. Doe v. Brandeis University, 177 F. Supp.3d 561, 571–572 (D. Mass. 2016).

58. *Id.* at 592.

59. *Id.*

60. *Id.*

61. White House Task Force to Protect Students from Sexual Assault, Not Alone: The First Report of the White House Task Force to Protect Students from Sexual Assault 14 (2014).

62. Wendy *McElroy, Title IX Group Resists Title IX Regulations*, Inside Sources (June 18, 2020), www.insidesources.com/title-ix-group-resists-title-ix-regulations/.

63. Phone conversation with university administrator on Mar. 3, 2015.

64. Withrow v. Larkin, 421 U.S. 35, 46 (1975) (quoting In re Murchison, 349 U.S. 133, 136 (1955)).

65. Gibson v. Berryhill, 411 U.S. 564, 579 (1973).

66. Withrow, 421 U.S. at 47 (quoting In re Murchison, 349 U.S. at 136).

67. *See* Walter Gellhorn, *The Administrative Procedure Act: The Beginnings*, 72 Va. L. Rev. 219, 231–232 (The Administrative Procedure Act: A Fortieth Anniversary Symposium: Mar. 1986) (internal citations omitted). I am indebted to Ed Rubin for this point.

68. *See* Administrative Procedure Act 5 U.S.C. § 554 (d)(2) and § 557.

69. *See id.* at 554 (d)(2).

70. Pub. L. 94–409, § 4(a), 90 Stat. 1246 (1976).

71. *See* Administrative Procedure Act, *supra* note 68.

72. Louis L. Jaffe, *The Report of the Attorney General's Committee on Administrative Procedure*, 8 U. Chi. L. Rev. 401, 402 (1941).

73. *Id.* at 418.

74. In re Larsen, 17 N.J. Super. 564, 574 (1952).

75. 333 U.S. 683, 702–703 (1948).

76. *Id.* at 701 (alteration in original).

77. 421 U.S. at 56.

78. *Id.* at 56–59.
79. *Id.* at 37 n.1.
80. For a comprehensive overview of studies showing bias in the courtroom, *see* Jerry Kang et al., *Implicit Bias in the Courtroom*, 59 UCLA L. Rev. 1124 (2012).
81. *See* John T. Jost et al., *The Existence of Implicit Bias is Beyond Reasonable Doubt: A Refutation of Ideological and Methodological Objections and Executive Summary of Ten Studies that No Manager Should Ignore*, 29 Res. Organizational Behav. 39, 51 (2009).
82. Michael L. Radelet & Glenn L. Pierce, *Race and Prosecutorial Discretion in Homicide Cases*, 19 L. & Soc'y Rev. 587, 617–618 (1985).
83. Samuel R. Sommers & Phoebe C. Ellsworth, *"Race Salience" in Juror Decision-Making: Misconceptions, Clarifications, and Unanswered Questions*, 27 Behav. Sci. & L. 599, 601 (2009). These effects were only detected in race neutral trials. When the trial was racially charged, researchers did not see this effect. The theory for this difference is that of "aversive racism," or the idea that whites are loath to appear racist, and so they are especially vigilant in racially charged settings. *Id.* at 601.
84. Jeffrey J. Rachlinski et al., *Does Unconscious Racial Bias Affect Trial Judges?* 84 Notre Dame L. Rev. 1195, 1208 (2009).
85. *Id.* at 1227.
86. Gordon B. Moskowitz, Amanda R. Salomon, & Constance M. Taylor, *Preconsciously Controlling Stereotyping: Implicitly Activated Egalitarian Goals Prevent the Activation of Stereotypes*, 18 Soc. Cognition 151, 155 (2000).
87. Eric Luis Uhlmann & Geoffrey L. Cohen, *"I Think it, Therefore It's True": Effects of Self-Perceived Objectivity on Hiring Discrimination*, 104 Organizational Behav. & Hum. Decision Processes 207, 210–211 (2007).
88. Samuel R. Sommers, *On Racial Diversity and Group Decision Making: Identifying Multiple Effects of Racial Composition on Jury Deliberations*, 90 J. Personality & Soc. Psychol. 597, 597 (2006).
89. A diverse hearing body has another benefit. Ultimately, whoever is deciding the case must assess the credibility of witnesses, which can be difficult when people come from different cultures. *See* Aldert Vrij, *Why Professionals Fail to Catch Liars and How They Can Improve*, 9 Legal & Criminological Psychol. 159, 167 (2004).
90. Raymond S. Nickerson, *Confirmation Bias: A Ubiquitous Phenomenon in Many Guises*, 2 Rev. Gen. Psychol. 175, 175 (1998).
91. Karl Ask, Anna Rebelius, & Par Anders Granhag, *The "Elasticity" of Criminal Evidence: A Moderator of Investigator Bias*, 22 Applied Cognitive Psychol. 1245, 1246 (2008) (internal citations omitted).

92. Nickerson, *supra* note 90, at 177.
93. Saul M. Kassin, Christine C. Goldstein, & Kenneth Savitsky, *Behavioral Confirmation in the Interrogation Room: On the Dangers of Presuming Guilt*, 27 L. & HUM. BEHAV. 187, 187 (2003).
94. Karl Ask & Par Anders Granhag, *Motivational Bias in Criminal Investigators' Judgments of Witness Reliability*, 37 J. APPLIED SOC. PSYCHOL. 561, 579 (2007).
95. Karl Ask, Anna Rebelius, & Par Anders Granhag, *The "Elasticity" of Criminal Evidence: A Moderator of Investigator Bias*, 22 APPLIED COGNITIVE PSYCHOL. 1245, 1257–1258 (2008).
96. Brandeis Univ., *supra* note 57, at 606.
97. Russlyn Ali, *"Dear Colleague" Letter: Sexual Violence*, U.S. DEP'T. OF EDUC. 11–12 (Apr. 4, 2011), www2.ed.gov/about/offices/list/ocr/letters/colleague-201104.pdf.
98. Dorian Hargrove, *San Diego Universities Botch Sexual Assault Investigations*, SAN DIEGO READER (Sept. 2, 2015), www .sandiegoreader.com/news/2015/sep/02/san-diego-universities-botch-sexual-assault-invest/#.
99. How detailed must the statement be? Must the accused discuss the entire history between the parties or just the incident in question? Must he discuss everything the complainant did, and if so, how can he do that if he hasn't read her statement?
100. Goldberg v. Kelly, 397 U.S. 254, 269 (1970).
101. Lilly v. Virginia, 527 U.S. 116, 124 (1999) (quoting California v. Green, 399 U.S. 149, 158 (1970)). Note that some venerable scholars disagree with the truth-seeking function of direct questioning, including, Christopher Slobogin. *See* Christopher Slobogin, *Lessons from Inquisitorialism*, 87 S. CAL. L. REV. 699, 705–707, 712 (2014).
102. Brandeis Univ., *supra* note 57, at 605.
103. Doe v. Univ. of Cincinnati, 872 F.3d 393, 402 (6th Cir. 2017).
104. *See* Vrij, *supra* note 89, at 166–167; *see also* Bella M. De Paulo et al., *Cues to Deception*, 129 PSYCHOL. BULL. 74 (2003) (conducting a meta-analysis of 120 independent samples and finding that behaviors commonly associated with deception such as unwillingness to maintain eye contact were not in fact related).
105. *See* Raymond LaMagna, *(Re)Constitutionalizing Confrontation: Reexamining Unavailability and the Value of Live Testimony*, 79 S. CAL. L. REV. 1499 (2006).
106. Chris William Sanchirico, *Evidence, Procedure, and the Upside of Cognitive Error*, 57 STAN. L. REV. 291, 332–344 (2004).
107. *See* De Paulo et al., *supra* note 104, at 95–96.

108. *See* Michael J. Saks, *What Do Jury Experiments Tell Us About How Juries (Should) Make Decisions*, 6 S. CAL. INTERDISC. L.J. 1, 21–22 (1997–1998).
109. *See* Chapter 4, Table 4.6.
110. *See* 34 C.F.R§106.45 (b)(5)(iv).
111. 407 U.S. 25, 31 (1972).
112. Johnston v. Zerbst, 304 U.S. 458, 462–463 (1938).
113. Powell v. Alabama, 287 U.S. 45, 69 (1932).
114. *See* Vrij, *supra* note 89, at 162; Lucy Akehurst et al., *Lay Persons' and Police Officers' Beliefs Regarding Deceptive Behavior*, 10 APPLIED COGNITIVE PSYCHOL. 461, 462 (1996).
115. Andrea DeSantis & Wesley A. Kayson, *Defendants' Characteristics of Attractiveness, Race, and Sex and Sentencing Decisions*, 81 PSYCHOL. REP. 679, 682 (1997).
116. Alvin G. Goldstein, June E. Chance, & Barbara Gilbert, *Facial Stereotypes of Good Guys and Bad Guys: A Replication and Extension*, 22 BULL. OF PSYCHONOMIC SOC'Y 549, 551–552 (1984); A. Daniel Yarmey, *Stereotypes and Recognition Memory for Faces and Voices for Good Guys and Bad Guys*, 7 APPLIED COGNITIVE PSYCHOL. 419, 419 (1993).
117. Rafaële Dumas & Benoît Teste, *The Influence of Criminal Facial Stereotypes on Juridic Judgements*, 65 SWISS J. PSYCHOL. 237 (Dec. 2006).
118. Telephone conversation with university administrator on Jan. 24, 2014.
119. Addington v. Texas, 441 U.S. 418, 423 (1979) (citing In re Winship, 397 U.S. 358, 370 (1970)).
120. *Id.*
121. *Id.*
122. *Id.*
123. *Id.* at 424.
124. *Id.*
125. *Id.*
126. *Id.*
127. *Id.*
128. *Id.* at 432.
129. *See* Michelle J. Anderson, *The Legacy of the Prompt Complaint Requirement, Corroboration Requirement, and Cautionary Instructions on Campus Sexual Assault*, 84 B.U. L. REV. 945, 1016–1017 (2004); Edward N. Stoner II & John Wesley Lowery, *Navigating Past the "Spirit of Insubordination": A Twenty-First Century Model Student Conduct Code with a Model Hearing Script*, 31 J.C. & U.L. 1, 48 (2004); Mathew R. Triplett, Note, *Sexual Assault on College Campuses: Seeking the Appropriate Balance Between Due Process and*

Victim Protection, 62 Duke L.J. 487, 516–519 (2012); Weizel, *supra* note 1.

130. Weizel, *supra* note 1, at 1642–1655; Triplett, *supra* note 129, at 516–519.
131. Anderson, *supra* note 129, at 1016.
132. Stoner & Lowery, *supra* note 129, at 48–49.
133. 34 C.F.R. §§ 99.31(13)–(14), (16).
134. *Id.* at § 99.31(a)(13).
135. *Id.* at C.F.R. § 99.31(a)(14).
136. Collin Binkley et al., *Students Easily Transfer After Violent Offenses*, Columbus Dispatch (Nov. 24, 2014, 8:05 AM), www.dispatch.com/content/stories/local/2014/11/24/hidden-on-campus.html.
137. Doe v Brandeis University, *supra* note 57 at 607.
138. *See* Gorman v. Univ. of R.I., 837 F.2d 7, 14 (1st Cir. 1988).
139. Dean G. Kilpatrick & Ron Acierno, *Mental Health Needs of Crime Victims: Epidemiology and Outcomes*, 16 J. Traumatic Stress 119, 126–127 (2003); Dean G. Kilpatrick et al., Rape Related PTSD: Issues and Interventions, Psychiatric Times, July 2007, at 50; Mary P. Koss, *Restoring Rape Survivors: Justice, Advocacy, and a Call to Action*, 1087 Annals N.Y. Acad. Sci. 206, 221 (2006).
140. *See* Carol E. Jordan, Jessica L. Combs, & Gregory T. Smith, *An Exploration of Sexual Victimization and Academic Performance Among College Women*, 15 Trauma, Violence, & Abuse 191 (2014).
141. *Id.* at 191.
142. *Id.* at 196.
143. *Id.* at 197.
144. Sofia Sinozich & Lynn Langton, Rape and Sexual Assault Victimization Among College-Age Females, U.S. Dept. of Just., 3 (Dec. 2014).
145. *Id.* at 1.
146. Dear Colleague Letter, *supra* note 97, at 2.
147. *See* Michele Gorman, *1 in 4 Women Experienced Sexual Assault while in College Survey Finds*, Newsweek (Sept. 21, 2015, 4:26 PM), www.newsweek.com/1-4-women-sexual-assault-college-374793; Richard Pérez-Peña, *1 in 4 Women Experience Sex Assault on Campus*, N.Y. Times (Sept. 21, 2015), www.nytimes.com/2015/09/22/us/a-third-of-college-women-experience-unwanted-sexual-contact-study-finds.html?_r=0; Kelly Wallace, *23% of Women Report Sexual Assault in College, Survey Finds*, CNN (Sept 23, 2015, 8:43 AM), www.cnn.com/2015/09/22/health/campus-sexual-assault-new-large-survey/.
148. Sinozich & Langton, *supra* note 144, at 4.
149. *See* Nat'l Research Council, Div. on Behav. and Soc. Sci. and Educ., Comm. on Nat'l Statistics, Estimating the Incidence

OF RAPE AND SEXUAL ASSAULT 55 (Candace Kruttschnitt et al., eds., 2014).

150. Sinozich & Langton, *supra* note 144, at 4.

151. CAMPUS CLIMATE SURVEY VALIDATION STUDY FINAL TECHNICAL REPORT, at ES-5 (2016), www.ojp.gov/pdffiles1/bjs/grants/249545.pdf at 103.

152. *Id.*

153. *See* Binkley et al., *supra* note 136; Kristen Lombardi, *A Lack of Consequences for Sexual Assault*, THE CTR. FOR PUB. INTEGRITY (July 14, 2014, 4:50 PM), www.publicintegrity.org/2010/02/24/4360/lack-consequences-sexual-assault; Corey Rayburn Yung, *Concealing Campus Sexual Assault: An Empirical Examination*, 21 PSYCHOL. PUB. POL'Y & L. 1, 6 (2015).

154. *See* Jody Clay-Warner & Callie Harbin Burt, *Rape Reporting after Reforms: Have Times Really Changed?*, 11 VIOLENCE AGAINST WOMEN 150, 165 (2005) (finding that a rape occurring after 1989 was 88% more likely to be reported than a rape that happened before 1975, which was when rape reforms began).

155. Cassia Spohn & Julie Horney, RAPE LAW REFORM 20–29 (Springer, 1992).

156. Clay-Warner & Burt, *supra* note 154, at 169.

157. *Id.* at 167.

158. *See* Meichun Mohler-Kuo et al., *Correlates of Rape While Intoxicated in a National Sample of College Women*, 9 J. OF STUD. ON ALCOHOL 37, 37–38 (2004) (discussing that one issue colleges should address is intoxication).

159. Gorman v. Univ. of R.I., 837 F.2d 7, 14–15 (1st Cir. 1988).

160. Doe v. Cincinnati, 872 F.3d 393, 403 (6th Cir. 2017).

161. Daniel S. Nagin, *Criminal Deterrence Research at the Outset of the Twenty-First Century*, 23 CRIME & JUST. 1, 3 (1998) (Reviewing studies on the impact of deterrence. "I now concur with Cook's more emphatic conclusion that the collective actions of the criminal justice system exert a very substantial deterrent effect.").

162. Tom R. Tyler & Jeffrey Fagan, *Legitimacy and Cooperation: Why Do People Help the Police Fight Crime in Their Communities?*, 6 OHIO ST. J. OF CRIM. L. 231, 235 (2008).

163. TOM R. TYLER, WHY PEOPLE OBEY THE LAW 103 (1990); *see also* TOM R. TYLER & YUEN J. HUO, TRUST IN THE LAW: ENCOURAGING PUBLIC COOPERATION WITH THE POLICE AND COURTS 7–18 (2002); Tom R. Tyler, *Psychological Perspectives on Legitimacy and Legitimation*, 57 ANN. REV. PSYCHOL. 375, 375–376 (2006).

164. *See* Raymond Paternoster et al., *Do Fair Procedures Matter? The Effect of Procedural Justice on Spouse Assault*, 31 LAW & SOC'Y REV. 163, 167–169 (1997).

165. Tom R. Tyler, *The Role of Perceived Injustice on Defendants' Evaluations of Their Courtroom Experience*, 18 LAW & SOC'Y REV. 51, 63–66 (1984).
166. *See* Joetta L. Carr, *Preventing Sexual Violence Through Empowering Bystanders*, SHIFTING THE PARADIGM: PRIMARY PREVENTION OF SEXUAL VIOLENCE 16, 16–18 (Aug. 2008), www.acha.org/documents/r esources/ACHA_PSV_toolkit.pdf.
167. *Id.* at 18.
168. *Id.* at 3.
169. Tyler & Fagan, *supra* note 162, at 267.
170. *Id.* at 252.
171. 42 U.S.C. § 2000e-5(b) (2012) ("Charges shall not be made public by the Commission.").
172. *Id.*
173. Civil Rights Act of 1991, Pub. L. No. 102–166, 105 Stat. 1071–1100 (codified as amended in scattered sections of 42 U.S.C.).
174. FED. R. CIV. P. 48.
175. *See* J.E.B. v. Alabama, 511 U.S. 127, 144–46 (1994) (holding that jurors should not be struck based on gender); Edmonson v. Leesville Concrete Co., 500 U.S. 614, 627–628 (1991) (holding that the prohibition against discriminatory peremptory challenges based on race applies in civil cases); Hernandez v. New York, 500 U.S. 352, 369–371 (1991); Batson v. Kentucky, 476 U.S. 79, 87–98 (1986).
176. 28 U.S.C. § 1870 (2012).
177. *Id.*
178. U.S. CONST. amend. VI.
179. FED. R. EVID. 101, 1101.
180. FED. R. CIV. P. 48(b). (Unless the parties stipulate otherwise...)
181. Dear Colleague Letter, *supra* note 97, at 11–12.
182. *Id.*
183. Gorman v. Univ. of R.I., 837 F.2d 7, 15 (citing Henry J. Friendly, Some Kind of Hearing, 123 U. Pa. L. Rev. 1276, 1276).
184. Doe v. Univ. of Cincinnati, 872 F.3d 393, 403 (6th Cir. 2017) (internal citations omitted).
185. "The pre-eminent generalization that emerges from this Court's precedents on an indigent's right to appointed counsel is that such a right has been recognized to exist only where the litigant may lose his physical liberty if he loses the litigation." Lassiter v. Dep't of Soc. Services, 452 U.S. 18, 25 (1981). *See generally* Benjamin H. Barton & Stephanos Bibas, *Triaging Appointed-Counsel Funding and Pro Se Access to Justice*, 160 U. PA. L. REV. 967, 968–972 (2012); Stan Keillor, James H. Cohen, & Mercy Changwesha, *The Inevitable, if Untrumpeted, March Toward "Civil Gideon,"* 64 SYRACUSE L. REV. 469, 481 (2014).

136 *Ready, Fire, Aim*

186. *See* Gabrilowitz v. Newman, 582 F.2d 100, 106 (1st Cir. 1978) (affirming that because of a pending criminal case, the denial to a student of the right to have a lawyer of the student's own choice consult with and advise him during a school disciplinary hearing without participating further in such proceeding would deprive the student of due process of law).
187. Lassiter, 452 U.S. at 27. Lassiter v. Dep't of Social Services, 452 U.S. 18, 27 (1981).
188. *Id.* at 31.
189. Turner v. Rogers, 564 U.S. 431, 438 (2011).
190. In Lassiter, the Court wrote: "[S]ince the *Eldridge* factors will not always be so distributed, and since 'due process is not so rigid as to require that the significant interests in informality, flexibility and economy must always be sacrificed,' neither can we say that the Constitution requires the appointment of counsel in every parental termination proceeding. We therefore adopt the standard found appropriate in Gagnon v. Scarpelli, and leave the decision whether due process calls for the appointment of counsel for indigent parents in termination proceedings to be answered in the first instance by the trial court, subject, of course, to appellate review." Lassiter, 452 U.S. at 31–32 (citation omitted).
191. *See generally* Weizel, *supra* note 1, at 1613.
192. Elevating the standard of proof could slow down the proceedings, which would result in the opportunity cost of how the participants could otherwise be spending their time.
193. *See* Slaughter v. Brigham Young Univ., 514 F.2d 622, 625 (10th Cir. 1975) (holding that the procedures utilized, including the standard of proof, satisfied procedural due process); Gomes v. Univ. of Me. Sys., 365 F. Supp. 2d 6, 16 (D. Me. 2005); Edwards v. Bd. of Regents of Nw. Mo. State Univ., 397 F. Supp. 822, 831 (W.D. Mo. 1975); Gagne v. Trs. of Ind. Univ., 692 N.E. 2d 489, 493 (Ind. Ct. App. 1998).
194. *See* Butler v. Oak Creek-Franklin Sch. Dist., 172 F. Supp. 2d 1102, 1119 (E. D. Wis. 2001) ("I observe here only that no lower standard of proof than 'preponderance of the evidence' could be acceptable.").
195. 398 F. Supp. 777 (W.D. Mich. 1975).
196. *Id.*
197. Goss v. Lopez, 419 U.S. 565, 581–582 (1975).
198. *Id.* at 582.
199. Rosa R. v. Connelly, 889 F.2d 435, 439 (2d Cir. 1989) (quoting Mullane v. Cent. Hanover Bank & Tr. Co., 339 U.S. 306, 314 (1950), *cert. denied*, 496 U.S. 941 (1990)).
200. Goss, 419 U.S. at 581.
201. *See* Dixon v. Ala. State Bd. of Educ., 294 F.2d 150, 159 (5th Cir. 1961) ("This is not to imply that a full-dress judicial hearing, with the right to cross-examine witnesses, is required.") and Jaksa v. Regents of Univ. of

Mich., 597 F. Supp. 1245, 1252 (E.D. Mich. 1984) ("The Constitution does not confer on plaintiff the right to cross-examine his accuser in a school disciplinary proceeding.").

202. *See* Dillon v. Pulaski Cnty. Special Sch. Dist., 468 F. Supp. 54, 58 (E.D. Ark. 1978), *aff'd* 594 F.2d 699 (8th Cir. 1979) (where a witness was known and present, and her "testimony was critical . . . [D]ue process clearly demanded that the plaintiff should have been given an opportunity to question her before the school board at its disciplinary hearing concerning the details of his alleged misconduct.").

203. *See* Gonzales v. McEuen, 435 F. Supp. 460, 469 (C.D. Cal. 1977) ("where the student is faced with the severe sanction of expulsion, due process does not permit admission of ex parte evidence by witnesses not under oath, and not subject to examination by the accused student.") and Flaim v. Med. College of Ohio, 418 F.3d 629, 636 (6th Cir. 2005) ("Some circumstances may require the opportunity to cross-examine witnesses, though this right might exist only in the most serious of cases.").

204. *See* Winnick v. Manning, 460 F.2d 545, 549–550 (2d Cir. 1972) ("The right to cross-examine witnesses generally has not been considered an essential requirement of due process in school disciplinary proceedings . . . [but] if this case had resolved itself into a problem of credibility, cross examination of witnesses might have been essential to a fair hearing.").

205. Doe v. Baum, 903 F.3d 575, 578 (6th Cir. 2018).

206. Haidak v. University of Massachusetts-Amherst, 933 F.3d 56, 69 (1st Cir. 2019).

207. *Id.* (internal citations omitted).

208. *Id.* at 406 (internal citation omitted).

209. *Id.*

210. *Id.* (internal citations omitted).

211. Plummer v. Univ. of Houston, 860 F.3d 767, 775 (5th Cir. 2017).

212. *Id.* at 776.

213. *See* Doe v. Baum, 903 F.3d 575, 581 (6th Cir. 2017) (". . . our circuit has made two things clear: (1) if a student is accused of misconduct, the university must hold some sort of hearing before imposing a sanction as serious as expulsion or suspension, and (2) when the university's determination turns on the credibility of the accuser, the accused, or witnesses, that hearing must include an opportunity for cross-examination."); Henson v. Honor Comm. of U. Va., 719 F.2d 69, 74 (4th Cir. 1983) ("Although *Dixon* was decided more than twenty years ago, its summary of minimum due process requirements for disciplinary hearings in an academic setting is still accurate today."); Dixon v. Ala.

State Bd. of Educ., 294 F.2d 150, 158–159 (5th Cir. 1961); Donohue v. Baker, 976 F. Supp. 136, 147 (N.D.N.Y. 1997).

214. Dixon, 294 F.2d at 158–159.
215. *Id.*
216. Doe v. Brandeis, 177 F. Supp. 3d 561, 601 (2016).
217. *Id.*
218. *Id.*
219. *Id.* at 602.
220. *Id.* at 603.
221. *Id.*
222. *Id.* at 604.
223. *Id.* at 605.
224. *Id.* at 606.
225. *Id.* at 607.
226. *Id.* at 607.
227. *Id.*
228. *Id.*
229. Doe v. Brown Univ. 166 F. Supp. 3d 177, 183 (R.I. Dist. Court, 2016).
230. *See* Jake New, *Court Wins for Accused*, INSIDE HIGHER ED. (Nov. 5, 2015), www.insidehighered.com/news/2015/11/05/more-students-pun ished-over-sexual-assault-are-winning-lawsuits-against-colleges.
231. Doe v. Regents of Univ. of Cal. San Diego, No. 37–2015-00010549-CU-WM-CTL, 2015 WL 4394597, at *6 (Cal. Super. Ct. July 10, 2015).
232. Doe v. Univ. of S. Cal., 200 Cal. Rptr. 3d 851, 877 (Ct. App. 2016).
233. Brandeis, *supra* note 216, at 608.
234. *Id.* at 573.
235. REPUBLICAN PLATFORM 2016, https://prod-cdn-static.gop.com/media/d ocuments/DRAFT_12_FINAL[1]-ben_1468872234.pdf?_ga=2.246164932.136 1714990.1608396976-27996157.1608396976 at 35.

6

There's a New Sheriff in Town

Fifteen days after his upset victory over Hillary Clinton, President-elect Trump nominated Betsy DeVos to be Secretary of Education after Jerry Falwell Jr. reportedly declined the position.[1] A billionaire philanthropist, DeVos used her money to push school voucher programs that diverted public funds into private and religious schools. Although she claimed that she was just trying to give families choice, past statements revealed that her goal was to "advance God's Kingdom."[2] Whatever her motives, DeVos' actions harmed children. As an article in the *Detroit Free Press* explained, "Largely as a result of DeVos' lobbying, Michigan tolerates more lower performing charter schools than just about any other state. And it lacks any effective mechanism for shutting down, or even improving, failing charters."[3]

With her distrust of public education and her long history of supporting anti-gay causes,[4] it was clear that DeVos would take the Trump Education Department in a new direction. At her confirmation hearing, DeVos indicated that she was likely to make significant changes to the way schools handled sexual misconduct.[5] When asked point blank by Senator Bob Casey of Pennsylvania whether she would keep the Dear Colleague Letter, DeVos responded: "It would be premature for me to do that today."[6] When pressed on whether she would maintain the preponderance standard, DeVos responded:

> Let me just say my mom's heart is really piqued on this issue. Assault in any form is never okay, and I just want to be clear on that. And so, if confirmed, I look forward to understanding the past actions and current situation better, and to ensuring that the intent of the law is actually carried out in a way that recognizes both the victim, the rights of the victims, as well as those who are accused.[7]

Citing DeVos' lack of experience in public education, two Republicans joined all forty-eight Democratic senators in voting against her confirmation.[8] With Vice President Pence voting in favor to break the tie – the first vice president to ever cast a tie-breaking vote for a cabinet nominee – DeVos was confirmed. Eight months later, the Department of Education (DOE) rescinded the 2011 Dear Colleague Letter.

This chapter discusses Title IX under Secretary DeVos. It begins by describing how the DOE quickly broke from its predecessor before turning to the two-year process of promulgating new regulations. It then takes a deeper dive into changes to Title IX enforcement made under the new rule. The discussion here focuses on when a school can be penalized for not responding to alleged misconduct. The next chapter delves into how a school is supposed to respond.

6.1 CHANGING THE RULES

6.1.1 *Every Sheriff Needs her Deputy – Candice Jackson*

On April 12, 2017, Secretary DeVos announced that she had hired Candice Jackson as the Deputy Assistant Secretary in the Office for Civil Rights – a role that did not require Senate confirmation.[9] She served as acting Assistant Secretary until Kenneth Marcus was confirmed.[10] Jackson was not an obvious choice for the job. While an undergraduate at Stanford, she complained of being discriminated against for being white, and she said of feminists on campus, "College women who insist on banding together by gender to fight for their rights are moving backwards, not forwards."[11] A rape survivor,[12] Jackson was an outspoken supporter of the women who had accused Bill Clinton of sexual assault, even escorting three of them to the second presidential debate where she sat with them in the front row.[13] Yet, she was dismissive of those who accused Donald Trump of sexual assault; she wrote that they were lying "for political gain" and called them "frankly, false victims."[14]

In a July interview with the *New York Times*, Jackson was asked about her plans for the department. She correctly criticized campus investigative processes for not being "fairly balanced between the accusing victim and the accused students."[15] However Jackson's further explanation was deeply problematic. "Men are labeled rapists," she said, "when the facts just don't back that up."[16] Instead of being cases in which a man overcame a woman's will, Jackson said: ". . . the accusations – 90 percent of them – fall into the category of 'we were both drunk,' 'we broke up, and six months later I found myself under a Title IX investigation because she just decided that our last sleeping together was not quite right.'"

Although false reporting is a real problem, no reputable study has *ever* documented anything close to 90 percent. Indeed, the best study I have seen regarding false reports of rape was done by Cassiah Spohn et al. in 2014.[17] They analyzed sexual assault cases that were reported to the Los Angeles Police in 2008. After studying the written reports and interviewing detectives, Spohn et al. estimated that 4.5 percent of rape reports were false.[18] Although this estimate is certainly too low given the fact that a false report may not become evident until further along in the criminal justice process, something Spohn et al. acknowledge, it is an indication that the rate of false reporting is much lower than the figure cited by Jackson.

Jackson later issued a statement stating that her remarks were "flippant"[19] and that "all sexual harassment and sexual assault must be taken seriously,"[20] but she had squandered any chance of gaining the trust of victims' groups. The president of the National Women's Law Center stated that she was "worried that the department will turn into apologists for the sort of violence that happens on campus."[21] Laura Dunn, the founder and former executive director of SurvJustice and a member of the ABA Criminal Justice Section Task Force on Campus Due Process and Victim Protection, said that the group was "deeply troubled that [Jackson's] apology does not admit how rare false reports are or admit how widespread the issue of campus sexual violence actually is based on research."[22] When later asked about Jackson's 90 percent claim, DeVos declined to comment.[23]

6.1.2 *Meetings with Stakeholders*

On June 28, Jackson and Thomas E. Wheeler, the Acting Assistant Attorney General in the Civil Rights Division at the Department of Justice, met with the National Association of College and University Attorneys (NACUA).[24] They started by emphasizing that they were committed to enforcing the nation's civil rights laws. "For those in the press and my friends with other political perspectives who have been expressing fear . . . OCR is scaling back or retreating from civil rights, that's just not the case." However, they made it clear that OCR would be handling things differently than under the Obama administration; they would be less confrontational and more collaborative. "OCR has fallen into a pattern and practice of overreaching," Jackson said, "of setting out to punish and embarrass institutions rather than appreciate their good faith and genuine desire to correct legitimate civil rights problems."

Two weeks later, DeVos hosted a closed-door summit with sexual assault victims, advocates for the rights of the accused, and campus representatives.[25] Some women objected to the inclusion of groups that were fighting for the rights of accused men, but DeVos was right to include them as they were primary stakeholders. However, DeVos should have thought twice about including a group like the National Coalition for Men, which publishes photographs, names, and biographical details of women they say have falsely accused men of rape.[26] Such a practice should be condemned for discouraging reporting and for falsely equating a finding of non responsibility with a finding that the complainant lied.

After the day of meetings, DeVos spoke with reporters.[27] "There are some things that are working," she said. "There are many things that are not working well. We need to get this right."

6.1.3 *Rescinding the 2011 Dear Colleague Letter*

On September 7, Secretary DeVos formally dashed the dreams of anyone who was holding out hope that the Obama era guidance would remain. "Through intimidating and coercion," De Vos proclaimed, "the failed system has clearly pushed schools to overreach. With the heavy hand of Washington tipping the balance of her scale, the sad reality is that Lady Justice is not blind on campuses today."[28] DeVos then pledged to do what the Obama administration had not – undergo a formal notice and comment process. "We will seek public feedback and combine institutional knowledge, professional expertise, and the experiences of students to replace the current approach with a workable, effective, and fair system."

Fifteen days later, on September 22, the DOE formally rescinded the 2011 Dear Colleague Letter and the Questions and Answers on Title IX Sexual Violence dated April 29, 2014.[29] In the letter formally announcing rescission, Candice Jackson wrote:

> The 2011 and 2014 guidance documents may have been well-intentioned, but those documents have led to the deprivation of rights for many students – both accused students denied fair process and victims denied an adequate resolution of their complaints. The guidance has not succeeded in providing clarity for educational institutions or in leading institutions to guarantee educational opportunities on the equal basis that Title IX requires. Instead, schools face a confusing and counterproductive set of regulatory mandates, and the objectives of regulatory compliance has displaced Title IX's goal of educational equity.[30]

DeVos announced that they would begin the formal rulemaking process in the coming months, and in the meanwhile would continue to rely on the 2001 Revised Sexual Harassment Guidance, which had gone through a public (albeit "truncated") notice and comment process,[31] and was discussed in Chapter 3.[32] The Department also released an interim Q&A to guide schools until the new regulations could be promulgated. Unlike the now defunct DCL, the Q&A allowed schools to use the clear and convincing standard of proof;[33] it required schools to provide written notice to the responding party of the allegations "including sufficient details and with sufficient time to prepare a response before any initial interview";[34] and it allowed schools to informally resolve allegations of sexual misconduct.[35]

6.1.4 *Challenging the Interim Rules*

In January 2018, the Victim Rights Law Center, SurvJustice, and Equal Rights Advocates filed a lawsuit to stop the DOE's 2017 interim guidance. The Department of Education, Betsy DeVos, and Candice Jackson were named defendants. The Victim Rights Law Center, SurvJustice, and Equal Rights Advocates argued that defendants had violated the Administrative Procedure Act (APA), the Fifth Amendment Equal Protection guarantee, and that it acted "ultra vires," meaning that it acted outside its legal authority. Jackson's comments to the *New York Times*, in addition to other actions and statements by DeVos and Jackson, were cited as evidence of discriminatory motivation.[36] In an amended complaint, they cited documents released by the DOE pursuant to a Freedom of Information Act request that showed Jackson actively reached out to, and was in regular contact with, advocates for accused male students.[37] "In contrast to the Department's solicitation of persons and organizations with views that female sexual assault survivors are prone to exaggerate or fabricate accusations, the Department met with organizations that advocate for Title IX's protections for survivors only after repeated, collective requests from those organizations."[38]

The lawsuit did not succeed. On October 1, 2018, a U.S. Magistrate Judge dismissed the APA claim with prejudice because the interim guidance did not constitute final agency action.[39] On March 29, 2019, the Court later dismissed the equal protection claim with prejudice for a lack of standing. Although there was a "concrete and particularized" injury, the plaintiffs weren't suffering the injury. The Court dismissed the ultra vires claim because the moving parties had not fixed the deficiencies with the original complaint, namely that it had "wholly conclusory allegations."[40]

6.1.5 *Confirming the Assistant Secretary of Civil Rights*

On June 7, 2018 the Senate voted 50 to 46 to confirm Kenneth L. Marcus as Assistant Secretary for Civil Rights.[41] Like Candice Jackson, whom he formally replaced, Marcus was distrusted by many civil rights groups. A coalition of more than 200 national organizations including the National Association for the Advancement of Colored People, the National Women's Law Center, and the Southern Poverty Law Center signed a letter opposing Marcus on multiple grounds; it emphasized "Mr. Marcus' own record of anti-civil rights positions and his failure to articulate clear support for robust civil rights enforcement during his confirmation hearing."[42]

6.1.6 *Promulgating New Rules*

Assistant Secretary Marcus did not waste any time. On November 16, 2018, the DOE released its proposed rules,[43] and soon after filed a notice of proposed rulemaking in the Federal Register.[44] It was the first time that DOE had ever promulgated Title IX regulations.[45] In the past it had relied on guidance documents.

The proposed regulations were enormously controversial. Although groups that advocated for the rights of accused students applauded the increased emphasis on due process, others were deeply critical. This included many Congressional Democrats. In a November 17 press release, House Speaker Nancy Pelosi proclaimed: "With wanton disregard, this Administration has cruelly codified their utter contempt for survivor justice by making schools unwelcoming and less safe."[46] Among the most disparaged parts were the change in the definition of sexual harassment, the change in what constituted notice for Title IX liability, and the increased procedural protections, especially the requirement that the complainant submit to cross-examination. "This draft proposal," Pelosi said, "enables schools to shirk responsibility, completely ignores harassment, denies survivors due process and discourages survivors to come forward."[47]

January 28, 2019 was set as the deadline for submitting comments,[48] and activists on both sides urged their constituents to participate.[49] Survivor advocates were particularly well organized. Two groups – *End Rape On Campus* and *Know Your IX* – announced a joint campaign called Hands Off IX "to encourage and enable people to submit comments with their opposition to the dangerous rule."[50] They created a special website that provided a template for making comments and then submitting them through the Federal eRulemaking Portal. Encouraging people to be heard is a noble endeavor but using misinformation to succeed is not. The Hands Off IX Notice and Comment Toolkit falsely stated that the new rules would "shut … out the thousands of survivors who are assaulted at parties held by fraternities …"[51] In fact, the proposed rules *explicitly* discussed why fraternities would be covered.[52]

Advocates for accused students also encouraged their constituents to formally respond. "We know we'll never match the number of comments of victims' advocates," Cynthia Garrett, co-president of Families Advocating for Campus Equality and a member of the ABA Criminal Justice Section Task Force on Campus Due Process and Victim Protection, told National Public Radio, "but the Department is smart enough to understand that quality is more important than quality."[53]

6.1.7 *The New Regulations*

On May 6, 2020, after almost a year and a half spent reviewing the over 124,000 public comments that were received, the DOE released its new rules on sexual harassment.[54] Its point-by-point explanation of the final rule totaled 2,033 pages. Without commentary, the new rule would have taken just eight pages! In a Brookings Institute Report, R. Shep Melnick described the rule-making process as "extraordinarily extensive" and the Education Department's response to comments as "meticulous."[55] Indeed, as the following discussion will show, the Department changed many of the final regulations in response to comments received.

Some celebrated the new rule. The Foundation for Individual Rights in Education (FIRE) released a statement that said: "Advocates for free speech and due process on campus won one of their biggest-ever victories today with the finalization of long-awaited new Department of Education Title IX Regulations."[56] Republican Senator Lamar Alexander said in in a written statement: "This final rule respects and supports victims and preserves due process rights for both the victim and the accused."[57]

Others were more critical. The advocacy group Know Your IX damned the new regulations: "Today the Department of Education released its final rule on Title IX, which guts student survivors' rights and tips the scales of school sexual misconduct cases in favor of perpetrators and schools that wish to sweep sexual violence under the rug." Democratic Senator Patty Murray released a similar statement: "Let me be clear, this rule is not about 'restoring balance,' this is about silencing survivors."[58] Then candidate Biden also took a firm stance against the new guidelines, ". . . Trump's Education Department – led by Betsy DeVos – is trying to shame and silence survivors, and take away parents' peace of mind."[59]

Critics promised to do everything they could to undo the new rule. "We will fight this rule in court, and we intend to win," said Emily Martin, a vice president at the National Women's Law Center.[60] Martin accused the law of being "arbitrary and capricious" and violating the Administrative Procedure

Act. Then candidate Biden vowed to change the new rules if elected. "It's wrong, and it will be put to a quick end in January 2021 because as President, I'll be right where I always have been throughout my career – on the side of survivors."[61]

Although four lawsuits were filed on the merits and to delay implementation of the new rule,[62] it went into effect as scheduled in August 2020. One of those lawsuits was later dismissed for a lack of standing,[63] and by October 2020, the other three were "still pending but ha[d] been largely unsuccessful."[64] On March 11, 2021 the Women's Student Union of Berkeley, California filed a lawsuit in federal court asking that the 2020 Regulations be declared unlawful and set aside.[65] That case is still ongoing.[66] On July 28, 2021, a federal District Court in Massachusetts ruled on one of the original four lawsuits.[67] It held that except for Section 106.45(b)(6)(i), "the Final Rule does not violate the APA or the Fifth Amendment."[68] That holding and the DOE's Response will be discussed in Chapter 7.

6.2 A DEEPER DIVE

The chapter now turns to the new regulations, which redefine the conditions under which a school's response to objectionable conduct violates Title IX. To set the stage, we need to return to the U.S. Supreme Court.

In *Gebser v. Lago Vista* (1998) and *Davis v. Monroe County Board of Education* (1999), which were discussed in Chapter 2, the Supreme Court ruled that a school cannot be held liable for monetary damages unless an official with authority to address the harassment has actual knowledge of it *and* is deliberately indifferent in responding to it. In *Davis*, the Court also adopted a heightened standard for monetary damages in peer harassment as opposed to employee harassment cases on the grounds that "schools are unlike the adult workplace and . . . children may regularly interact in a manner that would be unacceptable among adults."[69]

Davis adopted a three-part framework in peer sexual harassment cases: actionable sexual harassment, actual knowledge, and deliberate indifference. "We thus conclude," the Court wrote, "that funding recipients are properly held liable in damages only when they are deliberately indifferent to sexual harassment, of which they have actual knowledge, that is so severe, pervasive, and objectively offensive that it can be said to deprive the victims of access to the educational opportunities or benefits provided by the school."[70]

As discussed in Chapter 2, for twenty-one years the DOE used a broader definition than *Davis* for administrative enforcement. It did so by taking advantage of its power as a federal agency to "'promulgate and enforce requirements that effectuate [Title IX's] nondiscrimination mandate,' even in circumstances that would not give rise to a claim for money damages."[71] 2020 marked the end of dual standards. The DOE explicitly adopted the *Gebser/ Davis* framework in the new regulations, but in doing so, it "reasonably expands the definitions of sexual harassment and actual knowledge, and the deliberate indifference standard, to tailor the *Gebser/Davis* framework to the administrative context."[72]

In discussing the new regulations, I sometimes suggest how they could be improved. All of my recommendations in this chapter would constitute a change to existing law. For that reason, recipients would not be permitted to implement them on their own. Instead, the DOE would have to make these changes through formal or informal rulemaking, as described in Chapter 3. However, recipients can and should encourage DOE to make these changes.

Let's take a look.

6.2.1 *Sexual Harassment*

Under the new regulations, sexual harassment means conduct on the basis of sex that meets one or more of three definitions. It can be quid pro quo harassment, meaning that an employee of the recipient institution conditions aid, a benefit, or service on an individual's participation in an unwelcome sexual conduct.[73] It can be "unwelcome conduct determined by a reasonable person to be so severe, pervasive, and objectively offensive that it effectively denies a person equal access to the recipient's education program or activity."[74] It can also be any of four Clery Act/VAWA offenses: "sexual assault ... dating violence ... domestic violence ... or stalking."[75]

6.2.1.1 *Per se discrimination*

In some ways, the new regulations make sexual harassment *easier* to prove than prior guidance. As OCR explained in the 1997 Guidance Document, "a school will always be liable for even one instance of *quid pro quo* harassment. . .(but for other types of sexual harassment). . . (i)n order to give rise to a complaint under Title IX. . .(it) must be sufficiently severe, persistent, or pervasive that it adversely affects a student's education or creates a hostile or abusive educational environment."[76] It was possible that one incident could constitute sexual harassment under the law, but for that to happen, "it must be severe."[77] The new regulations, however, recognize not just quid pro quo but also Clery Act/VAWA offenses included in Section 106.30 as per se sex discrimination.[78] That means conditioning an educational benefit on submitting to unwanted sexual advances or "a *single* instance of sexual assault, dating violence, domestic violence, or stalking" constitutes sexual harassment.[79] Full stop. There is no longer a need to prove severity.

6.2.1.2 Denial of Equal Access to Education

In other ways, the new regulations are decidedly *more* restrictive. The Department eliminates "hostile environment" harassment, which under the 2001 Guidance Document was described as "unwelcome conduct of a sexual nature" that is "severe, persistent, or pervasive."[80] It replaces it with the more demanding standard put forth by the Supreme Court in *Davis v. Monroe County Board of Education*. For conduct that doesn't rise to the level of quid pro quo conduct or Clery violence, the relevant question is whether it is "[u]nwelcome conduct (on the basis of sex) determined by a reasonable person to be so severe, pervasive, and objectively offensive that it effectively denies a person equal access to the recipient's education program or activity."

GOAL: PROTECTING FREE SPEECH AND ACADEMIC FREEDOM. In making this change, the DOE seeks to ensure that ". . . free speech and academic freedom are not chilled or curtailed by an overly broad definition of sexual harassment."[81] Emphasizing the importance of free speech harkens back to Department guidance before the 2011 Dear Colleague Letter. The 2001 Guidance Document read in part: ". . . in regulating the conduct of its students and its faculty to prevent or redress discrimination prohibited by Title IX (e.g., in responding to harassment that is sufficiently serious as to create a hostile environment), a school must formulate, interpret, and apply its rules so as to protect academic freedom and free speech rights".[82] The 2003 Dear Colleague Letter was even written explicitly to address First Amendment concerns. "I want to assure you in the clearest possible terms," Former Assistant Secretary of Education, Gerald A Rebolds wrote, "that OCR's regulations are not intended to restrict the exercise of any expressive activities protected under the U.S. Constitution."[83]

Yet despite these pronouncements, overbroad and imprecise anti-harassment policies still infringed on constitutionally protected expression.[84] The advocacy group FIRE observed that "overly broad or vaguely constructed definitions of sexual harassment have served as a consistent justification for abuses of student free speech rights for more than two decades."[85] The Association of American University Professors (AAUP) published a 2016 report entitled, *The History, Uses, and Abuses of Title IX*, in which AAUP "argue[s] that questions of free speech and academic freedom have been ignored in recent positions taken by the Office for Civil Rights (OCR)."[86] Even worse, the AAUP writes, "in carrying out compliance reviews, the OCR has broadened its description of sexual harassment in ways that limit the scope of permissible speech."[87]

The AAUP report recounts notorious cases like that of former University of Colorado Sociology Professor Patty Adler. In 2013, university officials sat in on a lecture Adler was giving on prostitution in a popular course she taught on deviance. They witnessed assistant teaching assistants doing a voluntary role-playing exercise in which they dressed up as various kinds of sex workers and then answered questions about their lives. The Dean offered Adler a buyout for early retirement or staying but not teaching the course. He explained that there was "too much risk" having such an exercise in the "post-Penn state environment" (referring to convicted child molester Jerry Sandusky).[88] The case got a lot of pushback from outraged faculty, students, and advocacy groups like FIRE and the ACLU, and the University ended up backing down and allowing Adler to continue teaching the course.[89] She released a statement that said:

> Although it is gratifying that the Dean of Arts and Science has affirmed the Sociology Department Executive Committee's affirmation of the Ad Hoc Committee's decision to permit me to continue teaching a course that for 25 years had been held in high esteem with no reported complaints, the fact that it had to undergo this extraordinary scrutiny to reverse CU's initial jump to judgment is a sad statement on what is occurring in universities.[90]

Professor Adler stayed for one more semester and then retired.

Overbroad anti-harassment polices also undermine academic freedom. In a 2014 essay published in *The New Yorker*, Harvard Law Professor Jeannie Suk Gersen describes how the environment for teaching rape law is changing. Students are asking not to discuss subject matter that might trigger traumatic memories, and faculty are considering giving up the subject matter altogether. Gersen explains: "Even seasoned teachers of criminal law, at law schools across the country, have confided that they are seriously considering dropping rape law and other topics related to sex and gender violence. Both men and women teachers seem frightened of discussion, because they are afraid of injuring others or being injured themselves."[91]

I agree with the Department's strong position that protecting people from sexual harassment must be balanced against protection of freedom of speech and academic freedom.[92] Loosely worded policies silence potential speakers, which stifles campus discussion and debate.[93] There is value in "even seemingly low-value speech."[94] The solution put in place by the new regulations is to make quid pro quo conduct and sexual violence per se harassment but to have a much more demanding standard for other kinds of harassment, so speech and expression are less likely to be impacted. I will discuss the details of that more demanding standard now.

OBJECTIVELY PROBLEMATIC. The new rule requires a subjective viewpoint in determining the unwelcomeness of the conduct, but "as to elements of severity, pervasiveness, objective offensiveness, and denial of equal access, determinations are made by a reasonable person in the shoes of the complainant."[95] The 2011 Dear Colleague Letter, in contrast, seemed to take a solely subjective perspective. "When a student sexually harasses another student, the harassing conduct creates a hostile environment if the conduct is sufficiently serious that it interferes with or limits a student's ability to participate in or benefit from the school's program."[96] Without an objective component, a student can be punished for engaging in innocuous behavior simply because another student interpreted it as problematic. Even the 2001 Guidance Document had explicitly considered unwelcome conduct "from both a subjective and objective perspective."[97]

MORE THAN UNWELCOME. Requiring that the conduct be more than unwelcome is another step away from the 2011 Dear Colleague Letter, which described sexual harassment as "unwelcome conduct of a sexual nature" but removed all description of it having to be "severe, persistent, or pervasive." Advocates have contended that the new definition "represents a dramatic departure from the standard for sexual harassment that schools have been successfully applying for nearly two decades – that sexual harassment is 'unwelcome conduct of a sexual nature.'"[98] In fact, under the 2001 Guidance Document, sexual harassment was described as "unwelcome conduct of a sexual nature" that is "severe, persistent, or pervasive."[99] The 2001 Guidance Document further stated that in evaluating the severity and pervasiveness of the conduct, "OCR considers all relevant circumstances, i.e., 'the constellation of surrounding circumstances, expectations, and relationships.'"[100]

SO SEVERE, PERVASIVE, AND OBJECTIVELY OFFENSIVE THAT IT EFFECTIVELY DENIES A PERSON EQUAL ACCESS TO EDUCATION OR ACTIVITY. However, in mandating the conduct be "so severe, pervasive, and objectively offensive that it effectively denies a person equal access to the recipient's education program or activity,"[101] the Department has gone too far in trying to protect freedom of speech. 1. I agree that Title IX should not be a "Federal civility code that requires schools, colleges, and universities to prohibit every instance of unwelcome or undesirable behavior"[102] but requiring all three elements sets too high a bar, especially when combined with the requirement that it actually deny the person equal access to an education program or activity. Furthermore, it is clear from the discussion that the regulations appear more restrictive than the Department intends. For example, the Department writes:

> In line with this approach, the §106.30 definition does not apply only when a complainant has been entirely, physically excluded from educational opportunities but to any situation where the sexual harassment "so undermines and detracts from the victims' educational experience, that the victim-students are effectively denied equal access to an institution's resources and opportunities . . . Signs of enduring unequal educational access due to severe, pervasive, and objectively offensive sexual harassment may include, as commentators suggest, skipping class to avoid a harasser, a decline in a student's grade point average, or having difficulty concentrating in class; however, no concrete injury is required."[103]

SUGGESTION FOR IMPROVEMENT. The DOE should change the regulation from "and" to "or." It should also more carefully explain what it means by denial of access. The regulation should be changed to something like this: "Unwelcome conduct (on the basis of sex) determined by a reasonable person to be so severe, pervasive, or objectively offensive that it so undermines and detracts from the victim's educational experience that the victim student is effectively denied equal access to an institution's resources and opportunities. No concrete injury is required."

6.2.2 *Actual Knowledge*

Under the new regulations, a school must have "actual" knowledge of sexual harassment before it can be penalized by the DOE for not responding.[104] Actual knowledge requires that a designated person receive notice:

> Notice results whenever any elementary and secondary school employee, any Title IX Coordinator, or any official with authority: Witnesses sexual harassment; hears about sexual harassment or sexual harassment allegations from a complainant (i.e., a person alleged to be the victim) or a third party (e.g., the complainant's parent, friend, or peer); receives a written or verbal complaint about sexual harassment or sexual harassment allegations; or by any other means.[105]

This new definition marks a significant and problematic change. To understand why, it is necessary to delve deeper into what constitutes notice and knowledge under the new regulations.

6.2.2.1 Notice

Notice under prior guidance extended to almost any school employee, but under the new rule, it differs depending on the type of school. For elementary and secondary schools, actual knowledge refers to notice to *any* employee. The DOE adopted a broader definition in its final rules because it "is persuaded by commenters who asserted that students in elementary and secondary schools often talk about sexual harassment experiences with someone other than their teacher, and that it is unreasonable to expect your students to differentiate among employees for the purpose of which employees' knowledge triggers the school's response and which do not."[106] The DOE was also influenced by the doctrine of *in loco parentis*, meaning that schools "stand in the place of a parent with respect to certain authority over, and responsibility for, its students,"[107] and the fact that teachers are mandatory reporters of child abuse under state laws.

For institutes of higher education (IHEs), however, actual knowledge means notice to the Title IX Coordinator or any official who has the authority to institute corrective measures on behalf of the recipient IHE.[108] The regulations make it clear how narrowly defined authority to institute corrective measures is: "The mere ability or obligation to report sexual harassment or to inform a student about how to report sexual harassment, or having been trained to do so, does not qualify . . ."[109] Furthermore, if the only official with actual knowledge is the respondent, that does not count as notice. The Victim Rights Law Center, Equal Rights Advocates, Legal Voice, and Chicago Alliance Against Sexual Exploitation explained why limiting notice in this way is so problematic. "If the Final Rule had been in place earlier," they wrote, "institutions of higher education like Michigan State University would have had no responsibility to stop Larry Nassar – even though his victims reported their experiences to at least fourteen school employees over a twenty-year period-including athletic trainers, coaches, counselors, and therapists – merely because those employees were not school officials with the 'authority to institute corrective measures.'"[110]

One administrator I interviewed was deeply critical of this change in the law and contended that the only way to keep the community safe was by making everyone a mandatory reporter:

> I think everyone in the community should be a mandatory reporter. You can't control where students have a connection. Maybe it's a student who's also a student employee in the dining center, and they tell someone who they work with. . . . I am responsible for a lot of staff, and technically the way the new rule is written my RA's wouldn't have to report, and that's crap. They're

in a position to know things, and they should have to tell someone and they should have to make that report. Sometimes it's the only person the student tells. You want to know if there's potential harm; you want to respond, and you have a responsibility . . . Parents expect us to keep our students safe. If they find out we knew that we had a serial offender and did nothing, they will be very upset.

This same administrator emphasized that schools shouldn't have to file a formal complaint, but she still thought it was valuable to collect this information.

Another Title IX administrator that I spoke with was critical of the Obama era policy where reporting to any person would trigger university liability, but she also thought that the current rule went too far in the other direction:

I do think high student contact positions should be mandatory reporters to Title IX. It ensures that the right information is making it into the hands of the reporter because the faculty member may not have all the information or know all the information and even though we train all faculty members on this information, it is very difficult for them to be able to provide specific information and resources. It also allows us to identify trends on campus. If we have in a given semester five different students go to five different faculty members about inappropriate comments by one person . . . everyone thinks it's a one-time incident rather than happening many times. It allows us to see trends and identify repeat offenders . . .

Despite the fact that they had mandatory reporters, they didn't require that the name of the reporting student be disclosed:

We require that they tell us the Clery information, the what, when, and why, and we encourage them to obtain permission from the reporting party to share their name so we can reach out directly, but we don't reach out directly otherwise.

Although the final rule limits who is legally obligated to respond at the post-secondary school level, it requires that students be advised how to report if they want to do so. The goal is to give complainants at post-secondary institutions more control.

These final regulations ensure that all students and employees are notified of the contact information for the Title IX Coordinator and how to report sexual harassment for purposes of triggering a recipient's response obligations, and the Department believes that students at postsecondary institutions benefit from retaining control over whether, and when, the complainants want the recipient to respond to the sexual harassment that the complainant experienced.[111]

Giving more control to victims is a good thing, but it doesn't follow that notice should be narrowly circumscribed. The question is what best allows the Office for Civil Rights to enforce Title IX's nondiscrimination mandate, and for a variety of reasons, it's broader notice. Because notice triggers schools taking certain steps, a broader group of designated persons means that more victims will receive information and access resources from the Title IX office. Such information allows victims to make a more knowing and intelligent choice about how they want to proceed.

A broader notice requirement is also an acknowledgement of the power that professors and coaches have over victims or third parties. Sometimes they may unintentionally dissuade a victim or third party from triggering a formal process. Other times, they may do so intentionally. That's what happened at Michigan State University where coaches repeatedly told girls and women that they had misunderstood Larry Nassar and should trust him.[112] Requiring a professor or coach to report a basic summary of what they were told to an unbiased Title IX Coordinator better ensures that a victim will make an independent decision that reflects their own best interest.

Finally, a broader notice requirement means that the Title IX Coordinator will be able to see whether the accused student, faculty, or staff member has had any prior accusations against him. That may in turn influence whether the school should proceed with a formal investigation and adjudicatory process even if it's over the preferences of the complainant.

6.2.2.2 Actual versus Constructive Knowledge

The new rule only requires actual knowledge, but under prior guidance, the standard was constructive knowledge. The former meant a school was obligated to respond to sexual harassment if it "knew, or in the exercise of reasonable care, should have known' about the harassment,"[113] including harassment it would have learned about through a "reasonably diligent inquiry."[114] Actual knowledge is what the Supreme Court requires for Title IX liability in private Title IX lawsuits,[115] so why shouldn't it be the basis for administrative enforcement?

The issue, as pointed out more than twenty years ago by the four dissenting justices in *Gebser v. Lago Vista*, is that actual knowledge incentivizes willful ignorance.[116] Writing for the dissent, Justice Stevens explained: "As long as school boards can insulate themselves from knowledge about this sort of conduct, they can claim immunity from damages liability."[117] Under the new rule, the incentive to ignore by school employees and officials at all levels of education now exists in the context of administrative enforcement.

Granted, the DOE helps to abate the problem somewhat by having actual knowledge encompass "conduct that could constitute sexual harassment."[118] That means a school will have an affirmative duty to respond even if it hasn't received sufficient information for a reasonable person to determine that sexual misconduct occurred. The DOE provides the following discussion in the Federal Register:

> The Department acknowledges the commenter's question about how much detail is needed in order for the recipient to have actual knowledge triggering the recipient's obligation to provide a non-deliberately indifferent response, and whether a recipient with partial information about a sexual harassment allegation has a responsibility to notify the complainant that additional information is needed to further evaluate or respond to the allegation. In response, the Department notes that the definition of "complainant" under Section 106.30 is an individual who is alleged to be the victim of *conduct that could constitute sexual harassment*; thus the recipient need not have received notice of the facts that definitely indicate whether a reasonable person would determine that the complainant's equal access has been effectively denied in order for the recipient to be required to respond promptly in a non-deliberately indifferent manner under Section 106.44 (a). The definition of "actual knowledge," in Sect. 196.30, also reflects this concept as actual knowledge means notice of sexual harassment or *allegations* of sexual harassment.[119]

The Department also contends that by expanding notice to all employees in the elementary and secondary school context, it has effectively done away with the need for a constructive knowledge standard. It explains:

> In elementary and secondary schools, the final regulations charge a recipient with actual knowledge whenever any employee has notice. Thus, if sexual harassment is "so pervasive that some employees should have known" about it (e.g. sexualized graffiti scrawled across lockers that meets the definition of sexual harassment in Section 106.30), it is highly likely that at least one employee did know about it and the school is charged with actual knowledge.[120]

Even with the expansion of actual knowledge to include possible harassment and the extension of notice to every school employee at the primary and secondary school level, the new rule will still miss serious cases of sexual harassment. *Rost v. Steamboat Springs RE-2-School District* (2008) demonstrates why a constructive knowledge standard is necessary.[121] Rost sued for damages after her daughter, K.C., was coerced into performing various sexual acts with a number of boys beginning in seventh and continuing to eighth grade. She appealed to the Tenth Circuit after the District Court granted summary judgment for the School District on the grounds that they did not have actual knowledge of the abuse. The Tenth Circuit upheld the judgment even though K.C. had told the school counselor that the boys were "bothering her," and her mother had repeatedly urged both the principal and the school counselor that something was wrong with K.C. The fact that the school knew K.C. had a brain injury and thus might have difficulty communicating made no difference to the Court's decision. Indeed, K.C. actually testified that she did not know to use the word assault when she spoke with the school counselor. Nor did it make a difference that K.C.'s mother had told the principal that K.C. hated school, was afraid to go to school, and was afraid to go to a math class in which one of the boys who was assaulting her was enrolled. Under a constructive standard, these facts would have been enough for liability, but as the Court explained, "A negligent failure to investigate Ms. Rost's generalized complaints did not result in Title IX liability."[122] The question is whether it would meet the standard for knowledge under the new rules. Certainly, an experienced educator should have realized that K.C.'s conduct indicated that something serious was going on. But did it rise to the level of an allegation of sexual assault? I think not, which would mean no liability.

And of course, the new rule has a narrower definition of notice for IHEs. That means unless a Title IX Coordinator or official who has the ability to institute corrective measures learns about conduct that rises to an allegation of sexual harassment, they will have no duty to respond.

Under a constructive knowledge standard, the question is whether the person knew or should have known about sexual harassment. We use a negligence standard in tort law to make people more careful and products and workplaces safer. Why shouldn't we use a similar standard to keep students safe, especially in primary and secondary schools where, as DOE has acknowledged, schools take on some of the special functions and responsibilities of a parent (*in loco parentis*)? The merits of a constructive knowledge standard should also be considered within the context of other changes made by the new regulations. The new definition of sexual harassment means that schools would only be expected to know about conduct that is objectively problematic. That means a school can't be penalized for failing to respond to a problem that it had no reason to recognize as such.

6.2.2.3 Suggestion for Improvement

The DOE should change the rule in two ways. First, it should return to broader notice requirements in IHEs. Notice should be expanded from

Title IX Coordinators and officials with the ability to make corrective changes to include persons who have significant interaction with students, like professors and coaches. Second, the constructive knowledge standard should be reinstated at all levels of education. The modified rule would look something like this:

> Notice results whenever any elementary and secondary school employee, or at the post-secondary level, any Title IX Coordinator, official with authority, or employee with significant student interaction like a professor or coach: knows or should have known of the harassment, including harassment that person would have learned about through a reasonably diligent inquiry.

Regardless of what the DOE does, post-secondary schools should still institute broad reporting requirements. That doesn't mean they should necessarily file a formal complaint, but it's important that a centralized office knows so they can make a reasonable decision about how to proceed.

6.2.3 *Recipient's Response*

Under the new regulations, once a recipient has actual knowledge of sexual harassment, they "must respond promptly in a manner that is not deliberately indifferent."[123] Only responses that are "clearly unreasonable in light of the known circumstances" are deliberately indifferent.[124] The new response requirements are both meritorious and deeply problematic.

6.2.3.1 Deliberate Indifference

The most troubling change to this part of the new rule has to do with the standard DOE now uses for evaluating a school's response to a sex-based harassment complaint. Prior guidance required a "reasonable response," which differed depending on the circumstances.[125] The new rule demands far less of schools. Only a response that is "deliberately indifferent" will violate Title IX. By "deliberately indifferent," DOE means a response that is "clearly unreasonable in light of the known circumstances."[126]

Although the standard makes it seem like schools can get away with doing just about anything, DOE has actually spelled out "specific obligations that every recipient must meet as part of every response to sexual harassment."[127] They include offering supportive measures to complainants through the Title IX Coordinator (which DOE had not previously imposed as a legally binding requirement),[128] responding "promptly in a manner that is not deliberately indifferent,"[129] and following a detailed grievance process prior to imposing disciplinary sanctions. Indeed, the new rule is more explicit than former guidance on what schools are obligated to do in order to be in compliance with Title IX.

Unfortunately, as part of the deliberate indifference standard, DOE decided to give up significant oversight over a school's decision-making process and punishment. The Department justified this change on the ground that cases are fact specific, and schools know best how to respond:

> Sexual harassment incidents present context-driven, fact-specific needs and concerns for each complainant, and the Department believes that teachers and local school leaders with unique knowledge of the school climate and student body are best positioned to make decisions about supportive measures and potential disciplinary measures; thus unless the recipient's response to sexual harassment is clearly unreasonable in light of the known circumstances, the Department will not second guess such decisions.[130]

This change removes critical oversight. A school could follow all of the required processes, but if they always find respondents not responsible or vice versa then DOE should investigate. Likewise, if a student is found responsible for a serious offense like rape and the sanction is counseling, or if a person is found responsible for a trivial offense and they are expelled, DOE should step in. Requiring the complainant or respondent to prove the school's decisions were "clearly unreasonable in light of the known circumstances" makes such oversight unlikely.

The Supreme Court has made "deliberate indifference" the liability standard for private damages, but DOE does not need to use the same standard for administrative enforcement.[131] Indeed, as pointed out by the Victim Rights Law Center, Equal Rights Advocates, Legal Voice, and Chicago Alliance Against Sexual Exploitation, there is good reason to have an easier-to-meet standard here:

> The liability standard for private damages is restrictive so as not to expose schools to financial consequences except in cases that meet this notoriously high legal requirement. However the Department of Education's administrative mandate is not to hold schools financially liable, but rather to work with its recipient schools to achieve voluntary compliance with Title IX's anti-sex discrimination protections. The adoption of a standard that schools should be non-deliberately indifferent – suggesting that being indifferent is fine as long as it is not deliberate – is inappropriately restrictive in the administrative enforcement context.[132]

6.2.3.2 Suggestion for Improvement

The DOE should change the rule so it returns to the standard under prior guidance, which means schools would be required to provide a reasonable response to a sex-based harassment complaint. As part of that reasonable response, schools would have to meet detailed requirements like offering supportive measures to both parties through the Title IX Coordinator, responding promptly, and following a detailed grievance process prior to imposing disciplinary sanctions.

6.2.3.3 Complainants Have More Control

Another change for the better is giving complainants more control over how the case will be resolved. Under prior guidance, "[r]egardless of whether the student who was harassed, or his or her parent, decides to file a complaint or otherwise request action on the student's behalf ... the school must promptly investigate to determine what occurred and then take appropriate steps to resolve the situation."[33] The new regulations, in contrast, give complainants more power in deciding whether the case will be pursued. As the DOE explains in the preamble:

> These final regulations obligate a recipient to initiate a grievance process when a complainant files, or a Title IX Coordinator signs, a formal complaint, so that the Title IX Coordinator takes into account the wishes of a complainant and only initiates a grievance process against the complainant's wishes if doing so is not clearly unreasonable in light of the known circumstances.[134]

In making this change, the new regulations acknowledge the extensive literature showing how important it is to give victims control:

> What research does demonstrate is that respecting an alleged victim's autonomy, giving alleged victims control over how official systems respond to an alleged victim, and offering clear options to alleged victims are critical aspects of helping an alleged victim recover from sexual harassment. Unsupportive institutional responses increase the effects of trauma on complainants, and institutional betrayal may occur when an institution's mandatory reporting policies require a complainant's intended private conversation about sexual assault to result in a report to the Title IX Coordinator.[135]

Importantly, although the new rules give complainants more control, it is not absolute. At the primary and secondary school level parents and legal guardians have the right to act on behalf of a complainant, which includes discussing supportive measures and deciding whether to file a formal complaint.[136] In addition, the recipient school is allowed to go forward without the complainants' support "if doing so is not clearly unreasonable in light of the known circumstances." This flexibility is necessary because the school doesn't just have an obligation to respect the desires of complainants, it also has the duty to protect the safety and well-being of the community. It's worth noting that giving schools the right to proceed against the wishes of the complainant is a change that DOE made in response to comments provided during the notice and comment period.

6.2.3.4 More Protections for the Accused in Taking Interim Measures

Another change for the better is requiring that schools pay more attention to the rights of the accused when taking interim measures. Under the old rules, schools were required to take interim measures based on a report from a complainant, but there were no requirements that any attention be paid to the impact on the respondent. One student I spoke with was still required to comply with limitations to where he could eat even though he had been found not responsible!

Another was forced to move from his dorm room even though the complainant didn't even live in the same building. He described being treated as if he were guilty and receiving no resources from his school:

> I felt that some of the procedures that took place initially were those that should be done if someone was found guilty . . . I went to the Dean's office, and they said, "you have to move your stuff out by the end of tomorrow night." I was like, I have homework, exams, but they just disregarded everything I had going on. Engineering is a pretty tough major. You're talking about a lot of meat and potatoes as well as searching for a job. They just threw all of that out the window . . . They didn't help me move . . . They didn't give me any support in terms of an advisor. I had to reach out to a friend who referred me to another friend who referred me to my advisor. There was no given support.

I interviewed a former Deputy Title IX Coordinator from a large state school who was frustrated by the lack of resources available for accused students. She believed she had a responsibility toward all students, and she rejected the notion that supporting them betrayed victims:

> The services offered were definitely imbalanced; there was way more support for complainants and victims . . . I think it's a blind spot for higher education in student affairs . . . A student has to feel that the campus is for them at all times, so even if they are being accused of this conduct, they should be able to process it out with people. But there was a definite line drawn, if you were a respondent then you weren't able to access these resources . . . What we were seeing was that it was impacting these students: I'm taking you out of your community; I'm putting you over there; you

can't go back to where you lived, and people are going to ask. So then you're dealing with how do you say I was accused of something I didn't feel I did, or maybe something did happen, and you don't know how to make amends. For me there was a huge void and colleges need to do better. It doesn't mean that we're blaming the victim or not believing the victim. It just means that there are two human beings and we need to support both of them.

She cited her experience as a mother in explaining why she was committed to fair treatment of both sides:

Personally as a mother of a son, knowing that sons are at a higher rate named as respondents in sexual misconduct cases, I worry what does that mean for him. Will he have support in something like this if that ever happens.?

The new rule attempts to address the problems of unequal resources. It "ensures that recipients respond to sexual harassment by offering supportive measures designed to restore or preserve a complainant's equal educational access without treating a respondent as responsible until after a fair grievance process."[137]

Paying attention to the rights of accused students doesn't mean schools can't respond appropriately to risk. The new regulations allow schools to remove respondents from their education program or activity on an emergency basis "provided that the recipient undertakes an individualized safety and risk analysis, determines that an immediate threat to the physical health or safety of any student or other individual arising from the allegations of sexual harassment justifies removal, and provides the respondent with notice and an opportunity to challenge the decisions immediately following the removal."[138] This last part is particularly important as it allows schools to take immediate action while still preserving a student's right to challenge the decision.

6.2.3.5 Increased Procedural Protections

The new rules dramatically increase the procedural protections for both sides. This is a significant change for the better, and it will be the subject of the next chapter.

6.2.4 *Education Program or Activity*

The new regulations limit the reach of Title IX enforcement. Recipients are only required to respond to sexual harassment that occurs within a recipient's education program or activity. In making this change, DOE turns to the text of Title IX: "No person in the United States shall, on the basis of sex, be excluded from participation in, be denied the benefits of, or be subjected to discrimination under any education *program or activity* receiving Federal financial assistance." The Department emphasizes the words "program or activity" to highlight the scope of its authority. "Title IX does not authorize the Department to regulate sex discrimination occurring *anywhere* but only to regulate sex discrimination in education programs or activities."[139]

The Department then explains what it means by education program or activity. "[E]ducation program or activity," DOE writes, 'includes locations, events, or circumstances over which the recipient exercised substantial control over both the respondent and the context in which the sexual harassment occurs' and also includes 'any building owned or controlled by a student organization that is officially recognized by a postsecondary institution.'"[140]

6.2.4.1 Limit: In the United States

One of the most controversial parts of the new rule is that it limits Title IX enforcement to harassment that occurs within the United States.[141] Limiting enforcement of Title IX to American shores, DOE argues, is consistent with the recent U.S. Supreme Court case of *Morrison v. National Australian Bank* (2010) which pointed to the "longstanding principle of American law that legislation of Congress, unless a contrary intent appears, is meant to apply only within the territorial jurisdiction of the United States."[142] The DOE acknowledges a 2002 Federal District Court case cited by some commentators that applied Title IX outside of the United States, but that case was from 2002, eight years before *Morrison v. National Australian Bank*.[143] It also refers to a 2007 case, which held Title IX did not apply outside of the United States.[144] "Based on the presumption against extraterritoriality reinforced by Supreme Court decisions and the plain language in the Title IX statute limiting protections to persons 'in the United States,'" DOE writes, "the Department believes that the Department does not have authority to declare that the presumption against exterritoriality has been overcome, absent further congressional or Supreme Court direction on this issue."[145]

However, DOE emphasizes that the inapplicability of Title IX doesn't mean schools have no ability to respond. It writes:

> We emphasize that nothing in these final regulations prevents recipients from initiating a student conduct proceeding or offering supportive measures to address sexual misconduct against a person outside the United States. We have revised Section 106.45(b)(3) to explicitly state that even if a recipient must dismiss a formal complaint for Title IX purposes because the alleged sexual harassment did not occur against a person in the U.S., such a dismissal is only for purposes of Title

IX, and nothing precludes the recipient from addressing the alleged misconduct through the recipient's own code of conduct.[146] Suggestion for Improvement Schools should explicitly prohibit sexual and other misconduct by faculty, staff, or students that occurs outside of the United States.

Suggestion for Improvement

Schools should explicitly prohibit sexual and other misconduct by faculty, staff, or students that occurs outside of the United States.

6.2.4.2 Limit: Off-Campus Parties

At first it was unclear whether education program or activity would cover off-campus harassment. In response to comments made during the notice and comment period, DOE provided this clarification:

> The revisions to Section 106.44(a) clarify that where a postsecondary institution has officially recognized a student organization, irrespective of whether the building is on campus or off campus, and irrespective of whether the recipient exercised substantial control the recipient's Title IX obligations apply to sexual harassment that occurs in buildings owned or controlled by such a student organization, irrespective of whether the recipient exercised substantial control over the respondent and the context of the harassment outside the fact of officially recognizing the fraternity or sorority that owns or controls the building.[147]

The Department's interpretation of the statute seems reasonable even though it means that some misconduct – for example, a rape that occurs at an off-campus party that is not associated with a recognized student organization – will not be covered by the new rules. It bears reemphasizing that nothing about these rules precludes a school from prohibiting conduct that does not fall under Title IX. The Department explains:

> Title IX is not the exclusive remedy for sexual misconduct or traumatic events that affect students. As to misconduct that falls outside the ambit of Title IX, nothing in the final regulations precludes recipients from vigorously addressing misconduct (sexual or otherwise) that occurs outside the scope of Title IX or from offering supportive measures to students and individuals impacted by misconduct or trauma even when Title IX and its implementing regulations do not require such actions. The Department emphasizes that sexual misconduct is unacceptable regardless of the circumstances in which it occurs, and recognizing jurisdictional limitations on the purview of a statute does not equate to condoning any form of sexual misconduct.[148]

Suggestion for Improvement

Schools should explicitly prohibit sexual and other misconduct by faculty, staff, or students that occurs off campus but is not covered under Title IX.

6.2.4.3 Online Sexual Harassment

Although the new rule covers online harassment, it does not do so prominently or explicitly. A recipient would have to hunt through some 2,000+ pages to learn that "the statutory and regulatory definitions of 'program or activity' encompass 'all of the operations of' such recipients, and such 'operations' may certainly include computer and internet networks, digital platforms, and computer hardware or software owned or operated by, or used in the operations of the recipient."[149]

Making matters worse, DOE overly restricts online harassment which falls within a recipient's program or activity. The recipient must have both substantial control over the respondent *and* the context in which it occurs, which may even exclude online harassment during class time:

> [T]he final regulations revise §106.44 (a) to specify that an education program or activity includes circumstances over which the recipient exercised substantial control over both the respondent and the context in which the harassment occurred, such that the factual circumstances of online harassment must be analyzed to determine if it occurred in an education program or activity. For example, a student using a personal device to perpetrate online sexual harassment during class time may constitute a circumstance over which the recipient exercises substantial control.[150]

"Sexual harassment in cyberspace"[151] is a serious enough problem that it should be prominently and clearly discussed in the new rule. "Online harassment," Mary Anne Franks explains, "has various and wide-ranging harms: targets have committed suicide, lost jobs, dropped out of school, withdrawn from social activities, and decreased their participation in employment, educational, and recreational (including online) activities."[152] Recipients and students should not have to read the fine print to figure out that online sexual harassment is verboten. The Department should broaden what harassment falls under Title IX to include online harassment perpetrated over email servers/wifi belonging to the recipient or to a recognized student organization, as well as online harassment perpetrated from buildings, vehicles, or other property owned or controlled by the recipient or a recognized student organization. Suggestion for Improvement, Schools should explicitly prohibit sexual and other misconduct by faculty, staff, or students that occurs off campus but is not covered under Title IX.

Suggestion for Improvement

The DOE should change the rule to explicitly state that online sexual harassment violates Title IX. It should say something along these lines:

> [A]n education program or activity includes circumstances over which the recipient exercised substantial control over the respondent or the context in which the harassment occurred. It also includes online harassment perpetrated over recipient-controlled email servers/wifi or email servers/wifi of a recognized student organization and online harassment perpetrated from any buildings, vehicles, or other property owned or controlled by the recipient or a recognized student organization.

6.3 CONCLUSION

Title IX changed dramatically under Secretary DeVos. For the first time, the DOE went through formal rulemaking in Title IX sexual harassment enforcement. Many of these changes were improvements, but others, like limiting notice and requiring actual instead of constructive knowledge, were not. The next chapter focuses on what may be the most controversial part of the new rules – changes to Title IX adjudication.

NOTES

1. Katherine Stewart, *Betsy DeVos and God's Plan for Schools*, N.Y. TIMES (Dec. 13, 2016), www.nytimes.com/2016/12/13/opinion/betsy-devos-and-gods-plan-for-schools.html.
2. Benjamin Wermund, *Trump's Education Pick Says Reform Can "Advance God's Kingdom,"* POLITICO (Dec. 2, 2016), www.politico.com/story/2016/12/betsy-devos-education-trump-religion-232150.
3. Stephen Henderson, *Betsy DeVos and the Twilight of Public Education*, DETROIT FREE PRESS (Dec. 13, 2016), www.freep.com/story/opinion/columnists/stephen-henderson/2016/12/03/betsy-devos-education-donald-trump/94728574/.
4. Benjamin Wermund & Kimberly Hefling, *Trump's Education Secretary Pick Supported Anti-Gay Causes*, POLITICO (Nov. 15, 2016), www.politico.com/story/2016/11/betsy-devos-education-secretary-civil-rights-gay-transgender-students-231837.
5. Nick Anderson, *Under DeVos, Education Department Likely to Make Significant Shift on Sexual Assault*, WASHINGTON POST (Jan. 18, 2017), www.washingtonpost.com/news/grade-point/wp/2017/01/18/under-devos-education-department-likely-to-make-significant-shift-on-sexual-assault/.

6. *Id.*

7. *Id.*

8. Leigh Ann Caldwell, *Betsy DeVos Vote: Pence's History-Making Tie Breaker Confirms Controversial Education Secretary*, NBC NEWS (Feb. 7, 2017), www.nbcnews.com/politics/congress/mike-pence-casts-tie-breaking-vote-confirm-betsy-devos-education-n717836.

9. Press Release, *U.S. Department of Education, U.S. Secretary of Education Announces Chief of Staff and Additional Staff Hires* (Apr. 12, 2017), www.ed.gov/news/press-releases/us-secretary-education-announces-chief-staff-and-additional-staff-hires/.

10. Andrew Kreighbaum & Elizabeth Redden, *Issues for Trump's OCR Nominee: Sexual Assault and . . . Israel*, INSIDE HIGHER ED. (Oct. 30, 2017), www.insidehighered.com/news/2017/10/30/many-groups-are-reserving-judgment-trumps-pick-head-office-civil-rights-exception.

11. Annie Waldman, *DeVos Pick to Head Civil Rights Office Once Said She Faced Discrimination for Being White*, PROPUBLICA (Apr. 14, 2017), www.propublica.org/article/devos-candice-jackson-civil-rights-office-education-department.

12. Erica L. Green, *Some Hires by Betsy DeVos Are a Stark Departure from Her Reputation*, N.Y. TIMES (Jun. 2, 2017), www.nytimes.com/2017/06/02/us/politics/betsy-devos-education-secretary-hiring-diversity.html.

13. Waldman, *supra* note 11.

14. Tyler Kingkade, *The Lawyer Who Helped Bill Clinton's Rape Accusers May Have Scored a Top Civil Rights Job Under Trump*, BUZZFEED NEWS (Apr. 3, 2017), www.buzzfeednews.com/article/tylerkingkade/the-lawyer-who-helped-clinton-rape-accusers-may-have-scored#.ej6ZKYBG8X.

15. Erica L. Green & Sheryl Gay Stolberg, *Campus Rape Policies Get a New Look as the Accused Get DeVos's Ear*, N.Y. TIMES (July 12, 2017), www.nytimes.com/2017/07/12/us/politics/campus-rape-betsy-devos-title-ix-education-trump-candice-jackson.html.

16. *Id.*

17. Cassia Spohn, Clair White, & Katharine Tellis, *Unfounding Sexual Assault: Examining the Decision to Unfound and Identifying False Reports*, 48 LAW & SOCIETY REV., 161 (2014).

18. *Id.* at 174.

19. Andrew Kreighbaum, *DeVos Hints at Changes in Title IX Enforcement*, INSIDE HIGHER ED. (Jul. 14, 2017), www.insidehighered.com/news/2017/07/14/after-full-day-meetings-title-ix-devos-says-improvements-needed.

20. Green & Gay Stolberg, *supra* note 15.

21. *Id.*

22. Kreighbaum, *supra* note 19.

23. *Id.*

24. Doug Lederman, *"A New Day at OCR,"* INSIDE HIGHER ED. (June 28, 2017), www.insidehighered.com/news/2017/06/28/trump-administration-civil-rights-officials-promise-colleges-fairer-regulatory.

25. Kreighbaum, *supra* note 19.

26. Christina Cauterucci, *Betsy DeVos Plans to Consult Men's Rights Trolls About Campus Sexual Assault,* SLATE (Jul. 11, 2017), https://slate.com/human-interest/2017/07/betsy-devos-is-asking-mens-rights-trolls-to-advise-her-on-campus-sexual-assault.html.

27. Kreighbaum, *supra* note 19.

28. Susan *Svrluga, Transcript: Betsy DeVos's Remarks on Campus Sexual Assault,* WASHINGTON POST (Sept. 7, 2017), www.washingtonpost.com/news/grade-point/wp/2017/09/07/transcript-betsy-devoss-remarks-on-campus-sexual-assault/.

29. Press Release, Candice Jackson, U.S. Department of Education, Office for Civil Rights (Sept. 22, 2017), www2.ed.gov/about/offices/list/ocr/letters/colleague-title-ix-201709.pdf.

30. *Id.* at 2.

31. *See* R. SHEP MELNICK, THE TRANSFORMATION OF TITLE IX: REGULATING GENDER EQUALITY IN EDUCATION 192 (Brookings University Press, 2018). For an extended discussion, *see* note 58 in Chapter 2.

32. Press Release, U.S. Department of Education, *Department of Education Issues New Interim Guidance on Campus Sexual Misconduct* (Sept. 22, 2017), https://content.govdelivery.com/accounts/USED/bulletins/1b8b87c.

33. *Id.* at 5.

34. *Id.* at 4.

35. *Id.* at 4.

36. Comp. for Injunctive Relief at 26, SurvJustice, Inc., et al. v. Devos, 2018 WL 4770741 (Jan. 25, 2018), https://youthlaw.org/wp-content/uploads/2018/01/1-main.pdf.

37. Third Amended Comp. for Injunctive Relief, SurvJustice, Inc., et al. v. Devos, No. 3:18-cv-00535-JSC (Apr. 18, 2019), https://youthlaw.org/wp-content/uploads/2018/01/123-Third-Amended-Complaint.pdf.

38. *Id.* at 33–34.

39. Order Re: Def. ['s] Mot. to Dismiss, SurvJustice, Inc., et al. v. Devos, No. 3:18-cv-00535-JSC (Oct. 1, 2018), www.courtlistener.com/recap/gov.uscourts.cand.321800/gov.uscourts.cand.321800.81.0.pdf.

40. Order Re: Def. ['s] Mot. to Dismiss the Second Am. Comp., SurvJustice, Inc., et al. v. Devos, No. 3:18-cv-00535-JSC (Mar. 29, 2019), https://casetext.com/case/survjustice-inc-v-devos.

41. Valerie Strauss, *Divided Senate Confirms Controversial Figure to Head Education Department's Office for Civil Rights,* WASHINGTON POST

(Jun. 7, 2018), www.washingtonpost.com/news/answer-sheet/wp/2018/
06/07/divided-senate-confirms-controversial-figure-to-head-education-
departments-office-for-civil-rights/.

42. The Leadership Conference on Civil and Human Rights, Letter
    opposing confirmation of Kenneth Marcus for Assistant Secretary for
    Civil Rights (Jan. 11, 2018), http://civilrightsdocs.info/pdf/policy/letters/2
    018/SignOnLetterMarcusConfirmation011018.pdf.

43. Press Release, U.S. Department of Education, *Secretary DeVos:
    Proposed Title IX Rule Provides Clarity for Schools, Support for
    Survivors, and Due Process Rights for All* (Nov. 16, 2018), www.ed.gov/n
    ews/press-releases/secretary-devos-proposed-title-ix-rule-provides-clarity-
    schools-support-survivors-and-due-process-rights-all.

44. Nondiscrimination on the Basis of Sex in Education Programs or
    Activities Receiving Federal Financial Assistance, 83 Fed. Reg. 61462
    (proposed Nov. 29, 2018) (to be codified at 34 C.F.R. 106), www.govinfo
    .gov/content/pkg/FR-2018-11-29/pdf/2018-25314.pdf.

45. *Id.* at 61463.

46. Press Release, Nancy Pelosi, Speaker, House of Representatives, *Pelosi
    Statement on Trump-DeVos Draft Proposal to Roll Back Title IX* (Nov. 17,
    2018), www.speaker.gov/newsroom/111618-2.

47. *Id.*

48. But that was extended by two days to make up for lost time due to
    technical problems that temporarily shut down the federal rulemaking
    portal; Tyler Coward, *Comment Period for Department of Education's
    Proposed Title IX Rules Extended Two Days Due To Website Issues*, FIRE
    (Jan. 18, 2019), www.thefire.org/comment-period-for-department-of-
    educations-proposed-title-ix-rules-extended-two-days-due-to-website-
    issues/.

49. Tovia Smith, *Trump Administration Gets an Earful on New Campus
    Sexual Assault Rules*, NPR (Jan. 30, 2019), www.npr.org/2019/01/30/689
    879689/education-department-gathers-feedback-on-new-campus-sexual-
    assault-rules.

50. *End Rape on Campus & Know Your IX Announce Campaign to Rally
    Opposition to New Title IX Rule*, END RAPE ON CAMPUS (Dec. 6, 2018),
    https://endrapeoncampus.org/new-blog/2018/12/6/end-rape-on-campus-
    amp-know-your-ix-announce-campaign-to-rally-opposition-to-new-title-
    ix-rule.

51. *Hands Off IX Notice and Comment Toolkit*, https://actionnetwork.org/
    user_files/user_files/000/028/108/original/Hands_Off_IX_Notice_and_
    Comment_Toolkit.pdf.

52. Nondiscrimination on the Basis of Sex in Education Programs or
    Activities Receiving Federal Financial Assistance at 61468, *supra* note
    44, www.federalregister.gov/documents/2018/11/29/2018-25314/nondiscrimi

nation-on-the-basis-of-sex-in-education-programs-or-activities-receiving-federal#h-24.

53. Smith, *supra* note 49.
54. Nondiscrimination on the Basis of Sex in Education Programs or Activities Receiving Federal Financial Assistance, 85 Fed. Reg. 30026 (May 19, 2020) (codified at 24 C.F.R., pt. 106)., www.govinfo.gov/con tent/pkg/FR-2020-05-19/pdf/2020-10512.pdf
55. R. Shep Melnick, *Analyzing the Department of Education's Final Title IX Rules on Sexual Misconduct*, BROOKINGS (Jun. 11, 2020), www .brookings.edu/research/analyzing-the-department-of-educations-final-title-ix-rules-on-sexual-misconduct/.
56. *Education Dept. Issues New Title IX Regs with Crucial Campus Due Process Protections, Adopts Supreme Court Sexual Harassment Definition*, FIRE (May 6, 2020), www.thefire.org/breaking-education-dept-issues-new-title-ix-regs-with-crucial-campus-due-process-protections-adopts-supreme-court-sexual-harassment-definition/.
57. Greta Anderson, U.S. *Publishes New Regulations on Campus Sexual Assault*, INSIDE HIGHER ED. (May 7, 2020), www.insidehighered.com /news/2020/05/07/education-department-releases-final-title-ix-regula tions#:~:text=It%20took%20nearly%20a%20year,were%20published%20 in%20November%202018.
58. *Id.*
59. Bianca Quilantan, *Biden Vows "Quick End" to Devos' Sexual Misconduct Rule*, POLITICO (May 6, 2020), www.politico.com/news/2020/05/06/ biden-vows-a-quick-end-to-devos-sexual-misconduct-rule-241715.
60. Laura Meckler, *Betsy Devos Announces New Rules on Campus Sexual Assault Offering More Rights to the Accused*, WASHINGTON POST (May 6, 2020), www.washingtonpost.com/local/education/betsy-devos-announces-new-rules-on-campus-sexual-assault-offering-more-rights-to-the-accused/2020/05/06/4d950c7c-8fa0-11ea-a9c0-73b93422d691 _story.html.
61. Quilantan, *supra* note 59.
62. Greta Anderson, *Legal Challenges on Many Fronts*, INSIDE HIGHER ED (July 13, 2020), www.insidehighered.com/news/2020/07/13/understand ing-lawsuits-against-new-title-ix-regulations.
63. Bianca Quilantan, *Judge Tosses Lawsuit Challenging Devos' Sexual Misconduct Rule For Schools, Colleges*, POLITICO (Oct. 20, 2020, 9:07 PM EDT), www.politico.com/news/2020/10/20/betsy-devos-title-ix-lawsuit-430579.
64. *Id.*
65. The Women's Student Union v. U.S. Department of Education, U.S. District Court, Northern District of California, Case 3.21-cv-01626, file 3/8/ at 23.

66. University of Michigan Law School, Civil Rights Litigation Clearinghouse, www.clearinghouse.net/detail.php?id=18144&search= source%7Cgeneral%3BcaseCat%7CED%3Borderby%7CfilingYear%3B.

67. Victim Rights Law Ctr. v. Cardona, 2021 U.S. Dist. LEXIS 140982 (D. Mass. July 28, 2021).

68. *Id.* at 64.

69. Davis v. Monroe County Board of Education, 526 U.S. 629, 651 (1999).

70. *Id.* at 650.

71. U.S. Department of Education, Office for Civil Rights, *Revised Sexual Harassment Guidance: Harassment of Students by School Employees, Other Students, or Third Parties*, at ii (2001) (internal citations omitted).

72. *Id.* at 30033.

73. 34 C.F.R. § 106.30(a)(1) (2020).

74. 34 C.F.R. § 106.30(a)(2) (2020).

75. 34 C.F.R. § 106.30(a)(3) (2020).

76. *Sexual Harassment Guidance: Harassment of Students by School Employees, Other Students, or Third Parties*, 62 FED. REG. 12034, 12039 (Mar. 13, 1997), www.govinfo.gov/content/pkg/FR-1997-03-13/pdf/97-6373.pdf.

77. *Id.*

78. Nondiscrimination on the Basis of Sex in Education Programs, 85 Fed. Reg. at 30159.

79. Nondiscrimination on the Basis of Sex in Education Programs, 85 Fed. Reg. at 30036.

80. U.S. Department of Education, Office for Civil Rights, *supra* note 71, at 6 (citing 1997 Guidance Document) (internal citations omitted).

81. 20 U.S.C. § 1681 at 30159–30160.

82. U.S. Department of Education, Office for Civil Rights, *supra* note 71, at 22.

83. U.S. Department of Education, Office for Civil Rights, *First Amendment: Dear Colleague* (2003).

84. Nondiscrimination on the Basis of Sex in Education Programs, 85 Fed. Reg. at 30164. *See* footnote 747 and accompanying sources.

85. Azhar Majeed, *FIRE Issues Statement in Response to OCR "Dear Colleague" Letter on Universities' Obligations Regarding Sexual Harassment and Sexual Assault*, FIRE (April 4, 2011), www.thefire.org/fire-issues-statement-in-response-to-ocr-dear-colleague-letter-on-universities-obligations-regarding-sexual-harassment-and-sexual-assault/.

86. Risa L. Lieberwitz, et al., *The History, Uses, and Abuses of Title IX*, AMERICAN ASSOCIATION OF UNIVERSITY PROFESSORS 69, 70 (Jun. 2016), www.aaup.org/file/TitleIXreport.pdf.

87. *Id.* at 77.

88. Scott Jaschik, *Too Risky for Boulder?*, INSIDE HIGHER ED. (Dec. 16, 2013), www.insidehighered.com/news/2013/12/16/tenured-professor-boulder-says-she-being-forced-out-over-lecture-prostitution.

89. Matt Ferner, Patti Adler, *CU-Boulder Professor,* Will Continue to Teach *"Deviance" Class After Lecture Controversy*, THE HUFFINGTON POST (Jan. 10, 2014), www.huffpost.com/entry/patti-adler-cuboulder-pro_n_4575930.

90. *Id.*

91. Jeannie Suk Gersen, *The Trouble with Teaching Rape Law*, THE NEW YORKER (Dec. 15, 2014), www.newyorker.com/news/news-desk/trouble-teaching-rape-law.

92. Nondiscrimination on the Basis of Sex in Education Programs, 85 Fed. Reg. at 30165.

93. *Id.*

94. *Id.*

95. Nondiscrimination on the Basis of Sex in Education Programs, 85 Fed. Reg. at 30159.

96. Letter from Russlyn Ali, Assistant Sec'y for Civil Rights, Office for Civil Rights, U.S. Dep't. of Educ., to Title IX Coordinators (Apr. 4, 2011) at 3.

97. U.S. Department of Education, Office for Civil Rights, *supra* note 71, at 5 (citing *Davis*, 526 U.S. at 651; citing both *Oncale*, 523 U.S. at 82 and OCR's 1997 Guidance).

98. Victim Rights Law Center, Equal Rights Advocates, Legal Voice and Chicago Alliance against Sexual Exploitation v Elizabeth D. Devos, Kenneth L. Marcus, and U.S. Department of Education, Complaint for Declaratory and Injunctive Relief, in the U.S. District Court for the District of Massachusetts, p. 39.

99. U.S. Department of Education, Office for Civil Rights, *supra* note 71, at 6 (citing 1997 Guidance) (internal citations omitted).

100. U.S. Department of Education, Office for Civil Rights, *supra* note 71, at 5 (citing *Davis*, 526 U.S. at 651, citing both *Oncale*, 523 U.S. at 82 and OCR's 1997 Guidance Document).

101. 34 C.F.R. § 106.30(a)(2) (2020).

102. Nondiscrimination on the Basis of Sex in Education Programs, 85 Fed. Reg. at 30170.

103. *Id.* at 30169–30170 (internal citations omitted).

104. 34 C.F.R. § 106.30(a).

105. Nondiscrimination on the Basis of Sex in Education Programs, 85 Fed. Reg. at 30040; U.S. Department of Education, Office for Civil Rights, *supra* note 71, at 13.

106. Nondiscrimination on the Basis of Sex in Education Programs, 85 Fed. Reg. at 30039.

107. *Id.* at 30039.

108. "Determining whether an individual is an 'official with authority' is a legal determination that depends on the specific facts relating to a recipient's administrative structure and the roles and duties held by officials in the recipient's own operations." 20 U.S.C. § 1681 at 30039.

109. *Id.*

110. Victim Rights Law Center, Equal Rights Advocates, Legal Voice, & Chicago Alliance Against Sexual Exploitation, Complaint for Declaratory and Injunctive Relief, District Court of Massachusetts, June 10, 2020 at 42–43.

111. Nondiscrimination on the Basis of Sex in Education Programs, 85 Fed. Reg. at 30040.

112. Tracy Connor and Sarah Fitzpatrick, *Gymnastics Scandal: 8 times Nassar Could Have Been Stopped*, NBC News (Jan. 2, 2018) (updated Jan. 28, 2018), www.nbcnews.com/news/us-news/gymnastics-scandal-8-times-larry-nassar-could-have-been-stopped-n841091.

113. 2001 Guidance Document at 13.

114. *Id.*; Office for Civil Rights; Sexual Harassment Guidance: Harassment of Students by School Employees, Other Students, or Third Parties, 62 Fed. Reg. at 12039–12040, 12042 (Mar. 13, 1997).

115. Gebser v. Lago Vista Independent. School District, 524 U.S. 274 (1998).

116. *Id.*

117. Davis, 526 U.S. at 300–301.

118. Nondiscrimination on the Basis of Sex in Education Programs, 85 Fed. Reg. at 30047.

119. *Id.* at 30192.

120. *Id.* at 30047.

121. Rost ex rel. K.C. v. Steamboat Springs RE-2-School District, 511 F.3d 1114 (10th Cir. 2008).

122. *Id.* at 1119.

123. 34 C.F.R. § 106.44.

124. *Id.*

125. 2001 Guidance Document at 15.

126. *Id.*

127. Nondiscrimination on the Basis of Sex in Education Programs, 85 Fed. Reg. at 30086.

128. *Id.* at 3088.

129. *Id.*

130. *Id.* at 30091–30092.

131. *Id.* at 30091.

132. Victim Rights Law Center, *supra* note 98 at 53.

133. U.S. Department of Education, Office for Civil Rights, *supra* note 71, at 15.

134. Nondiscrimination on the Basis of Sex in Education Programs, 85 Fed. Reg. at 30045.
135. *Id.* at 30042–30043.
136. *Id.* at 30193.
137. *Id.* at 30034.
138. 34 C.F.R. § 106.44(c).
139. Nondiscrimination on the Basis of Sex in Education Programs, 85 Fed. Reg. at 30196.
140. *Id.*
141. 34 C.F.R. § 106.44(a).
142. Nondiscrimination on the Basis of Sex in Education Programs, 85 Fed. Reg. at 30205. (citing Morrison v. National Australian Bank, 561 U.S. 247 (2010) (internal citations omitted).
143. King v. Board of Control of Eastern Michigan University, 221 F.Supp.2d 783 (E.D. Mich. 2002).
144. Phillips v. St. George's University, No. 07-CV-1555, 2007 WL 3407728, at *1 (E.D.N.Y. Nov. 15, 2007).
145. Nondiscrimination on the Basis of Sex in Education Programs, 85 Fed. Reg. at 30206.
146. *Id.*
147. *Id.* at 30197.
148. *Id.* at 30199.
149. *Id.* at 30202.
150. *Id.*
151. Mary Anne Franks, *Sexual Harassment* 2.0, 71 MD. L. REV. 655, 659 (2012).
152. Franks, *supra* note 151 at 658.

7

Due Process at Last!

The most controversial part of the new Title IX regulations is the increase in due process for accused students. At a news briefing the day the rule was released, Betsy DeVos claimed that these changes would not interfere with the Department's responsibility to victims. "Today we release a final rule that recognizes we can continue to combat sexual misconduct without abandoning our core values of fairness, presumption of innocence and due process."[1] Some, like the Foundation for Individual Rights in Education (FIRE) applauded the change. "Advocates for free speech and due process on campus won one of their biggest-ever victories today with the finalization of long-awaited Department of Education Title IX regulations," FIRE wrote. "The regulations guarantee critical due process protections that Americans recognize as essential to securing justice, but that have for too long been denied to students accused of sexual misconduct on college campuses."[2]

Others claimed the new procedures would harm women. The advocacy group Know Your IX released a statement the day the new rule went into effect: "This rule with (sic) deter survivors from reporting, allow schools to sweep sexual violence under the rug with impunity, and stacks (sic) the deck against survivors who try and seek support from their school following violence."[3] National Organization for Women President Toni Van Pelt made a similar claim: "The new Trump/DeVos rule," she said, "is unfair, discriminatory, and places all students in danger. It not only makes it harder for survivors to achieve proper justice, it favors the side of the accused, further silencing and traumatizing the victim."[4]

This chapter looks carefully at the procedures required by the new regulations. It explains how they differ from those under the 2011 Dear Colleague Letter, and it considers whether they adequately protect both sides. In considering the fairness of the new procedures, it compares them to the consensus recommendations of the 2017 American Bar Association Criminal Justice

Section Task Force on Campus Due Process and Victim Protection. Along the way, it offers suggestions for how schools can implement the new regulations in a way that is compliant but better protects the rights of victims and the accused.

Because the Task Force is being used as a benchmark for comparison, the chapter will begin there.

7.1 2017 ABA CRIMINAL JUSTICE SECTION TASK FORCE ON CAMPUS DUE PROCESS AND VICTIM PROTECTION

In November 2016, the Executive Committee of the American Bar Association (ABA) Criminal Justice Section (CJS) commissioned a task force to develop best practices for ensuring due process for victims and the accused.[5] Andrew S. Boutros, a former Assistant US Attorney in the Chicago Office and partner at Seyfarth Shaw LLP, was selected to chair the task force, and I agreed to be the reporter. We invited a diverse set of stakeholders to become members, and the Task Force was fully constituted in the winter of 2017. Two voting members were originally liaisons from the ABA Section of Civil Rights and Social Justice (CRSJ) and the ABA Commission on Domestic and Sexual Violence. They were elevated in recognition of their significant contributions to the Task Force.

The legitimacy of the Task Force's work depends on the degree to which we actually included the perspectives of victim/survivors and the accused, so it's worth introducing the members. This inclusiveness is especially important for those readers who would otherwise dismiss the new Rule simply because it was put out by Secretary DeVos and the Trump Administration.

The Task Force had members who advocated for victim/survivors. Carrie Bettinger-Lopez, my colleague at the University of Miami, is a human rights professor who served as White House Advisor on Violence Against Women and Senior Advisor to Vice President Joe Biden. Laura Dunn, Founder and then Executive Director of SurvJustice, is a nationally recognized victim rights attorney.[6] Robin Rachel Runge, Professorial Lecturer in Law at George Washington University, is a longtime consultant and activist on violence against women and gender equality. Brenda V. Smith, Professor at American University Washington College of Law, is the Director of the Project on Addressing Prison Rape.

We also had members who fought for the accused: Robert M. Cary, a partner at Williams & Connolly, represented one of the defendants in the infamous *Duke Lacrosse* case. Cynthia P. Garrett, Co-President of Families Advocating for Campus Equality (FACE), met extensively with legislators in trying to change Title IX disciplinary procedures. Marcos Hasbun, a partner at

Zukerman Spaeder LLP, represented students accused of sexual misconduct in campus proceedings. I am a former deputy public defender who has advised both accused students and complainants in Title IX hearings and appeals.

We also had members with significant administrative experience applying Title IX: Pamela J. Bernard is Vice President & General Counsel at Duke University. Janet P. Judge, President Sport Law Associates LLC and co-author of the NCAA Manual on Gender Equity, advised over 400 colleges, universities, and conferences in connection with Title IX compliance. Bridget M. Maricich, Counsel, Seyfarth Shaw LLP, served as E.O. Officer for Policy and Legal Compliance and Deputy Title IX Coordinator at the University of Virginia. Lauren Schoenthaler is Senior Associate Vice Provost for Institutional Equity and Access at Stanford University.

Finally, we had two recognized experts in sexual assault who served as liaisons: the world-renowned Mary P. Koss, Regents' Professor and Elise Lopez, Assistant Director, Relationship Violence Program, both at the Mel and Edit Zuckerman College of Public Health, University of Arizona. Koss has conducted some of the most influential research on the incidence, causes, and best way to respond to, campus sexual assault. Her 1987 study is discussed in Chapter 1.

The Task Force met for the first time on March 4, 2017. In preparation for our meeting, we read several articles that were recommended by Task Force members. To make our discussion as efficient as possible, we had a due process check list that we worked through systematically, and we drafted language in real time on a large screen. After that first meeting, we collaborated via email. We met again on March 25, where we finished drafting most of our recommendations. We then continued to jointly edit our recommendations via email, and we had a lengthy conference call on April 1 in which we hammered out lingering areas of disagreement including the standard of proof. We carried on with our work via email before presenting our recommendations in early May to the CRSJ, which unanimously approved them.

How were we able to reach consensus on such detailed recommendations so quickly? Certainly, there was uneasiness in the beginning. As Laura Dunn put it, "Walking in, I was very wary. There was apprehension on all sides that it would be challenging and hard and frustrating and possibly resulting in zero agreement at all."[7] It helped that we had tacos and margaritas together the night before our first meeting and then spent eight hours crammed into one conference room. The presence of Carrie's son, Casey, at the second meeting also made a difference. It's easier to get along when you have an adorable baby to hold.

The Task Force was also extremely motivated. We believed the new administration would likely release new guidance on Title IX adjudication, and we wanted to have the chance to impact national policy. Our goal was always to finish our recommendations by the ABA Criminal Justice Section Task Force meeting in March. We each prioritized the work of the Task Force. We adjusted personal and professional schedules to attend meetings and participate in conference calls. Emails were responded to almost immediately instead of sitting in inboxes for days or even weeks.

Transparency also helped build trust. We drafted language on a large screen as we went. I wrote up a working draft of the recommendations, which I sent to all members. I used screen shots to compile all of their comments and criticisms into one document, made suggested fixes via track changes, and recirculated the document. No change was made without full approval from the group.

Most importantly, we genuinely respected one another, and we quickly realized that *everyone* wanted the proceedings to be fair. Members who were "pro victim" understood that not all complainants were telling the truth, and those who were "pro accused" recognized that not all respondents were innocent. Many of us had first-hand experience with biased hearings, and so we agreed that both sides benefitted from transparency and robust procedural protections. We also knew that consensus recommendations would be more credible, but the only way to get there was to yield. As Cynthia Garrett articulated, "Nobody gets everything they want. I understood I had to compromise just like every other person in the room did."

7.1.1 *Politics at the ABA*

We had hoped to receive the endorsement of the CRSJ and the ABA Commission on Domestic and Sexual Violence, but this proved impossible. The explanation we got from the CRSJ was disheartening. They criticized the Task Force because it "was put together very quickly and met few times on an extremely tight timelines (sic) and without any Title IX experts or input from other ABA entities with expertise in the area."[8] They also voiced "substantial concern that the current membership of the Task Force is comprised in large measure of members of the defense bar, with insufficient representation from those involved in representing victims".[9] In making these criticisms, CRSJ devalued the intense time commitment Task Force members had made, and misrepresented who was on the committee. They also ignored the fact that we had elevated liaisons from CRSJ and the Commission on Domestic and Sexual Violence to be full voting members of our Task Force.

We attempted in good faith to make some modifications that might allow CRSJ to support our proposal, but they never responded. Ultimately, we decided to move forward with just the support of the Criminal Justice Section. After many more emails and another conference call we reached consensus on our final report and recommendations. Both were published on June 17, 2017.

7.1.2 *Influence of Our Work*

The Task Force *Recommendations* have been enormously influential. Secretary DeVos cited our work in a September 2017 address.[10] "The American Bar Association established a task force comprised of lawyers and advocates from diverse backgrounds and varying perspectives," DeVos said. "They found consensus and offered substantive ideas on how we can do better. Schools should find their recommendations useful."[11] The Department of Education (DOE) then explicitly acknowledged that they had reviewed our work in coming up with the proposed regulations.[12]

In 2018, California Governor Jerry Brown created a working group to make recommendations for how best to address allegations of student sexual misconduct on college and university campuses. The group was comprised of three members: UC Berkeley Political Science Professor Wendy Brown, retired California Supreme Court Justice Carlos R. Moreno, and Lara Stemple, Assistant Dean, UCLA School of Law. On November 14, 2018, the California Working Group adopted many of the Task Force's *Recommendations* (either wholly or in part) and cited to the Task Force's work twenty-two times.[13]

In the preamble to the final Title IX rule, the DOE compared the final regulations to the recommendations of the California Working Group, which it noted had relied on the work of the ABA Task Force. "That working group released a memorandum detailing those recommendations," the Department wrote, "and many of those recommendations are consistent with the approach taken in these final regulations."[14]

I will now turn to the grievance procedures put in place by the new regulations.

7.2 THE NEW GRIEVANCE PROCEDURES

The new rules lay out robust procedural protections with which all federal funding recipients must comply. I will discuss many of these procedures and point out where they are consistent with the consensus recommendations of the ABA Task Force and/or the Governor Brown Working Group. I will also provide my own suggestions for how the regulations can be improved.

Unless otherwise noted, these suggestions can be implemented by schools because they do not change existing law. Indeed, they are explicitly contemplated by the new regulations which allow schools to have "provisions, rules or practices other than those required" as long as they "apply equally to both parties."[5] Other suggestions, as discussed in Chapter 3, can only be implemented if the regulation is changed by the DOE through formal or informal rulemaking. Recipients can always lobby DOE to make those changes.

7.2.1 *Treat Parties Equitably*

The new regulations require that schools provide remedies to a complainant where a determination of responsibility has been made and follow a grievance procedure that meets certain requirements before disciplinary sanctions can be imposed on a respondent.[16] This is an appropriate and obvious rule, and it is consistent with recommendations of the ABA Task Force and the Governor Brown Working Group.

7.2.2 *Objective Evaluation of the Evidence*

The new regulations require that all relevant evidence, both inculpatory and exculpatory, be objectively evaluated.[17] They also require that credibility determinations not be based on a person's status as a complainant, respondent, or witness. This is also a no-brainer, and it is consistent with the recommendations of the ABA Task Force.

7.2.3 *Decision-makers Must Be Trained and Impartial*

The new regulations require that any person designated as the Title IX Coordinator, Investigator, decision-maker, or facilitator of an informal resolution be impartial and well trained. They accomplish this goal in multiple ways. To begin with, they explicitly state that these persons "not have a conflict of interest or bias for or against complainants or respondents generally or an individual complainant or respondent."[18] It should be a given that those who implement a Title IX policy be impartial. It is a basic requirement for a fair adjudicatory system, and it is consistent with both the ABA recommendations and those of the Governor Brown Working Group.

Second, they require that these persons "receive training on the definition of sexual harassment in Section 106.30, the scope of the recipient's education program or activity, how to conduct an investigation and grievance process including hearings, appeals, and informal resolution processes, as applicable, and how to serve impartially, including by avoiding prejudgment of the facts at issue, conflicts of interest and bias."[19] Regardless of whether you agree with the definition of harassment or the scope of the recipient's education program or activity under the new regulations, understanding the rules is a necessary step for following them and applying them consistently.

They also require schools to:

> receive training on any technology to be used at a live hearing and on issues of relevance of questions and evidence, including when questions and evidence about the complainant's sexual predisposition or prior sexual behavior are not relevant . . . A recipient must also ensure that investigators receive training on issues of relevance to create an investigative report that fairly summarizes relevant evidence . . .[20]

Again, understanding how to implement the rules is a necessary step for a fair procedure.

The new regulations also mandate that training materials be fair. "Any materials used to train Title IX Coordinators, investigators, decision-makers and any person who facilitates an informal resolution process, must not rely on sex stereotypes and must promote impartial investigations and adjudications of formal complaints of sexual harassment."[21] The Governor Brown Working Group discusses the dangers of "trauma-informed" training.[22] They acknowledge that it's important to train investigators "so they can avoid re-traumatizing complainants during the investigation." However, they acknowledge the dangers of a trauma-informed approach in evaluating testimony. "The use of trauma-informed approaches to evaluating evidence can lead adjudicators to overlook significant inconsistencies on the part of complainants in a manner that is incompatible with due process protections for the respondent." For that reason, they recommend "investigators and adjudicators should consider and balance noteworthy inconsistencies (rather than ignoring them altogether) and must use approaches to trauma and memory that are well grounded in current scientific findings."

A former Title IX Investigator/current Title IX Coordinator whom I spoke with explained the mistake that many trauma-informed Investigators make:

> If you are asking why they don't remember this, you're not going to question them or use it against them, but you are not going to fill in the blanks with information on your own to reach a result that's not there. You can still provide a safe and empowering environment and be understanding, but a trauma informed approach is not filling in the blank that this information

would have been there but for the trauma. I think that's where a lot of people get confused.

7.2.3.1 Suggestion for Improvement

I agree with the new regulations and the Governor Brown Working Group. Both investigators and adjudicators must be trained in how to ask questions in a way that doesn't cause harm, but at the same time, they need to be willing and able to identify deficiencies in a person's account. Doing so is complicated by preconceptions about how "true" victims behave. For example, many believe that a real victim would resist her assailant, but in fact some "freeze with fright" or disassociate from what is happening.[23] Another expectation is that a true victim would report quickly, but studies show that most do not report. The revised 2020 AAU Campus Climate Survey on Sexual Assault and Misconduct study of thirty-three schools, for instance, found that just 15 percent of victims reported to the police or some other program.[24]

Just as criminal courts allow evidence that corrects false stereotypes about victims, so should schools. Such evidence doesn't mean that investigators and factfinders should disregard conduct that calls into question the complainant's claims. It just allows them to better assess the significance of such evidence, so they don't simply jump to the conclusion that the complainant must be lying. Should the school decide to educate factfinders in this way, that process should take place during the hearing itself, so the respondent has the chance to ask questions or present contradictory research.

7.2.4 *Burden Is on the School and Not the Parties*

The new regulations make it clear that it is the school's responsibility to "gather evidence sufficient to reach a determination regarding responsibility."[25] In the commentary, the Department explains that "such a presumption reinforces that the burden of proof remains on recipients (not on the respondent, or the complainant) and reinforces correct application of the standard of evidence."[26]

The school is the recipient of Title IX funding, and it is the school's responsibility to respond promptly and effectively to allegations of sexual misconduct that fall under the law. Consequently, it should be the school's burden to prove that misconduct has occurred. This should be a non-controversial change to the law, and I don't know of any major victim's right group that's challenging it.

7.2.5 *Presumption of Nonresponsibility*

One of the more contentious parts of the new regulations is that the respondent is presumed to be not responsible until a determination is made at the end of the grievance process.[27] On January 30, 2019, Josh Shapiro, the Attorney General of Pennsylvania; Xavier Becerra, the Attorney General of California; and Gurbir S. Grewal, Attorney General of New Jersey sent a comment on the proposed new rule to Secretary DeVos. Among other concerns, they wrote: "[T]he presumption contradicts the regulation's stated goal of promoting impartiality by inherently favoring the respondent's denial over the complainant's allegation."[28] The advocacy group Know Your IX made a similar critique saying that the presumption "means schools must start by disbelieving survivors . . ."[29]

But this argument is misleading. The presumption of innocence instructs the factfinder as to what mental state they must have at the start of the hearing. It tells them that unless and until the school presents evidence that convinces them otherwise, they must find the accused student not responsible. It codifies the irrefutable fact that just because a person stands accused of an offense doesn't mean he committed it. As the Honorable Judge J. Harvie Wilkinson III of the Fourth Circuit Court of Appeals put it in a recent article, "Explicit recognition of a presumption of civil innocence will help to temper the subliminal sense to which, unfortunately, we are all sometimes prone that the truth lies in the accusation."[30]

Importantly, a presumption of innocence is not the same as saying that the complainant is probably lying. Nor is it saying that the defendant is probably telling the truth. Even in criminal cases, this is not how the presumption works. The jury instruction from California is instructive. It tells jurors that they must presume the defendant innocent until the State proves him guilty. It states: "The fact that a criminal charge has been filed against the defendant is not evidence that the charge is true. You must not be biased against the defendant just because he has been arrested, charged with a crime, or brought to trial." In determining whether the State has met its burden, jurors are explicitly told to weigh the evidence in an impartial fashion. They are *never* told to assume that one side is telling the truth and the other is not. "In deciding whether the People have proved their case beyond a reasonable doubt," the instruction reads, "you must impartially compare and consider all the evidence that was presented throughout the entire trial."[31]

If that seems too theoretical, then consider this. The school has the burden of proof in Title IX hearings, but they can meet that burden in different ways. They could call the complainant to testify, but they could rely instead on eyewitness testimony or security footage. The new regulations allow schools to go forward against the wishes of the complainant and even when the complainant testifies on behalf of the accused! This should make it clear that the presumption of innocence is not a comment on whether the complainant is telling the truth; it is instead a statement about the school's burden to prove the accused student is responsible based only on the evidence presented, without relying on the fact that he has been accused. Indeed, although the ABA Task Force did not discuss a presumption of innocence, it did explicitly recommend that, "[i]f there is insufficient credible, reliable, and relevant evidence for the decision-maker(s) to find that a violation occurred then the student must be found not responsible."[32]

7.2.6 *Preponderance or Clear and Convincing Evidence*

The 2011 Dear Colleague Letter mandated that the standard of proof be set at preponderance of the evidence, but the new rule allows schools to use clear and convincing evidence.[33] However, it requires schools to use the same standard for complaints against students as complaints against employees, and it requires schools to use the same standard of evidence for all formal complaints of sexual harassment.[34] Many have publicly spoken against the clear and convincing standard. Some of these criticisms have been misleading. For example, an article on College Media Network stated that raising the standard of proof would place "the burden on the victim to *prove* the guilt of the accused."[35] Such a statement is false because whatever the standard of proof, the burden to prove responsibility remains on the school.

Many criticisms, however, have been on the merits of the change. In a letter filed on the rulemaking portal during the notice and comment period, the ACLU notes that preponderance is the standard used in civil litigation involving discrimination under Title IX, Title VII (which prohibits employment discrimination), and Title VI (which prohibits racial discrimination in federally funded programs).[36] "[W]e are aware of no other circumstance," the ACLU writes, "in which discrimination claims are subjected to a 'clear and convincing standard.'"[37] The ACLU also contends that preponderance treats the complainant and respondent equitably whereas "(a) 'clear and convincing' standard tips the scale against the complainant."[38] Although the ACLU concedes that "[s]erious disciplinary sanctions will undoubtedly affect a respondent's access to education," it points out that "a school's failure to address sexual harassment or assault will affect that complainant's access to education."[39]

As discussed in Chapter 5, to evaluate the proper standard of proof, it is necessary to remember the purpose it plays. In *Addington v. Texas* (1979), the Court said that the function of the standard of proof is to "instruct the factfinder concerning the degree of confidence our society thinks he should have in the correctness of factual conclusions for a particular type of adjudication."[40] Setting a high or low standard is a way "to allocate the risk of error between the litigants and to indicate the relative importance attached to the ultimate decision."[41]

At one end of the spectrum lies the archetypal civil case involving a pecuniary dispute between private parties. "Since society has a minimal concern with the outcome of such private suits, plaintiff's burden of proof is a mere preponderance of the evidence. The litigants thus share the risk of error in roughly equal fashion."[42] This is to be contrasted with criminal cases in which "the interests of the defendant are of such magnitude that historically and without any explicit constitutional requirement they have been protected by standards of proof designed to exclude as nearly as possible the likelihood of an erroneous judgment."[43]

In the middle are cases that use the intermediate standard of clear and convincing evidence. This standard is typically used in civil cases involving "quasi-criminal wrongdoing" like fraud.[44] The rationale for this intermediate standard is that the interests at stake are "more substantial than mere loss of money."[45] The Court noted that it also used this higher standard in certain civil proceedings as a way of "protect[ing] particularly important individual interests."[46]

The question then is whether it is appropriate for schools to use the intermediate standard of proof in Title IX proceedings. In answering this, it bears emphasizing that the question isn't whether sexual assault is bad; it clearly is. Our job is to compare the consequences on access to education of a false positive (an innocent student being found responsible) with a false negative (a "guilty" student being found not responsible).

The impact of an innocent student being found responsible for a rape he didn't commit is serious. He can get expelled, which will make it difficult to transfer to a new school, enroll in higher education, or get a good job. He may be labeled a rapist, which can alienate him from friends, family, and prospective employers. Although a school can't sentence a student to prison time, the consequences are still devastating.

As long as the victim/survivor is not harassed during the hearing, the impact of a false negative is likely to be less pernicious. The new regulations explicitly allow schools to continue offering supportive measures, even after a finding of nonresponsibility.[47] That means victims can still be provided access to nonpunitive remedial measures like counseling or accommodations regarding classes and housing. Contrary to the ACLU's assertion, there is no reason that a victim/survivor can't maintain their access to education should a respondent be found not responsible.

7.2.6.1 Suggestion for Improvement

Given the difference in harm that the parties suffer from a mistake, schools should make the burden clear and convincing evidence. Indeed, they should use this higher standard in *all* proceedings where students face the possibility of expulsion, even if they aren't facing the stigma of being found responsible for a sex crime. If schools do use this higher standard, they should clearly instruct the factfinder, ideally in writing before deliberations begin, what it means. It is a demanding standard, but it is not daunting. The CJS Task Force recommended such a higher standard of proof but only when schools did not afford certain procedural protections, like a live hearing. This is that instruction:

> The decision-maker should first evaluate the quality of the evidence. The decision-maker should consider all of the evidence regardless of who provided it. Any evidence the decision-maker finds to be of high quality should be given more weight than any evidence the decision-maker finds to be of low quality. Quality may, or may not be identical with quantity, and sheer quantity alone should not be the basis for a finding of responsibility. The testimony of a single party or witness may be sufficient to establish a fact.
>
> After assessing the quality of the evidence, the decision-maker should only find the respondent responsible for alleged misconduct if the evidence firmly convinces the decision-maker to reasonably conclude that a finding of responsibility is justified. That is, the decision-maker should find that there is sufficient evidence that is relevant, probable, and persuasive to firmly convince him or her that the respondent engaged in the alleged misconduct, and that the evidence supporting a finding of responsibility significantly outweighs any evidence that the respondent is not responsible for the alleged misconduct.[48]

Should a school opt to keep the lower preponderance standard – which the new regulations allow – they should only do so under an adjudicatory model with at least a three-person panel of decision-makers, a unanimity requirement, and other robust procedural protections. In addition, they should provide a written instruction, which clearly articulates what preponderance of the evidence means. The CJS Task Force agreed that a lower standard of proof was appropriate as long as specified procedures (including unanimity) were in place. Moreover, we were careful to define the standard in a way that emphasized its rational basis, so that a mere feather would not be enough to tip the scales. Here is that instruction, with the first paragraph omitted because it is identical to the one above:

> After assessing the quality of the evidence, the decision-makers should only find the respondent responsible for alleged misconduct if the evidence unanimously convinces them to reasonably conclude that a finding of responsibility is justified. That is, the decision-makers should find that there is sufficient evidence that is relevant, probable, and persuasive to convince them that the respondent engaged in the alleged misconduct, and that the evidence supporting a finding of responsibility outweighs any evidence that the respondent is not responsible for the alleged misconduct.[49]

7.2.7 *Legally Protected Privileges*

The new regulations require schools to respect legally protected privileges unless waived by the person who has them. "Not require, allow, rely upon, or otherwise use questions or evidence that constitute, or seek disclosure of, information protected under a legally recognized privilege, unless the person holding such privilege has waived the privilege."[50] This rule means that a school can't use a person's medical or psychological records unless they have waived the privilege. Indeed, the rules later explicitly state just that:

> the recipient cannot access, consider, disclose, or otherwise use a party's records that are made or maintained by a physician, psychiatrist, psychologist or other recognized professional or paraprofessional acting in the professional's or paraprofessional's capacity, or assisting in that capacity, and which are made and maintained in connection with the provision of treatment of the party unless the recipient obtains that party's voluntary, written consent to do so for a grievance process under this section . . .[51] This rule clearly protects both complainants and the accused, and it should be seen as noncontroversial.

7.2.8 *Written Notice*

The new regulations require all recipients, upon receipt of a formal complaint, to provide written notice to the complainant and the respondent, informing the parties of the recipient's grievance process and providing sufficient details of the sexual harassment allegations being investigated "includ (ing) the identities "of the parties involved in the incident, if known, the conduct allegedly constituting sexual harassment . . . and the date and location of the alleged incident, if known".[52] This is a welcome change from the old guidance, which did not require adequate notice. It is also consistent with the Task Force Recommendations.[53]

7.2.9 *Dismissal*

The new regulations require schools to dismiss allegations if they would not constitute sexual harassment.[54] Importantly, although schools must dismiss the allegations for Title IX purposes, they are still allowed to pursue them under their own codes of conduct. The regulations are explicit as to that point, stating: "[S]uch a dismissal does not preclude action under another provision of the recipient's code of conduct."[55]

7.2.10 *Witnesses*

Under the new regulations, schools must "provide an equal opportunity for the parties to present witnesses, including fact and expert witnesses, and other inculpatory and exculpatory evidence."[56] This is a very important change because there have been multiple cases in which schools did not allow respondents to defend themselves. It also helps to protect complainants in cases where a school has a vested interest in not finding a particular respondent responsible, such as if they are a prominent athlete.

7.2.11 *No Gag Rule*

Under the old regime, schools often prohibited students from discussing the case. So called gag rules made it difficult for people to defend themselves because they would have a difficult time gathering evidence. The new rues explicitly bar schools from restricting "the ability of either party to discuss the allegations under investigation or to gather and present relevant evidence."[57]

7.2.11.1 Suggestion for Improvement

The right to discuss allegations should not include the right to harass the other party, and schools should explicitly prohibit such harassment. One of the students I interviewed described how after he was found not responsible, his accuser went to his fraternity and various sororities on campus and told everyone that he was a rapist. He described the way it made him feel:

> I literally walked around campus thinking everyone thought I was a rapist. This is coming from me who's a very social, extroverted person. I usually like to smile or say hi, but after that I didn't want to see anyone, and I didn't want to be seen.

7.2.12 *Advisor of Their Choice*

The former guidelines did not give students the right to an advisor of their choice, and schools often barred attorneys from the proceedings. The new rules allow students to have an advisor of their choice, including an attorney, however schools are allowed to limit the degree to which the advisor may participate in the proceedings as long as the restrictions are the same for both sides.[58]

The ABA Task Force's recommendation on this point was in line with the new rules. Indeed, the ABA Task Force noted that the Violence Against Women Authorization Act of 2013 explicitly gives both parties in sexual assault cases the right to an advisor of their choice.[59] Both recommended that the advisor at a minimum "should have the right to communicate with the party in oral or written form during all meetings and proceedings."[60]

When a university is deciding whether to allow more robust representation, it should consider – as I did in Chapter 5 – why the right to counsel is enshrined in the Sixth Amendment of the U.S. Constitution. In *Argersinger v. Hamlin* (1972), the Supreme Court wrote: "The assistance of counsel is often a requisite to the very existence of a fair trial."[61] This is because of the "obvious truth that the average defendant does not have the professional legal skill to protect himself when brought before a tribunal with power to take his life or liberty ..."[62] Of course, university grievance procedures are not as complicated as jury trials, but the stakes are still high.

I have mixed feelings about allowing robust participation by lawyers. I worry that they may obfuscate and make it harder for the panel to learn the truth. Indeed, I agree with the concerns articulated by one of the Title IX coordinators I interviewed who supported direct questioning between the parties but did not think it should be conducted by lawyers. She worried about whether a proceeding could be fair if one party had a lawyer, and the other did not. She also pointed out that without trained judges or the rules of evidence, lawyer-conducted cross was especially likely to complicate and confuse.

> I think the new rules requiring that there can be cross examination conducted by an attorney are very detrimental. Attorneys try to take over the process [and] it becomes a lot more trying on the parties without adding much value. It takes away from student involvement, and it creates unfairness ... Now if a party doesn't have an advisor/attorney, how are you going to compete? You need training and practice; you can't just have a regular advisor do it. The fact that we are now in a position where we have to provide an advisor who is going to conduct cross ... we had a person who was a great advisor, but they don't have the training to stand against the cross of a trained litigator ...,

I think direct questioning should be part of every process, but the manner and form of cross and having it done by attorneys – that's something I would take away. It makes the process less fair When you are conducting a cross, you are dictating the narrative, you are taking it away from students and putting it in the hands of an attorney. Judges, good and bad as they are, have gone through ample training. They have a good understanding of cross examination, and they can see through attorney tricks, but a decisionmaker in [a Title IX hearing] doesn't have that level of training, and I don't think it's realistic to have it. [Cross by lawyers] takes away from truth, the theatrics of lawyering, especially when you don't have a judge who will call them out and the rules of evidence don't apply, cross really clouds the story and manipulates the narrative.

At the same time, I am concerned about students who may not be able to adequately represent themselves. One of the students I spoke with felt comfortable with a silent advisor, but he acknowledged that not everyone would feel the same way:

I think it's important they see how I am and that they see me telling my story. But then again, some people are afraid to talk publicly, are bad at speaking, and they might look worse if they had severe anxiety. They might look worse and less credible because it is a high-pressure situation.

Another student described how difficult but also worthwhile it was to have a silent advisor:

In terms of having to be an advocate for myself, I'm much better at sticking up for my friends, but I'm not very good at doing that for myself, and so I found this process incredibly difficult. I wish that I had had, I wish someone would have done it for me. Because I don't do that for my own self. But in the alternative, it taught me how to start sticking up for myself, and how to ask questions when I needed answers, it was also helpful in the sense of the hearing in a couple of levels. I had my own guilt about the incident, because in some ways this furthered the guilt, because I was attacking this man, I had to tell people what he did to me, and it furthered my own guilt about the consequences, but at the same time, the more I talked about it, the angrier I got, so it alleviated the guilt. Being an advocate for my own self, and not having an advocate who was aggressive, was difficult but necessary … As much as I hated being an advocate for myself, I liked that better than my advisor doing everything.

7.2.13 *Inspection of Evidence*

The prior guidance did not give either party the right to review evidence at any point in the adjudicatory process, but most especially not before the investigation report was finalized. This made it difficult for the complainant to ensure that the school was fully pursuing their case, and it made it hard for the accused to represent himself at the hearing. The new regulations give both parties

> an equal opportunity to inspect and review any evidence obtained as part of the investigation that is directly related to the allegations raised in a formal complaint, including the evidence upon which the recipient does not intend to rely in reaching a determination regarding responsibility and inculpatory or exculpatory evidence whether obtained from a party or other source so that each party can meaningfully respond to the evidence prior to the conclusion of the investigation.[63]

This evidence must be provided to the parties before the investigation report has been completed. They are then given "at least 10 days to submit a written response which the investigator will consider prior to completion of the investigative report."[64] This is important because it gives both parties the opportunity to meaningfully respond to the evidence. The school then must make "all such evidence subject to the parties' inspection and review available at any hearing to give each party equal opportunity to refer to such evidence during the hearing, including for purposes of cross examination . . . "[65] That means that the parties are allowed to refer to the evidence in presenting their side or questioning the other.

7.2.14 *Investigation Report*

The recipients are required to create an investigation report that "fairly summarizes relevant evidence" and provide it to the parties at least ten days before the hearing for their review and written response.[66] Since the investigation is a summary of the relevant evidence as seen by the recipient, this gives both parties the chance to read and respond. If, for instance, one party thinks the school has left out relevant inculpatory or exculpatory evidence, they can formally request that it be added and/or be prepared to present that evidence themselves. This prevents unfair surprises at the hearing.

Requiring schools to create a written investigation report is a significant change. Prior Guidance mandated that schools conduct an "[a]dequate, reliable, and impartial investigation of complainants, including the opportunity to present witnesses and other evidence,"[67] but there was no requirement that it be written. Nor were there any specifics about what an "adequate, reliable, and impartial" investigation entailed. The new regulations spell out what a school must do, and the requirements are substantially similar to those recommended by the ABA Task Force.[68]

7.2.15 *Live Hearings*

One of the most significant changes is that the new regulations require post-secondary schools to have a live hearing. This is a tremendous improvement from the old guidance which did not require live hearings, and which permitted the single investigatory method where the same person listens to the evidence and comes to a decision. Live hearings allow the fairest shake of the evidence, and they were endorsed by the ABA Task Force, which wrote: "In considering the differences between the adjudicatory and investigatory model, the Task Force has a preference for the adjudicatory model because it can offset any potential for investigator bias, and it allows the decision-maker(s) to hear live testimony from the parties."[69]

7.2.15.1 Suggestions for Improvement

There are several ways in which schools can improve upon this part of the new regulations.

RELEVANT EVIDENCE. The parties should explicitly be allowed to introduce relevant evidence at the hearing, which includes calling witnesses. The right to present evidence is implied by the right to cross-examine, but it should be spelled out. Furthermore, relevant evidence should be defined, so a decision-maker has some basis for deciding about the admissibility of certain evidence. The ABA Task Force provided a good definition, which I've combined with the Rule's statement regarding a complainant's prior sexual history to provide a model instruction:

> Evidence is relevant if (1) it bears on a fact of consequence in the case, or (2) it reflects on the credibility of a testifying party or witness in a material way. Evidence may be excluded if it is unfairly prejudicial or if it is needlessly duplicative.[70] Questions about a complainant's sexual history are only allowed where they would provide evidence that someone else had committed the offense or to show consent.[71]

SPECIAL REQUIREMENTS FOR ADMISSIBILITY OF COMPLAINANT'S SEXUAL HISTORY. Evidence of a complainant's sexual history is sometimes essential for a fair hearing. For example, if a respondent claims the sex was consensual, evidence that the two had an ongoing sexual relationship is critical. Because of the sensitivity of this evidence, however, schools should create a special protocol for its admissibility that is modeled on Federal Rule of Evidence

Section 412. First, the respondent should have to provide notice that he is intending to admit this evidence. Notice can be met by his statement to the Title IX Investigator. Second, if the complainant objects, there should be a hearing that takes place in advance of the formal adjudicatory hearing where a hearing chairperson (but preferably not a decision-maker) determines whether the evidence should be admitted. At that pre-hearing, both parties should have the chance to speak.

PANEL SIZE AND DIVERSITY. Schools should have a panel of at least three people, who are ideally diverse across gender, race, and sexual orientation. I discussed the problem of implicit bias and how to combat it at length in Chapter 5, and I explained that having a larger and more diverse hearing body has been shown to increase the quality of deliberation and reduce bias. One study looked at the effects of having a racially homogeneous versus a heterogeneous jury.[72] It found that on every relevant measure, racially heterogeneous groups outperformed homogeneous ones. Not only did racially mixed groups spend more time deliberating, but they discussed a wider range of case facts and personal perspectives. They also made fewer factual errors than all-white juries.[73] This recommendation is consistent with that of the ABA Task Force.[74]

7.2.16 *Cross-Examination*

Perhaps the most controversial part of the new regulations is that they require schools to allow cross-examination. In an essay in *Time Magazine*, Nicole Bedera, a doctoral student in sociology; Seth Galanter, Senior Director of Legal Advocacy at the National Center for Youth Law; and Sage Carson, manager of Know Your IX, strongly condemned this change to the law, writing: "Live cross-examination is known to be traumatic to survivors of sexual violence."[75] At the hearing, each party's advisor must be given the chance to ask the other party and any witnesses "all relevant questions and follow-up questions, including those challenging credibility. Such cross-examination at the live hearing must be conducted directly, orally, and in real time by the party's advisor of choice and never by a party personally . . ."[76] As explained in Chapter 5, the fact that questioning is direct, oral, and in real time makes it more difficult to lie.

Although cross-examination can no doubt be upsetting, the new regulations take significant measures to reduce stress and eliminate harassment. First, they do not allow the parties to directly question one another. If a party does not have their own advisor, the recipient will provide the party with an advisor of the recipients' choice.

The new regulations also permit the parties to be in separate rooms with technology allowing them to still "simultaneously see and hear the party or the witness answering questions."[77] Although this separation is no doubt intended to reduce stress on the parties, a complainant I spoke with did not like it. Her hearing took place over Zoom, and the only people who could be seen at all times were the adjudicator and the person presenting evidence. That meant when she told her side of the story, the respondent's camera was turned off. And vice versa. She said it made her uncomfortable not knowing what the respondent was doing while she spoke, and she felt it deprived the adjudicators of important evidence for proving that she was telling the truth:

> I didn't like the way our cameras had to be off. I thought that was bizarre. I can see their reasoning behind doing it. Maybe they thought it would make me more comfortable telling my story. He was probably having visible reactions by me telling the story and I think if I had seen those, maybe it would have made me upset. But I think it would have been more helpful to see him, because I'm not very good at advocating for myself, but if I'm angry I'm better. If I had been able to see him, it might have made it more powerful on my end. But I don't know, it just felt awkward, talking about this person, knowing he's listening to you, but I can't see him. It felt awkward and uncomfortable and distant. I'm not sure how to put it into words. I just didn't like it. It might have been harder, but I would have rather seen his face. I would have rather seen the face of the man who had done these things to me. Especially because we were over Zoom, it makes things impersonal. It's hard to get across what you want to say when you don't have any body language. And I don't think that he should have had the luxury of having his camera off while I was speaking. I had the luxury of having it off, but then the administrator couldn't see that I was crying, and those were cues that were important. I didn't think he deserved the luxury of having the camera off while I was telling the trauma of what had happened.

Another change that should be seen as noncontroversial is that the new regulations limit the content of the questions to "relevant cross examination and other questions." Just as in court, decision-makers are tasked with ensuring that questions are relevant. "Before a complainant, respondent, or witness answers a cross-examination or other question, the decision-makers(s) must first determine whether the question is relevant and explain any decision to exclude a question as not relevant."[78] Questions about a complainant's sexual history are only allowed where it would provide evidence that someone else had committed the offense or to show consent. That means that parties may not simply try and shame a complainant for her sexual history or mode of dress. "Questions and evidence about the complainant's sexual predisposition or prior sexual behavior are not relevant, unless such questions and evidence about the complainant's prior sexual behavior are offered to prove that someone other than the respondent committed the conduct alleged by the complainant, or if the questions and evidence concern specific incidents of the complainant's prior sexual behavior with respect to the respondent and are offered to prove consent."[79]

Recipients must also keep an audio or audiovisual recording or transcript of any live hearing and make it available for the parties to review.[80] This is critical for parties who are considering appealing.

7.2.16.1 Suggestion for Improvement

Schools should explicitly prohibit harassment during the hearing including during cross-examination. Schools should have a hearing chairperson who will function like a judge. She will decide whether questions are relevant and will prohibit questions that are irrelevant, duplicative, or that stray into areas of the complainant's sexual history that have been determined to be off-limits at the hearing on evidence admissibility described earlier in the chapter.

It should be noted that the ABA Task Force recommended against direct questioning but said that the parties "should be given an ongoing opportunity during the proceeding to offer questions to be asked through the decision-maker(s), who will determine whether to ask them."[81]

I also agree with the complainant that unless schools have a very good reason for turning off the cameras that they should remain on for all parties during the hearing. The purpose of live hearings is to better assess witness and party credibility, and turning off the cameras undermines that purpose.

7.2.17 *Elementary and Secondary Schools*

Importantly, the new rules put in place different requirements for elementary and secondary schools.[82] They are not required to have live hearings; however, they still must provide the investigative report to the parties before reaching a determination of responsibility and allow the parties to respond. They must also give parties the chance to submit written, relevant questions, and to ask follow-up questions. As with postsecondary institutions, questions about the complainant's prior sexual history are limited. If a decision-maker decides not to ask a question, however, they must explain why.

7.2.18 *Limited Admissibility of Witness and Party Statements*

The new regulations do not require parties to submit to questions, but if they don't, their prior statements cannot be considered:

> If a party or witness does not submit to cross-examination at the live hearing, the decision-maker(s) must not rely on any statement of that party or witness in reaching a determination regarding responsibility; provided, however that the decision-maker(s) cannot draw an inference about the determination regarding responsibility based solely on a party's or witness's absence from the live hearing or refusal to answer cross examination or other questions.[83]

This rule change is consistent with the recommendations of the ABA Task Force,[84] and it is loosely modeled on the constitutional rights afforded to criminal defendants and the restriction on the admissibility of a party's own statements under the Federal Rules of Evidence. Specifically, allowing the accused student to remain silent and not holding that silence against him is consistent with the Fifth Amendment right against self-incrimination. Likewise, the ban on admitting statements when the declarant refuses to submit to questioning is based on a criminal defendant's Sixth Amendment right to confront and cross-examine their accuser.[85] Finally, the bar on a party introducing his own self-serving statements is consistent with 801(d)(2)(b) of the Federal Rules of Evidence, which prohibits a party from introducing his own statement as an admission.

In *Victim Rights Law Center v. Cardona* (2021), the United States District Court for the District Court of Massachusetts identified several serious problems with this section of the new regulations.[86] It allows a respondent to "further a disruptive agenda" by scheduling the hearing "at an inopportune time for third-party witnesses ... or even ... persuad[ing] other witnesses not to attend the hearing."[87] It keeps out relevant evidence: "no police reports, no medical history, no admissions by the respondent, no statements by anyone who witnessed the incident and either could not attend or was dissuaded from attending by the respondent."[88] It gives the respondent the power to suppress any inculpatory statements he had made to the police or anyone else by simply declining to show up at the hearing.[89] For these reasons, the Court held that "in the absence of evidence that the Department adequately considered section 106.45(b)(6)(i)'s prohibition on statements not subject to cross-examination, this Court finds and rules said prohibition arbitrary and capricious."[90] It then remanded the section to the DOE for further consideration and explanation.[91] In accordance with the Court's order, on August 24, 2021, the DOE issued a bulletin stating that they would immediately cease enforcement of this part of the section.[92]

7.2.18.1 Suggestion for Improvement

The Massachusetts District Court is right; this section does need to change. First, just as in a criminal court, the ban on out-of-hearing statements by nontestifying witnesses should be limited to self-serving statements by the respondent and testimonial statements by the complainant or other witnesses. That means a school should be able to introduce *any* statement by the respondent, but the respondent shouldn't be able to introduce his own statement unless he agrees to be questioned. Such a rule is fair because the respondent can always choose to testify and explain his response.

Furthermore, consistent with the Sixth Amendment, the school shouldn't be able to introduce testimonial statements unless the declarant agrees to be cross-examined. Testimonial statements, as the Supreme Court explained in *Crawford v. Washington* (2004), are "statements that were made under circumstances which would lead an objective witness reasonably to believe that the statement would be available for use at a later trial."[93] This includes, "material such as affidavits, custodial examinations, prior testimony that the [respondent] was unable to cross-examine, or similar pretrial statements that declarants would reasonably expect to be used prosecutorially."[94]

Let there be no misunderstanding: Limiting the ban to testimonial statements means that *most* out-of-hearing statements could still be admitted. Text messages, emails to friends and family members, diary entries, and medical records would all be fair game. Introducing an out-of-hearing statement like the complainant's interview with the Title IX Investigator, however, would require the complainant to submit to questioning unless the respondent waived his right.

Lastly, if there is any evidence that either party dissuaded a witness from testifying or scheduled the hearing to prevent a witness from testifying, that witness' statement should be admitted regardless of whether they testify. Similarly, if there is any evidence that either party tried to prevent the other from testifying, that party's statement should be admitted. Full stop.

Because such a limit would change existing law, a school would not be able to implement it on their own. The Office for Civil Rights would have to make this change via formal rulemaking or through the informal, notice and comment process; OCR should prioritize making this change.

7.2.19 *The Decision-maker Cannot Be the Title IX Coordinator or Investigator*

One of the important changes made by the new rules is that they prohibit the Title IX Coordinator or Investigator from being the decision-maker in the case.[95] This is a huge improvement because it means that a school cannot use the single Investigator model, and it helps to offset the problem of confirmation bias, which was described at length in Chapter 5. It is also consistent with the recommendations of the ABA Task Force: "It was the consensus of the Task Force that the single investigator model, which consists of having an investigator also serve as the decision-maker, carries inherent structural fairness risks especially as it relates to cases in which suspension or expulsion is a possibility."[96]

7.2.20 *A Written Determination*

The new regulations require that schools issue a written determination that explains the allegations, the procedural steps taken, the findings of fact, a rationale for each result, the disciplinary sanctions, and the permissible bases for appeal. All of it must be provided to the parties simultaneously.[97] Although this is a more onerous burden for schools, it also makes it more likely that they will take the process seriously. The written record makes it easier to handle an appeal. And it also gives the process more legitimacy.

7.2.21 *Appeal*

For the first time, parties are given an automatic right to appeal for the following grounds: procedural irregularity, new evidence that was not reasonably available that could affect the outcome, conflict of interest, or bias.[98] Recipients may also broaden the right to appeal, as long as it is available to both parties equally.[99] For all appeals, the schools must notify both parties in writing, if and when an appeal is filed; ensure that the person hearing the appeal is not the same as the decision-maker; give both parties the chance to submit a written statement; issue a written decision describing the result; and provide it simultaneously to both parties.[100] The stakes are high for both sides in these proceedings, and so it's important to have a procedure in place in case there are any problems.

7.2.22 *Informal Resolution*

The new rule allows schools to informally resolve allegations of sexual misconduct. However, both parties must consent, and any party may withdraw prior to agreeing to a resolution.[101]

7.2.22.1 Suggestion for Improvement

Schools should follow the ABA Task Force in limiting options for alternative adjudication. "Where appropriate, the Task Force encourages schools to consider non mediation alternatives to resolving complaints that are research or evidence-based, such as Restorative Justice [RJ] processes."[102]

As Tom Tyler explains: "Restorative Justice argues that the social goal that should dominate reactions to transgressions is to resolve the dispute via reintegrative shaming [which] ... combines strong disapproval of bad conduct with respect for the person who committed those bad acts. The goal is restoring victims, offenders and the community."[103] Unlike mediation, which "provides neutrality and treats parties as equal partners in the resolution process," the starting point for RJ is that "harm has been done and someone is responsible for repairing it."[104]

Although RJ is geared toward reintegrating the transgressing student back into the community, it is also dedicated to helping the victim heal and move forward. "A consensus of published studies is that sexual assault victims need to tell their own stories about their own experiences, obtain answers to questions, experience validation as a legitimate victim, observe offender remorse for harming them, [and] receive support that counteracts isolation and self-blame."[105] Restorative Justice responds to these needs. In conferencing (the most widely used model of RJ), the first meeting begins with the responsible person (otherwise known as the respondent or the accused) describing and taking responsibility for what he did and the victim describing the impact of the violation.[106] Family and friends of both are present for support and are given the opportunity to explain the impact of the harm.[107] A written redress plan is later formalized that describes "the concrete means through which the responsible person will be held accountable and remedy the impacts on victims and the community."[108] This can include counseling (sex offender treatment, drug and alcohol interventions, and anger management); community service; and victim restitution.[109] A one-year supervision period is put in place to monitor the responsible person and make sure that he meets his commitments.[110]

Restorative Justice has been shown to be effective at lowering recidivism and empowering victims in both academic and nonacademic settings. A 2014 study by David Karp and Casey Sacks compared outcomes across three different college disciplinary processes: model code (a term used for the more traditional hearing conducted by a single hearing officer or panel),[111] restorative justice, and a combination of the two.[112] Karp and Casey used data from the STARR project, which has a total of 659 complete cases,[113] gathered from eighteen colleges and universities across the United States.[114] Although they cautioned that their results may be limited by the fact that they had few suspension-level cases, their findings showed that RJ provided a positive alternative to more traditional disciplinary proceedings. They "consistently found that restorative justice practices have a greater impact on student learning than model code hearings."[115]

Furthermore, RJ has been successfully adopted for juvenile sex offenses and adult sex crimes. RESTORE is one such program that uses conferencing.[116] Mary Koss evaluated RESTORE using a sample of sixty-six cases involving sex crimes. Although caution is necessary due to the small sample size, the results are promising. Koss found that 63 percent of victims and 90 percent of responsible persons chose RJ; 80 percent of responsible persons completed all elements of their redress plan within one year (12 months), and postconference surveys showed that in excess of 90 percent of all participants, including the victims, agreed that they felt supported, listened to, treated fairly and with respect, "and believed that the conference was a success."[117] Importantly, there were no incidents involving physical threats, and standardized assessments showed decreases in victim posttraumatic stress disorder symptoms from intake to post conference.[118]

Prominent scholars like Koss[119] and Donna Coker[120] have called for universities to include RJ in addressing allegations of sexual assault. Koss has outlined how RJ can be used not solely as an alternative resolution process but also as a complement to a formal adjudicatory hearing.[121] For instance, it could be used to determine the appropriate sanction after a finding of responsibility has been made and/or as a reintegration process once the responsible student has finished his sanction. In whatever way RJ is used, Coker emphasizes that the responsible person's statements during RJ proceedings must be protected so that they cannot be used by the State in a future prosecution, otherwise RJ will just become a discovery-gathering opportunity for the State.[122]

7.2.23 *Recordkeeping*

Schools must maintain a record for seven years.[123] This rule change is important in case there is an appeal or legal challenge.

7.2.24 *Retaliation*

The regulations also make significant changes to the section on retaliation. They explicitly extend the right against retaliation to complainants, witnesses, participants, and respondents:

> No recipient or other person may intimidate, threaten, coerce, or discriminate against any individual for the purpose of interfering with any right or privilege

secured by title IX or this part, or because the individual has made a report or complaint, testified, assisted, or participated or refused to participate in any manner in an investigation, proceeding, or hearing under this part.[124]

Extending the umbrella of protection beyond complainants is important, as evidenced by the experience of one of the students I interviewed for this book who described being assaulted and called a rapist by a friend of the complainant's after he was found not responsible.

In order to prevent retaliation from occurring, the regulations require schools to keep confidential the names of any complainant, witness, or respondent except as permitted by law or statute.

The Department acknowledges that a school can file additional charges as retaliation.[125] They discuss research cited by commentators, which found that fear of disciplinary action for collateral misconduct deterred many victims of sexual assault in the military from reporting.[126] To address this kind of retaliation, the new regulations prohibit code of conduct violations that arise from the same facts or circumstances "for the purpose of interfering with any right or privilege secured by title IX or this part."[127] They provide the following example as guidance, "If a recipient always takes a zero tolerance approach to underage drinking in its code of conduct and always imposes the same punishment for underage drinking, irrespective of the circumstances, then imposing such a punishment would not be 'for the purpose of interfering with any right or privilege secured by' Title IX . . . and thus would not constitute retaliation."[128]

The new regulations create two "specific circumstances." The first involves resolving the potential conflict between retaliation and freedom of expression. "The exercise of rights protected under the First Amendment does not constitute retaliation prohibited under . . . this section."[129] In making this change, the Department acknowledges that "the First Amendment does not restrict the activities of private elementary and secondary schools or private postsecondary institutions . . . [however, the Department] is subject to the First Amendment and may not administer these regulations in a manner that violates or causes a recipient to violate the First Amendment."[130]

Clarifying that First Amendment protected expression doesn't constitute retaliation is important given high-profile cases like that of Northwestern Professor Laura Kipnis.[131] Kipnis was formally investigated for Title IX retaliation after she wrote an essay in *The Chronicle of Higher Education* in which she questioned the legitimacy of accusations against a professor who had been disciplined for sexual harassment.[132] One of the accusers filed a Title IX complaint against Kipnis alleging that her essay constituted retaliation, even though Kipnis had never called the student by name. Kipnis was allowed to bring a faculty support person to the meeting, and when that faculty member later voiced concerns to the Faculty Senate about how the investigation was undermining Kipnis' academic freedom, the same student filed a retaliation claim against him and another against Kipnis. Both complaints were dismissed after Kipnis published an essay on her treatment during the Title IX process.[133] Kipnis then wrote a book about the experience,[134] and the same student, along with four Northwestern faculty, accused Kipnis of retaliation. Once again, Northwestern found her not responsible.[135] Although Kipnis ultimately prevailed, the impact of these multiple investigations should not be underestimated. Indeed, it would be no surprise if faculty who shared Kipnis' views decided not to criticize Title IX proceedings out of fear that doing so could ruin their career.

The second "special circumstance" involves false accusations. The new regulations give schools the right to charge a person with making a false report, but importantly they state that a finding of nonresponsibility is not enough to prove a person made a false report.[136] Although research by Spohn et al., which was discussed in Chapter 6, indicates that the number of false reports is small, it is not an insignificant number. When they do occur, it is appropriate for schools to respond.

7.2.24.1 Suggestion for Improvement

Explicitly recognizing that protected expression can't constitute retaliation for Title IX purposes is important, however it may have unintended consequences. Students may feel emboldened to harass, and schools may be reluctant to respond. To protect against either, schools should remind community members that First Amendment rights are not absolute. Speech may constitute prohibited quid pro quo language, defamation, or libel. Schools are also allowed to institute content-neutral time, place, and manner restrictions. Finally, courts are often deferential to schools in terms of their ability to prohibit speech that interferes with the mission of the school.

7.3 CONCLUSION

The new regulations changed Title IX adjudication in innumerable ways, and mostly for the better. Although most think of procedural protections as only benefitting the accused, in fact they help complainants as well. The new rule allows the factfinder to make fairer and more accurate decisions because her decision is based on evidence instead of preconceptions or an incomplete view of the evidence.

NOTES

1. Teresa Watanabe, Students *Accused of Sexual Misconduct Get Stronger Protections Under New Federal Rules*, L.A. TIMES (May 6, 2020, 1:25 PM EST), www.latimes.com/california/story/2020-05-06/students-accused-of-sexual-misconduct-get-stronger-protections-under-new-federal-rules/.

2. Daniel Burnett, *Education Dept. Issues New Title IX Regs with Crucial Campus Due Process Protections, Adopts Supreme Court Sexual Harassment Definition*, FIRE (May 6, 2020), www.thefire.org/breaking-education-dept-issues-new-title-ix-regs-with-crucial-campus-due-process-protections-adopts-supreme-court-sexual-harassment-definition/.

3. Sage Carson, *Press Releases*, KNOW YOUR IX (Oct. 21, 2020), www.knowyourix.org/press-room/press-releases/.

4. Maia Brockbank et al., *NOW President Says New Trump/Devos Title IX Rule Endangers All Students*, NOW (July 20, 2020), http://now.org/issues/economic-justice/now-president-says-new-trump-devos-title-ix-rule-endangers-all-students/.

5. ABA, ABA *Forms Task Force to Study Due Process Rights in College Sexual Misconduct Cases*, ABA (Jan. 18, 2017), www.americanbar.org/news/aba news/aba-news-archives/2017/01/aba_;forms_;task_;force/.

6. Dunn was executive director of SurvJustice from October 2014 to March 2018. She left SurvJustice in March 2020, two months before the final rule was released. She is the founding partner of the L.L. Dunn Law Firm, PLLC, www.linkedin.com/in/lauraldunn/.

7. Tovia Smith, *Is There A "Better Way" To Handle Campus Sexual Assault?*, WBEZ CHICAGO (Sept. 19, 2017, 10:17 AM CT), www.wbez.org/stories/is-there-a-better-way-to-handle-campus-sexual-assault/3ed48178-9df6-49cc-a451-c216e28867bc/.

8. Email on file with author.

9. Email on file with author.

10. Susan Svrluga, *Transcript: Betsy DeVos's Remarks on Campus Sexual Assault*, WASHINGTON POST (Sept. 7, 2017, 2:08 PM EDT), www.washingtonpost.com/news/grade-point/wp/2017/09/07/transcript-betsy-devoss-remarks-on-campus-sexual-assault/.

11. Press Office, *Secretary DeVos Prepared Remarks on Title IX Enforcement*, U.S. DEP'T. OF EDUC. (Sept. 7, 2017), www.ed.gov/news/speeches/sec retary-devos-prepared-remarks-title-ix-enforcement/.

12. Dep't. of Educ., *Title IX of the Education Amendment*, U.S. DEP'T. OF EDUC., 10, www2.ed.gov/about/offices/list/ocr/docs/title-ix-nprm.pdf/.

13. Governor Edmund G. Brown, Jr.'s Working Group to Address Allegations of Student Sexual Misconduct on College and University Campuses in California, Recommendations of the Post-SB 169 Working Group (Nov. 14, 2018) [hereinafter "Recommendations of the Post-SB 169 Working Group"].

14. Nondiscrimination on the Basis of Sex in Education Programs or Activities Receiving Federal Financial Assistance, 85 Fed. Reg. 30026, 30050 (May 19, 2020) (codified at 24 C.F.R. pt. 106).
15. *Id.* at 30575.
16. 34 C.F.R. §106.45 (b).
17. 34 C.F.R. §106.45(b)(1)(ii).
18. 34 C.F.R. §106.45(b)(1)(iii).
19. *Id.*
20. *Id.*
21. *Id.*
22. Recommendations of the Post-SB 169 Working Group, *supra* note 13, at 3.
23. Carol E. Tracy et al., *Rape and Sexual Assault in the Legal System: Presented to the National Research Council of the National Academies Panel on Measuring Rape and Sexual Assault in the Bureau of Justice Statistics Household Surveys Committee on National Statistics*, June 5, 2012, at 8 (internal citations removed).
24. DAVID CANTOR ET AL., REPORT ON THE AAU CAMPUS CLIMATE SURVEY ON SEXUAL ASSAULT AND MISCONDUCT, ASSOC. OF AMERICAN UNIVERSITIES (Jan. 17, 2020), Table 44, www.aau.edu/sites/default/files/AAU-Files/Key-Issues/Campus-Safety/Revised%20Aggregate%20report%20%20and%20appendices%201–7_(01–16–2020_;FINAL).pdf/. Victims included those of harassing behavior, intimate partner violence, stalking, or sexual contact involving physical force, inability to consent or stop what was happening, coercion, or without voluntary agreement.
25. 34 C.F.R. §106.45 (b)(5)(i).
26. Nondiscrimination on the Basis of Sex in Education Programs, 85 Fed. Reg. at 30103.
27. 34 C.F.R. §106.45(b)(1)(iv).
28. Letter by Commonwealth of Pennsylvania Office of Attorney General Josh Shapiro, State of California Office of the Attorney General, Xavier Becerra, Attorney General and State of New Jersey Office of the Attorney General Gurbir S. Grewal, Attorney General Letter on behalf of the Commonwealths of Pennsylvania and Kentucky and the States of New Jersey, California, Delaware, Hawai'i, Illinois, Iowa, Maine, Maryland, Minnesota, Nevada, New Mexico, North Carolina, Oregon, Rhode Island, Vermont, Washington, and the District of Columbia (Jan. 30, 2019), at 35, www.nj.gov/oag/newsreleases19/Title-IX_;Comments.pdf.
29. *What to Know About the Title IX Rule*, KNOW YOUR TITLE IX, www.knowyourix.org/hands-off-ix/basics/.
30. J. Harvie Wilkinson, *The Presumption of Civil Innocence*, 104 VIRGINIA L. REV. 589, 596 (2018).

31. Judicial Council of California, *CALCRIM No. 220. Reasonable Doubt Judicial Council of California Criminal Jury Instructions (2020 edition)*, JUSTIA (Oct. 2020), www.justia.com/criminal/docs/calcrim/200/220/.

32. ABA Criminal Justice Section Task Force on College Due Process Rights and Victim Protections, *Recommendations for Colleges and Universities in Resolving Allegations of Campus Sexual Misconduct* (June 2017) at 7 [hereinafter "Recommendations of the ABA Task Force"]. https://www.americanbar.org/content/dam/aba/publications/criminaljustice/due_process_tf_recommendations.pdf

33. 34 C.F.R. § 106.45 (b)(1)(vii).

34. *Id.*

35. *Betsy DeVos Reinterprets Title IX: Victims Must Bear the Burden of Proof*, COLLEGE MEDIA NETWORK, www.collegemedianetwork.com/betsy-devos-reinterprets-title-ix-victims-must-bear-the-burden-of-proof/ (emphasis in original).

36. Brittany Bull, RE: *ACLU Comments in Response to Proposed Rule, "Nondiscrimination on the Basis of Sex in Education Programs or Activities Receiving Federal Financial Assistance,"* ACLU (Jan. 20, 2019), at 22, www.aclu.org/letter/aclu-comments-title-ix-proposed-rule/.

37. *Id.*

38. *Id.*

39. *Id.*

40. Addington v. Texas, 441 U.S. 418, 423 (1979) (citing In re Winship, 397 U.S. 358, 370 (1970)).

41. *Id.*

42. *Id.*

43. *Id.*

44. *Id.*

45. *Id.*

46. *Id.*

47. Nondiscrimination on the Basis of Sex in Education Programs, 85 Fed. Reg. at 30183.

48. Recommendations of the ABA Task Force, *supra* note 32 at 8.

49. Recommendations of the ABA Task Force, *supra* note 32 at 8.

50. 34 C.F.R. § 106.45 (b)(1)(x).

51. 34 C.F.R. §106.45(b)(5)(i).

52. 34 C.F.R. §106.45(b)(2)(i)(B).

53. Recommendations of the ABA Task Force, *supra* note 32 at 4.

54. 34 C.F.R. § 106.45 (3).

55. *Id.*

56. 34 C.F.R. §106.45(b)(5)(ii).

57. 34 C.F.R. §106.45(b)(5)(iii).

58. 34 C.F.R. §106.45(b)(5)(iv).

59. Federal Register, Vol. 79, No. 202, Part 668, Section 668.46, pg. 62789, (k)(1)(iv)(2)(iii).
60. Recommendations of the ABA Task Force, *supra* note 32 at 4.
61. Argersinger v. Hamlin, 407 U.S. 25, 31 (1972).
62. Johnston v. Zerbst, 304 U.S. 458, 462–463 (1938).
63. 34 C.F.R. §106.45(b)(5)(iv).
64. *Id.*
65. *Id.*
66. 34 C.F.R. §106.45(b)(5)(vii).
67. U.S. Department of Education, Office for Civil Rights, *Revised Sexual Harassment Guidance: Harassment of Students by School Employees, Other Students by School Employees, Other Students, or Third Parties,* January 2001 at 20, www.govinfo.gov/content/pkg/FR-2001-01-19/pdf/01-1606.pdf.
68. Recommendations of the ABA Task Force, *supra* note 32 at 4.
69. *Id.* at 3.
70. *Id.* at 6.
71. 34 C.F.R. §106.45(b)(6)(i).
72. Samuel R. Sommers, *On Racial Diversity and Group Decision Making: Identifying Multiple Effects of Racial Composition on Jury Deliberations,* 90 J. PERSONALITY & SOC. PSYCHOL. 597, 597 (2006).
73. A diverse hearing body has another benefit. Ultimately, whoever is deciding the case must assess the credibility of witnesses, which can be difficult when people come from different cultures. *See* Aldert Vrij, *Why Professionals Fail to Catch Liars and How They Can Improve,* 9 LEGAL & CRIMINOLOGICAL PSYCHOL. 159, 167 (2004).
74. Recommendations of the ABA Task Force, *supra* note 32 at 7.
75. Nicola Bedera et al., *A New Title IX Rule Essentially Allows Accused Sexual Assailants to Hide Evidence Against Them,* TIME (Aug. 14, 2020, 12:58 PM EDT), https://time.com/5879262/devos-title-ix-rule/.
76. 34 C.F.R. §106.45(b)(6)(i).
77. *Id.*
78. *Id.*
79. *Id.*
80. *Id.*
81. Recommendations of the ABA Task Force, *supra* note 32 at 7.
82. 34 C.F.R. §106.45(b)(6)(ii).
83. 34 C.F.R. §106.45(b)(6)(i).
84. Recommendations of the ABA Task Force, *supra* note 32 at 6.
85. The Sixth Amendment right only applies to testimonial statements if the declarant is unavailable and was subject to prior cross-examination.

86. Victim Rights Law Ctr. v. Cardona, 2021 U.S. Dist. LEXIS 140982 (D. Mass. July 28, 2021).

87. *Id.* at 49.

88. *Id.* at 50.

89. *Id.* at 51.

90. *Id.* at 52–53.

91. *Id.* at 64.

92. U.S. Department of Education, Bulleting: Update on Court Ruling about the Department of Education's Title IX Regulations, 8/24/2021, https://content.govdelivery.com/accounts/USED/bulletins/2ee0a5d.

93. Crawford v. Washington, 541 U.S. 36, 52 (2004).

94. Crawford v. Texas, 541 U.S. 36 (2004).

95. 34 C.F.R. §106.45(b)(7)(i).

96. Recommendations of the ABA Task Force, *supra* note 32 at 3.

97. 34 C.F.R. §106.45(b)(7)(ii)(iii).

98. 34 C.F.R. §106.45(b)(8)(i)(A)(B)(C).

99. 34 C.F.R. §106.45(b)(8)(C)(iii).

100. 34 C.F.R. §106.45(b)(8)(iii)

101. 34 C.F.R. §106.45(b)(9).

102. Recommendations of the ABA Task Force, *supra* note 32 at 3.

103. *See* Tom R. Tyler, *Restorative Justice and Procedural Justice: Dealing with Rule Breaking: Dealing with Rule Breaking*, 62 J. Soc. Just. 307, 315 (2006).

104. Mary P. Koss et al., *Campus Sexual Misconduct: Restorative Justice Approaches to Enhance Compliance with Title IX Guidance*, 15 Trauma, Violence, & Abuse 242, 246 (2014). Koss argues that this distinction is important: Judicial "responses to sexual misconduct must acknowledge and obviate the negative effects of societal and individual norms that operate to silence victims and create opportunities for re-abuse. When someone has been harmed by another person, mediation that provides neutrality and treats parties as equal partners in the resolution process is inappropriate."
Id. at 245–246. Koss also argues that because of this difference, colleges can adopt RJ and not be in violation of the DCL. *Id.* at 246.

105. Koss et al., *supra* note 104, at 246–247.

106. *Id.* at 248.

107. *Id.*

108. *Id.*

109. *Id.*

110. *Id.*

111. David R. Karp & Casey Sacks, *Student Conduct, Restorative Justice, and Student Development: Findings from the STARR Project: A Student Accountability and Restorative Research Project*, 17 Contemp. Just. Rev. 154, 156 (2014). "The model code calls for a hearing process that

is conducted by a single hearing officer or a volunteer board, often composed of students, faculty, and staff. While proponents of the model code highlight that the hearing is not a criminal trial, it has many of the similarities to the courtroom process." *Id.*

112. *See id.*
113. *Id.* at 162.
114. *Id.* at 160.
115. *Id.* at 169.
116. Koss et al., *supra* note 104, at 248.
117. *Id.* (internal citation omitted).
118. *Id.*
119. *See generally id.*
120. *See* Donna Coker, *Crime Logic, Campus Sexual Assault, and Restorative Justice*, 49 Texas Tech L. Rev. 147 (2016).
121. Koss et al., *supra* note 104, at 250, 252–253.
122. *See* Coker *supra* note 120, at 203–206.
123. 34 C.F.R. §106.45(b)(10).
124. 34 C.F.R. §106.71(a).
125. Nondiscrimination on the Basis of Sex in Education Programs, 85 Fed. Reg. at 30536.
126. *Id.*
127. *Id.*
128. *Id.*
129. 34 C.F.R. § 106.71 (b).
130. Nondiscrimination on the Basis of Sex in Education Programs, 85 Fed. Reg. at 30537.
131. Jeannie Suk Gersen, *Laura Kipnis's Endless Trial by Title IX*, The New Yorker (Sept. 20, 2017), www.newyorker.com/news/news-desk/laura-kipniss-endless-trial-by-title-ix/.
132. Laura Kipnis, *Sexual Paranoia Strikes Academe*, Chronicle of Higher Education (Feb. 27, 2015), www.chronicle.com/article/sexual-paranoia-strikes-academe/.
133. Laura Kipnis, *My Title IX Inquisition*, Chronicle of Higher Education (May 29, 2015), www.chronicle.com/article/my-title-ix-inquisition/.
134. Laura Kipnis, Unwanted Advances Sexual Paranoia Comes to Campus (Harper Collins, 2017).
135. Will Haskill & Graham Piro, *Northwestern Professor Charged with Title IX Harassment After Critiquing Title IX Policy*, The Free Speech Project (Aug, 15, 2019), https://freespeechproject.georgetown.edu/tracker-entries/northwestern-professor-charged-with-title-ix-harassment-after-critiquing-title-ix-policy/.
136. 34 C.F.R. §106.71(b)(2).

Conclusion

Critics have attempted to undo the new Title IX rule ever since it became law in May 2020. Multiple lawsuits were filed to stop implementation of the law, and when they were unsuccessful, litigation commenced to halt its enforcement.[1]

Now that Joe Biden is President, opponents of the law are optimistic that they will succeed. After all, candidate Biden condemned the Trump Administration's Education Department for "trying to shame and silence survivors."[2] "Instead of protecting women," Biden wrote on his campaign website, "they have rolled back the clock and given colleges a green light to ignore sexual violence and strip survivors of their civil rights under Title IX."[3] Biden promised to "restore the Title IX guidance for colleges, including the 2011 Dear Colleague Letter."[4] Hours after the 2,000+ page Rule was released, Biden condemned it and vowed to put it to a "quick end."[5]

Just three months into his presidency and in the middle of a global pandemic and economic crisis, Biden started making good on his promise. He signed an executive order directing the Department of Education (DOE) to conduct a comprehensive review of the new rule.[6] Soon after, the Assistant Secretary announced that they would begin gathering feedback, and a public hearing would happen soon.[7] In an ominous sign that he wants to return to Obama-era guidance, Biden announced in May 2021 that he intended to nominate Catherine Lhamon to be Assistant Secretary for Civil Rights.[8] Lhamon, of course, was the author of the infamous 2011 Dear Colleague Letter. On October 20, 2021, Lhamon was confirmed in a 51–50 party-line vote, with Vice President Kamala Harris casting the deciding vote.[9]

Distrust of the new rule is understandable. It was initiated by an acting head of OCR who dismissed 90 percent of rape allegations as next-morning regret, under a Secretary of Education who put her own religious views over the best interests of students, during the presidency of a man who bragged about committing sexual assault.[10] But whatever your thoughts about the Trump

Administration, Secretary DeVos should be applauded for following the law in promulgating the new rule, something the Obama DOE failed to do with the 2011 Dear Colleague Letter. Not only are the new regulations the product of a legally sanctioned rulemaking process, as described in Chapter 6, but they demonstrate careful regard for the 124,000 comments that were made during the notice and comment process. Indeed, the new regulations contain changes that were *explicitly* made in response to criticisms received.

Make no mistake. The Biden DOE is undermining the rule of law by moving so quickly to completely undo regulations painstakingly enacted pursuant to the Administrative Procedure Act. It teaches stakeholders that instead of earnestly working toward a difficult compromise they can instead dig in their heels and wait for a new administration to give them everything they want. But advocates beware. You may be willing to sacrifice procedural niceties when they get in the way of policies to which we are committed, but two can play at that game. It may be OK when it's the Biden Administration overturning Trump Title IX regulations, but it's going to feel different when it's a Republican administration overturning cherished regulations protecting the environment or workplace safety.

That doesn't mean there isn't room for improvement. Substantively, as I discuss in Chapters 6 and 7, the new regulations are a mixed bag. Among other advancements, the new rule recognizes quid pro quo and Clery Act/VAWA offenses as per se discrimination. That means a school employee conditioning an aid, benefit, or service on an individual's unwelcome sexual conduct or "a single instance of sexual assault, dating violence, domestic violence, or stalking" constitutes sexual harassment.[11] The new rule also requires that other kinds of harassment be objectively unreasonable, which is an improvement over the Obama-era guidance, which made harassment purely subjective. However, the new regulations also significantly narrow what counts as non Clery Act/VAWA or quid pro quo discrimination. Now the unwelcome conduct must be severe, pervasive, *and* objectively offensive, which would seem to exclude, for instance, a student passing around nonconsensual pornographic images of his ex-girlfriend during class on the grounds that it wasn't pervasive enough, regardless of how devastating it was for her.[12]

Not only do the new regulations narrow what counts as sexual harassment, but they make it easier for schools to get away with doing nothing in response. The recipient must have had notice (actual knowledge of sexual harassment), which at the postsecondary level is limited to the Title IX Coordinator or someone who has the authority to institute corrective measures. That means there will be no Title IX consequences if a coach or professor witnesses a violent rape but takes no action. Primary and secondary schools allow any school employee to count for notice purposes, but they still require that person have actual knowledge, which incentivizes willful ignorance. Even assuming that a recipient has notice, the standard for their response under the new rule is deliberate indifference. That means the DOE will not step in unless their response is clearly unreasonable in light of the known circumstances. Although DOE mandates that schools follow certain enumerated procedures, it yields too much oversight over decisions like supportive measures and punishment.

In contrast, the procedural protections put in place by the new rule constitute a dramatic improvement over what existed before. They rectify the due process wasteland that existed in the wake of the 2011 Dear Colleague Letter, which is discussed at length in Chapters 4 and 5. Requiring adjudicatory hearings with live testimony and witness questioning is hands down the most significant reform because it advances a fair, unbiased process especially as compared with the single investigatory model that was being used by some schools. Importantly, as discussed in Chapter 7, many of these new procedural regulations are based on consensus recommendations of a diverse ABA Criminal Justice Section Task Force, which contained members who were pro-victim and pro-accused. These recommendations were in turn endorsed by a special working group appointed by the Governor of one of the most progressive states in the country.

Biden is right that the law isn't perfect, but the solution isn't to return to the injustice of the 2011 Dear Colleague Letter. Doing that means disregarding the rights and vulnerabilities of accused students. Biden should know better, especially since he himself was recently accused of sexual assault that his supporters immediately dismissed as false.[13] It also wrongly assumes that victim/survivors won't benefit from having robust procedures when in truth there are schools that, whether it's because the accused is a football star or a popular professor, would not otherwise take their allegations of sexual assault seriously.

I now recap my recommendations for reforming the new regulations from Chapters 6 and 7. Unless otherwise noted, both schools and the DOE are allowed to make these changes because they are interpretations of existing rules. Other suggestions could only be implemented by the DOE through formal or informal rulemaking because they would change existing law. However, recipients can and should advocate that these changes be made.

1. RELAX THE STANDARD FOR NON/CLERY ACT/QUID PRO QUO HARASSMENT

The new regulations set a high bar for non Clery Act/quid pro quo harassment. In order to be actionable, it must be "[u]nwelcome conduct (on the basis of sex) determined by a reasonable person to be so severe, pervasive, and objectively offensive that it effectively denies a person equal access to the recipient's education program or activity." This standard is too demanding because it will exclude conduct that meets one but not all of the elements. Since the new rule creates a reasonable person standard, there is no need to require all three elements. Instead, the DOE should change the regulation from "and" to "or." It should also more carefully explain what it means by denial of access. The regulation should thus be changed to something like the following: "Unwelcome conduct (on the basis of sex) determined by a reasonable person to be so severe, pervasive, or objectively offensive that it so undermines and detracts from the victim's educational experience that the victim-student is effectively denied equal access to an institution's resources and opportunities. No concrete injury is required."

Making this change will require going through formal or informal rulemaking.

2. CHANGE TO WHAT CONSTITUTES KNOWLEDGE

Return to Constructive Knowledge Standard

The new rule changes the standard from constructive to actual knowledge for Title IX liability. Now a school must have "actual" knowledge of sexual harassment before it can be penalized by DOE for not responding.[14] This new standard is deeply problematic. It incentivizes willful ignorance, and as I show in Chapter 6, it misses serious cases of sexual misconduct that a school should have known about. Returning to a constructive knowledge standard will require going through formal or informal rulemaking.

Notice Should Be Broadened at the Post-Secondary Level

For elementary and secondary schools, actual knowledge refers to notice to *any* employee. For institutes of higher education (IHEs), however, actual knowledge means notice to the Title IX Coordinator or any official who has the authority to institute corrective measures on behalf of the recipient IHE.[15] As discussed in Chapter 6, restricting notice in this way means a school would have no accountability under Title IX even if multiple coaches and doctors were informed of the kind of sexual assault that Larry Nassar perpetrated against athletes at Michigan State University.

The DOE should change the rule in two ways. First, it should return to broader notice requirements in IHEs. Notice should be expanded from Title

IX Coordinators and officials with the ability to make corrective changes to include persons who have significant interaction with students, like professors and coaches. Second, the constructive knowledge standard should be reinstated at all levels of education. The modified rule would look something like this:

> Notice results whenever any elementary and secondary school employee, or at the postsecondary level, any Title IX Coordinator, official with authority, or employee with significant student interaction like a professor or coach: knows or should have known of the harassment, including harassment that person would have learned about through a reasonably diligent inquiry.

Making this change would require going through formal or informal rulemaking.

3. REPLACE THE DELIBERATE INDIFFERENCE STANDARD

Under the new regulations, once a recipient has actual knowledge of sexual harassment, they "must respond promptly in a manner that is not deliberately indifferent."[16] Only responses that are "clearly unreasonable in light of the known circumstances" are deliberately indifferent.[17] As part of the deliberate indifference standard, the new rule removes all oversight from the judgement of responsibility and the punishment if a respondent is found responsible.[18]

The DOE should change the rule so it returns to the standard under prior guidance, which means schools would be required to provide a reasonable response to a sex-based harassment complaint. As part of that reasonable response, schools would have to meet detailed requirements like offering supportive measures through the Title IX Coordinator, responding promptly, and following a detailed grievance process prior to imposing disciplinary sanctions. Making this change could only be done through formal or informal rulemaking.

4. EXPLICITLY PROHIBIT MISCONDUCT THAT FALLS OUTSIDE THE AMBIT OF TITLE IX

The new rule limits Title IX enforcement to harassment that occurs within the United States, and it only covers off-campus harassment that occurs in buildings owned or controlled by an officially recognized student organization. Schools should explicitly prohibit sexual and other misconduct by faculty, staff, or students that occurs (1) outside of the United States, and /or (2) off campus but is not covered under Title IX.

5. BEEF UP PROTECTIONS AGAINST ONLINE HARASSMENT

Although the new rule covers online harassment, it does not do so prominently or explicitly. Making matters worse, DOE has a narrow definition of when online harassment would fall within a recipient's program or activity. The recipient must have both substantial control over the respondent *and* the context in which it occurs, which may even exclude online harassment during class time.

The DOE should change the rule to explicitly state that online sexual harassment violates Title IX. It should say something along these lines:

> [A]n education program or activity includes circumstances over which the recipient exercised substantial control over the respondent or the context in which the harassment occurred. It also includes online harassment perpetrated over recipient-controlled email servers/wifi or email servers/wifi of a recognized student organization and online harassment perpetrated from any buildings, vehicles, or other property owned or controlled by the recipient or a recognized student organization.

This change would have to be made through formal or informal rulemaking.

6. INVESTIGATORS AND ADJUDICATORS SHOULD BE INFORMED ABOUT COMMON RAPE MYTHS

The new rule states: "Any materials used to train Title IX Coordinators, Investigators, decision-makers and any person who facilitates an informal resolution process, must not rely on sex stereotypes and must promote impartial investigations and adjudications of formal complaints of sexual harassment."[19] Research shows that rape victims often don't act the way people expect; for example, they delay reporting, or they aren't highly emotional when describing what happened to them. Correcting those misperceptions should not constitute sex stereotyping. However, to the extent that a school decides to educate decision-makers, it should happen at the hearing, so the respondent has the chance to ask questions or present contradictory research. Since schools are interpreting but not changing existing regulations, they should be able to make this change.

7. WRITTEN INSTRUCTIONS ON STANDARD OF PROOF

The new rule gives schools the right to set the standard of proof at preponderance of the evidence or clear and convincing evidence.[20] Given the harm that the parties suffer from a mistake, schools should make the burden clear and convincing evidence. Indeed, they should use this higher standard in *all* proceedings where students face the possibility of expulsion, even if they aren't facing the stigma of being found responsible for a sex crime.

Whatever standard they use, however, they should provide the factfinder with a written instruction before deliberations begin. For clear and convincing evidence, I recommend the following instruction, which is from the 2017 ABA Criminal Justice Section Task Force:

> The decision-maker should first evaluate the quality of the evidence. The decision-maker should consider all of the evidence regardless of who provided it. Any evidence the decision-maker finds to be of high quality should be given more weight than any evidence the decision-maker finds to be of low quality. Quality may, or may not be identical with quantity, and sheer quantity alone should not be the basis for a finding of responsibility. The testimony of a single party or witness may be sufficient to establish a fact.
>
> After assessing the quality of the evidence, the decision-maker should only find the respondent responsible for alleged misconduct if the evidence firmly convinces the decision-maker to reasonably conclude that a finding of responsibility is justified. That is, the decision-maker should find that there is sufficient evidence that is relevant, probable, and persuasive to firmly convince him or her that the respondent engaged in the alleged misconduct, and that the evidence supporting a finding of responsibility significantly outweighs any evidence that the respondent is not responsible for the alleged misconduct.

Should a school opt to use the lower preponderance standard – which the new regulations allow – they should only do so under an adjudicatory model with at least a three-person panel of decision-makers, a unanimity requirement, and other robust procedural protections. In addition, they should provide a written instruction, which clearly articulates what preponderance of the evidence means. I recommend the 2017 CJS Section instruction, which has the first paragraph omitted because it is identical to the one above:

> After assessing the quality of the evidence, the decision-makers should only find the respondent responsible for alleged misconduct if the evidence unanimously convinces them to reasonably conclude that a finding of responsibility is justified. That is, the decision-makers should find that there is sufficient evidence that is relevant, probable, and persuasive to convince them that the respondent engaged in the alleged misconduct, and that the evidence supporting a finding of responsibility outweighs any evidence that the respondent is not responsible for the alleged misconduct.[21]

Providing written instructions does not change existing law, and so schools should be able to do this on their own.

8. PROHIBIT HARASSMENT

The new rule explicitly bars schools from restricting "the ability of either party to discuss the allegations under investigation or to gather and present relevant evidence."[22] This is a welcome change; however, it can be abused. The right to discuss allegations should not include the right to harass the other side, and schools should explicitly prohibit such harassment. Schools should be able to do so on their own because it would not change existing law.

9. RELEVANT EVIDENCE

The new rule requires a live adjudicatory hearing for postsecondary schools, but it never explicitly gives parties the right to present relevant evidence. Schools should explicitly grant that right, but they should also define what relevant evidence means. The ABA Task Force provided a useful definition, which I've combined with the Rule's statement regarding a complainant's prior sexual history to provide a model instruction:

> Evidence is relevant if (1) it bears on a fact of consequence in the case, or (2) it reflects on the credibility of a testifying party or witness in a material way. Evidence may be excluded if it is unfairly prejudicial or if it is needlessly duplicative.[23] Questions about a complainant's sexual history are only allowed where it would provide evidence that someone else had committed the offense or to show consent.[24]

Again, schools should be permitted to make this change.

10. SPECIAL RULES FOR COMPLAINANT'S PRIOR SEXUAL HISTORY

Evidence of a complainant's sexual history is sometimes essential for a fair hearing. Because of the sensitivity of this evidence, however, schools should create a special protocol for its admissibility that is modeled on Federal Rule of Evidence Section 412. First, the respondent should have to provide notice that he is intending to admit this evidence. Second, if the complainant objects, there should be a hearing that takes place in advance of the formal adjudicatory hearing where a hearing chairperson (but preferably not a decision-maker) determines whether the evidence should be admitted. At that pre-hearing, both parties should have the chance to speak.

    This is an interpretation of existing law, so schools should be able to make this change.

11. INCREASE PANEL SIZE AND DIVERSITY

Schools should have a panel of at least three people, who are diverse across gender, race, and sexual orientation to reduce bias and increase accuracy. This recommendation is consistent with that of the ABA Task Force,[25] and it does not require a formal rule change.

12. PROHIBIT HARASSMENT DURING THE HEARING

Schools should explicitly prohibit harassment during the hearing including during cross-examination. Schools should have a hearing chairperson who will function like a judge. She will decide whether questions are relevant and will prohibit questions that are irrelevant, duplicative, or that stray into areas of the complainant's sexual history that have been determined to be off-limits at the hearing on evidence admissibility described earlier. This is an interpretation of existing law, so schools should be able to make this change.

13. FINE-TUNE ADMISSIBILITY OF WITNESS AND PARTY STATEMENTS

The new regulations do not require parties to submit to questions, but if they don't, their prior statements cannot be considered:

> If a party or witness does not submit to cross-examination at the live hearing, the decision-maker(s) must not rely on any statement of that party or witness in reaching a determination regarding responsibility; provided however that the decision-maker(s) cannot draw an inference about the determination regarding responsibility based solely on a party's or witness's absence from the live hearing or refusal to answer cross examination or other questions.[26]

This rule change is consistent with the recommendations of the ABA Task Force,[27] and it is loosely modeled on the constitutional rights afforded to criminal defendants and the restriction on the admissibility of a party's own statements under the Federal Rules of Evidence. However, this ban goes too far. It should be limited to self-serving statements by the respondent and testimonial statements by the complainant or other witnesses, unless the right to question is waived. Furthermore, if there is any evidence that either party dissuaded a witness from testifying or scheduled the hearing to prevent a witness from testifying, that witness' statement should be admitted regardless of whether they testify. Similarly, if there is any evidence that either party tried to prevent the other from testifying, that party's statement should be admitted.

This would constitute a change to existing law, so it could only be implemented if the DOE went through formal or informal rulemaking.

14. RESTORATIVE JUSTICE

The new rule allows schools to informally resolve allegations of sexual misconduct. However, both parties must consent, and any party may withdraw prior to agreeing to a resolution.[28] Schools should follow the ABA Task Force in limiting options for alternative adjudication. "Where appropriate, the Task Force encourages schools to consider non mediation alternatives to resolving complaints that are research or evidence-based, such as Restorative Justice processes."[29] Schools are given the right to informally resolve allegations of sexual misconduct, and they should be able to limit informal resolution to RJ.

15. HARASSMENT CAN CONSTITUTE RETALIATION

The regulations explicitly extend the right against retaliation to complainants, witnesses, participants, and respondents:

> No recipient or other person may intimidate, threaten, coerce, or discriminate against any individual for the purpose of interfering with any right or privilege secured by title IX or this part, or because the individual has made a report or complaint, testified, assisted, or participated or refused to participate in any manner in an investigation, proceeding, or hearing under this part.[30]

In resolving the potential conflict between retaliation and freedom of expression, the new rule falls firmly on the side of the latter. "The exercise of rights protected under the First Amendment does not constitute retaliation prohibited under . . . this section."[31]

Explicitly recognizing that protected expression can't constitute retaliation for Title IX purposes may have unintended consequences. Students may feel emboldened to harass, and schools may be reluctant to respond. To protect against either, schools should remind community members that First Amendment rights are not absolute. Speech may constitute prohibited quid pro quo language, defamation, or libel. Schools are also allowed to institute content neutral time, place, and manner restrictions. Finally, courts are often deferential to schools in terms of their ability to prohibit speech that interferes with the mission of the school. Schools should be permitted to make these changes on their own.

CONCLUSION – THE LIMITS OF DUE PROCESS

The adjudicatory procedures put in place by the new regulations are a significant improvement over what existed before, but we shouldn't fool ourselves. A fair process is important; indeed, it's paramount, but it is not a panacea. The students I spoke with still voiced pain about the process even when they thought it was fair, and even when they prevailed. One woman, a complainant whose assaulter was found responsible, said:

> Even if you have the right process, are there really any winners here? I still feel like shit. He feels like shit . . . You keep asking me was the process fair; overall it was OK, but processes are just that, they're processes, there are real people and real people's lives and feelings that are affected by going through these processes and without taking that human component into account you are doing everyone a disservice. It could be the most fair process in the world, and mine was pretty fair, and I still wouldn't put myself through it again. I don't really have any complaints about how they handled anything, but I still don't think I would do it again.

The processes recommended in this book are just a first step. Schools must also support students after the hearing. They may need to get an extension, delay exams, receive psychological counseling, or take a voluntary leave of absence. One person I spoke with – a man who had been accused of sexual assault but ultimately found not responsible – talked about how much it helped to discuss what he had gone through even though the hearing happened years before:

> I did not think that this [interview] would take two hours without taking a breath, it definitely helps to talk about it. It is a traumatic experience . . . After any traumatic experience, you have to talk about it with someone. There's such value, self-benefit, in talking with someone because you start to come to these realizations and start to identify next steps and you start to have closure.

But schools should also consider alternatives to traditional adjudication, especially restorative justice (RJ), which I discussed in Chapter 7. Restorative Justice works from a completely different paradigm than traditional adjudication, which seeks to determine whether a person violated a formal code of conduct, and if so, what sanction they should receive. As Wenzel et al. explain, in traditional adjudication, "once a punishment is imposed, justice is often considered done."[32] With RJ, however, the *starting* point is that a harm has occurred, and the objective is to "best repair the acknowledged hurt."[33]

The process by which that harm is repaired is critical to RJ. In traditional adjudication, victim/survivors are participants in a process, but in restorative justice, they control the process. This control, Koss and Chisholm explain, is essential to recovery:

> Those who experience sexual misconduct frequently feel stripped of power and control, and conventional, adversarial responses can create what has been called the second rape. But a study of restorative justice has shown that victims who participate in the process and speak face to face with the person who caused them harm feel they have reclaimed their power. Restoring a sense of empowerment is crucial to recovering from these harmful and deflating experiences.[34]

Choosing RJ doesn't mean that the offender gets off scot-free. There is no reason a person couldn't be suspended or even expelled if his wrongdoing was serious enough. But the ultimate goal isn't punishment; it's healing the harm to the victim/survivor, the offender, and the community. As Wenzel et al. explain:

> While punishment can be, and often is, part of restorative justice practices, it is not central. Crucial for proper restorative justice is a process of deliberation that places emphasis on healing rather than punishing: healing the victim and undoing the hurt; healing the offender by rebuilding his or her moral and social selves; healing communities and mending social relationships.[35]

The fact that punishment isn't central to RJ may make it particularly suitable for some campus sexual assault cases. The studies I discussed in Chapter 1 uniformly show that most victim/survivors did not report to authorities. When asked why, the majority said that they did not think it was serious enough to report. Probing further, the 2015 AAU Campus Climate Survey found that a sizable percentage (23.3% of those who experienced penetration by force and 27% who experienced penetration by incapacitation) did not want the person to get into trouble. Restorative Justice would offer a meaningful alternative to those victim/survivors.

There are, however, some important caveats before a school can use RJ. It is only appropriate if both parties consent to participate. Additionally, the offender must first admit that he harmed the victim/survivor. However, that admission can take place after a person is found responsible at a hearing with the kind of robust procedural rights put in place by the new regulations. Last, RJ is not the same as mediation, and schools should not offer it unless they have trained facilitators and can provide the appropriate supportive structure. When RJ is not appropriate, the default must be an adjudicatory hearing with robust procedural protections.

Campus sexual assault is a serious problem in the United States, but it must be handled fairly. Schools can't simply decide that because a woman said she was raped that she is telling the truth or because a man said he didn't do it that she is lying. Schools must protect *everyone*, both the Ericas and the Franciscos. That protection requires robust procedural protections, but it also demands that schools acknowledge the limits of those proceedings. A fair adjudicatory process doesn't mean that the harm is healed. Justice, in the broadest sense, requires more than just a fair process.

NOTES

1. *See* Chapter 6.
2. *The Biden Agenda for Women,* JOEBIDEN.COM, https://joebiden.com/womens-agenda/.
3. *Id.*
4. *The Biden Plan to End Violence Against Women,* JOEBIDEN.COM, https://joebiden.com/vawa/.
5. *Id.*
6. *Executive Order on Guaranteeing an Educational Environment Free from Discrimination on the Basis of Sex, Including Sexual Orientation or Gender Identity,* THE WHITE HOUSE (Mar. 8, 2021), www.whitehouse.gov/briefing-room/presidential-actions/2021/03/08/executive-order-on-guaranteeing-an-educational-environment-free-from-discrimination-on-the-basis-of-sex-including-sexual-orientation-or-gender-identity/; Rebecca Shabad, *Biden to order review of changes to college sexual misconduct rules under Trump,* NBC News (Mar. 8, 2021, 7:47 AM EST).
7. Letter from Suzanne B. Goldberg, Acting Assistant Secretary for Civil Rights, to U.S. Dept. of Educ., Office for Civil Rights (Apr. 6, 2021), www2.ed.gov/about/offices/list/ocr/correspondence/stakeholders/20210406-titleix-eo-14021.pdf.
8. Press Release, White House, President Biden Announces His Intent to Nominate Catherine Lhamon (May 13, 2021), www.whitehouse.gov/briefing-room/statements-releases/2021/05/13/president-biden-announces-his-intent-to-nominate-catherine-lhamon-for-assistant-secretary-for-civil-rights-at-the-department-of-education/
9. Jeremy Bauer-Wolf, *Catherine Lhamon Narrowly Survives Senate Confirmation, Will Head Ed Dept's Civil Rights Arm,* HIGHER ED. DIVE (Oct. 20, 2021), www.highereddive.com/news/catherine-lhamon-narrowly-survives-senate-confirmation-will-head-ed-depts/608600/.
10. *See* Chapter 6. *See US Election: Full transcript of Donald Trump's obscene videotape,* BBC NEWS (Oct. 9, 2016), www.bbc.com/news/election-us-2016-37595321/.
11. Nondiscrimination on the Basis of Sex in Education Programs or Activities Receiving Federal Financial Assistance, 85 Fed. Reg. 30026, 30036 (May 19, 2020) (codified at 24 C.F.R. pt. 106).
12. The DOE discussed whether disseminating so-called revenge porn could meet the pervasiveness requirement. DOE wrote that it "may meet the

elements of the Davis standard including pervasiveness, particularly where the unwelcome sex-based conduct involves widespread dissemination of offensive material …" (Nondiscrimination on the Basis of Sex in Education Programs, 85 Fed. Reg. at 30166). If "widespread dissemination" is required then the classroom scenario probably doesn't count.

13. Lisa Lerer & Sydney Ember, *Examining Tara Reade's Sexual Assault Allegation against Joe Biden*, N.Y. TIMES (Apr. 12, 2020) (Updated, Sept. 28, 2020).
14. 34 C.F.R. §106.30(a).
15. "Determining whether an individual is an 'official with authority' is a legal determination that depends on the specific facts relating to a recipient's administrative structure and the roles and duties held by officials in the recipient's own operations." Nondiscrimination on the Basis of Sex in Education Programs, 85 Fed. Reg. at 30039.
16. 34 C.F.R. §106.44(a).
17. *Id.*
18. Nondiscrimination on the Basis of Sex in Education Programs, 85 Fed. Reg. at 30034.
19. 34 C.F.R. §106.45(b)(1)(iii).
20. 34 C.F.R. § 106.45 (b)(1)(vii).
21. ABA Criminal Justice Section Task Force on College Due Process Rights and Victim Protections, *Recommendations for Colleges and Universities in Resolving Allegations of Campus Sexual Misconduct* (June 2017) at 8 [hereinafter "Recommendations of the ABA Task Force"].
22. 34 C.F.R. §106.45(b)(5)(iii).
23. Recommendations of the ABA Task Force, *supra* note 21 at 6.
24. 34 C.F.R. §106.45(b)(6)(i).
25. Recommendations of the ABA Task Force, *supra* note 21 at 7.
26. 34 C.F.R. §106.45(b)(6)(i).
27. Recommendations of the ABA Task Force, *supra* note 21 at 6.
28. 34 C.F.R. §106.45(b)(9).
29. Recommendations of the ABA Task Force, *supra* note 21 at 3.
30. 34 C.F.R. §106.71(a).
31. 34 C.F.R. § 106.71 (b).
32. Michael Wentzel et al. *Retributive and Restorative Justice*, 32 Law & Hum. Behav. 375, 375 (2008).
33. Mary P. Koss & Kate Chisholm, *The Time Is Now: Restorative Justice for Sexual Misconduct*, CHRONICLE OF HIGHER ED. (February 16, 2020), www.chronicle.com/article/the-time-is-now-restorative-justice-for-sexual-misconduct/.
34. Id.
35. *Id.* at 376 (internal citations omitted).

Index

For EU product safety concerns, contact us at Calle de José Abascal, 56–1°, 28003 Madrid, Spain or eugpsr@cambridge.org.

www.ingramcontent.com/pod-product-compliance
Ingram Content Group UK Ltd.
Pitfield, Milton Keynes, MK11 3LW, UK
UKHW020353140625

459647UK00020B/2446